JOHN PIERCE HAWLEY

LIFE AND TIMES OF
JOHN PIERCE HAWLEY

A MORMON ULYSSES OF THE AMERICAN WEST

Melvin C. Johnson

Greg Kofford Books
Salt Lake City, 2019

Copyright © 2019 Melvin C. Johnson

Cover design copyright © 2019 Greg Kofford Books, Inc.

Cover design by Loyd Isao Ericson

Published in the USA.

All rights reserved. No part of this volume may be reproduced in any form without written permission from the publisher, Greg Kofford Books. The views expressed herein are the responsibility of the author and do not necessarily represent the position of Greg Kofford Books.

ISBN 978-1-58958-764-9 (paperback); 978-1-58958-765-6 (hardcover) Also available in ebook.

Greg Kofford Books
P. O. Box 1362
Draper, UT 84020
www.gregkofford.com
facebook.com/gkbooks
twitter.com/gkbooks

Library of Congress Cataloging-in-Publication Data

Names: Johnson, Melvin C., 1949- author.
Title: Life and times of John Pierce Hawley : a Mormon Ulysses of the American West / Melvin C. Johnson.
Description: Salt Lake City : Greg Kofford Books, 2019. | Includes bibliographical references and index.
Identifiers: LCCN 2018056657| ISBN 9781589587649 (pbk.) | ISBN 9781589587656
  (hardcover)
Subjects: LCSH: Hawley, John Pierce, 1826-1909. | Mormons--Biography. | Church of Jesus Christ of Latter-day Saints--Biography. | Church of Jesus Christ of Latter-day Saints (Wightites)--Biography. | Reorganized Church of Jesus Christ of Latter Day Saints--Biography. | Mormon missionaries. | Ex-church members--Church of Jesus Christ of Latter-day Saints.
Classification: LCC BX8695.H38 J64 2019 | DDC 289.3092 [B] --dc23
LC record available at https://lccn.loc.gov/2018056657

Contents

Preface, vii
Prologue: The Start of a Trek, xi

1. On The Borderlands of America, 1826–1842, 1
2. Wisconsin Territory to the Republic of Texas, 1843–1851, 13
3. Mormon Mills, Texas to The Indian Nations, 1851–1856, 29
4. Wagons West to Utah Territory, 1856, 45
5. Welcome to Zion, 1856–1857, 63
6. The Hawleys of Pine Valley, Part I, 81
7. The Racial Divide and Theocracy in Greater Dixie, 95
8. The Hawleys of Pine Valley, Part II, 113
9. A Pine Valley Missionary to Iowa, 1868, 129
10. Return to Utah and Conversion to the RLDS Church, 1868–1870, 141

Epilogue: End of a Trek, 1870, 155

Appendix A: John Hawley, Letter to Joseph Smith III, June 12, 1884, 167
Appendix B: Temple Lot Case, 171
Appendix C: Chronology of John Pierce Hawley, 185

Bibliography, 189
Index, 205

Preface

    History and baseball are my passions and have counseled me through the years. The first may describe the story of a person: his people, his tribe; and the myth and action of the second offer a window into American culture. John Pierce Hawley's forty-year odyssey in the American interior was in pursuit of his dream to find a true Mormon restoration faith. The story describes John Pierce Hawley and Mormonism, particularly the Latter-day Saints and the Wightites, and their cultural and geographic landscapes as the multitude of sects compete one with the other for converts and land. This story finishes in 1870 as John Pierce Hawley finds his final place in theological Mormonism, as the Mormon Diaspora has been permanently situated in the American landscape from the upper Midwest to the Rocky Mountains. During his odyssey, John has recorded his own myth and rationale for his life's religious journey in his writings.

    As a Latter-day Saint convert from California, I knew very little about western Mormonism when I entered Dixie College in St. George, Utah. Dixie was then a two-year school, a very small world of academia, and Professor Pansy L. Hardy was my first professional mentor. She took kindly to me and guided me academically. I grew to love her, as so many of her students would over the years. She instilled in me a love for the English language. She also introduced me to an older cousin named Juanita L. Brooks. I had no idea who she was. I did think she was 'old.' Now I am almost the age she was then. I had no idea where Mountain Meadows was located or what had occurred there, although the killing fields were but some thirty miles north of St. George. A friend from college took me fishing at the reservoir in Pine Valley. I thought the little hamlet quaint as I did the house on the southeast corner of the burg's main intersection. I was not aware that George Hawley, a brother of John Pierce Hawley, had built it, or that George had three wives, or that John would struggle with plural marriage for decades before rejecting it and Utah Mormonism. Hawley took his large family away from Pine Valley, and George and his family as well, to Iowa and RLDS Mormonism (Reorganized Church of Latter Day Saints of Jesus Christ, now called Community of Christ) in 1870.

After Dixie College, my four years at Utah State University found a much larger academic domain and new mentors: Ty Booth, Dean Skabelund, the great folklorists Austin E. and Alta S. Fife, Hector B. Lee, and Barre Tolkien. Gary Snyder convinced me I should never, ever consider being a poet. They all taught me about a larger world beyond Dixie and Logan and Utah. Twelve years followed in the United States Army. During those years I played baseball and softball, read a lot, and finally felt the need for graduate school in Nacogdoches, Texas. I earned graduate degrees in English and history at Stephen F. Austin State University. Archie L. McDonald mentored and guided me and helped me get my first professional history job with the Texas Forestry Museum at Lufkin, Texas. Carol Riggs, its director, was kind and generous, allowing me to develop the milltown and logging tram database research projects founded by Jon L. Gerland, now senior archivist of the Temple History Center in Diboll, Texas.

The database projects allowed me to unknowingly cross paths with John Pierce Hawley. The Mormon millers in the Hill County in pre-Civil War Texas became at first an intriguing side note in the museum's database collection. However, the Mormon millers' narrative fanned my need to know more. I read and researched and began writing. My fascination with Lyman Wight and his schismatic runaway Mormon colony from Wisconsin to Texas led to a series of papers and finally the work and publication of *Polygamy on the Pedernales: Lyman Wight's Mormon Villages in Antebellum Texas, 1845–1858* in 2006, published by Utah State University Press. That work featured at times John Pierce Hawley (1826–1909), whose personality and character fascinate me. His fluidity and interchangeability within the sectarianism and denominationalism that have dominated Restoration groups from 1845 until now have intrigued me. Just as importantly, John R. Alley, my editor at USU Press for the Wight book, taught me how to be a writer of history, and became my lifelong friend.

This book would not have happened without the dedication and friendship of John Alley and Brian Whitney. Will Bagley, my oldest friend from early days in Carlsbad and Oceanside, California, has inspired me, analyzed my work, and supported me in tough times, as I hope I have for him. Susan Louise Petty, the mother of my children and now long for the ages, always told me that my greatest challenge was to be "honest with yourself" and to the work I do. Time has proven her right. Art, Ben, Amber, and Julie, now with her mom, has their mother's glow. They are my heroes. Bill Shepherd, Mike Marquardt, Paul Reeve, Todd Compton, Joseph Johnstun, Chris Smith, Chris Blythe, Bill Russell, Ron Romig,

Lach Mackay, Steve Snow, Larry Morse, Rick Turley, and many others have contributed to forming, guiding, and encouraging the direction of my historical pursuits. Jenny Lund and Jen Barkdull at the LDS Church History Library have taken notice of my needs and provided critical assistance. Most of all, Halli Wren Johnson has supported me, listened to me, traveled with me, and never once have her eyes glazed over; she always has spoken the needed words when deserving, "Well done, Mel." She has been my Liahona, my guide to my true path, without whom I would have lost my way a long time ago.

All errors and mistakes in this work are, of course, my sole responsibility.

PROLOGUE

The Start of a Trek

"THE MOST IMPORTANT REASON OF ALL THAT [BIOGRAPHY] IS AN IMPOSSIBLE CRAFT IS THAT YOU CANNOT KNOW WHAT SOMEONE ELSE'S LIFE WAS LIKE."

Life and Times of John Pierce Hawley: A Mormon Ulysses of the American West fits within the latter day religious movement of Joseph Smith Jr. That is where John defined his identity. The more I researched Lyman Wight and his colonies in Wisconsin and Texas, the more the Pierce Hawley family story and that of John Pierce Hawley emerged from the Wightite story. I became intrigued by John P. Hawley. His record in the West and his interaction with major sects of Mormonism rival that of Bishop George Miller and Zenas Hovey Gurley Sr. Hawley exemplified ordinary peoples' struggles of the Mormons in the nineteenth century. Although he had his secrets and did not easily share them, I believe I have uncovered most of them.

A biographer wants to tell the whole story and clarify the narrative's important details. And most importantly, he or she must accept that one cannot know completely what someone else's life was like. The historian can only hope to come close. Because biography is an art, conclusions will be imprecise. Gathering data is critical. Just as important is that the quality of this type of research and writings develops with the laborer's growing skill over the decades in appraising the data and interpreting the story. The historian should quarry all evidence, no matter how contrary or opposed or kindly or reassuring, and fairly assess it. Not all the evidence, most likely, will be found about a complex subject. Thus, the writer's objective professionalism and experience and talent can only mitigate the inexactness of biography.

An incredible assemblage of writers and researchers have stepped forward these last decades in the field of Restoration Studies. They have produced wonderful readings. Many have overcome the tendency to create dualistic interpretations of belief and experience, and many surrendered to the desire to separate "us" from "them." Dualism regrettably satisfies some readers, the kind who will agree to take evidence screwed onto a preconceived position, rather than alter the viewpoint to fit the data. A history of the faithful, a category into which John Hawley fits, can too often devolve into a faithful history. Such a concept of barrel and hoops will constrain the arts of history and biography and trap the dialogue of both readers and writer in corners of classification that warp interpretation.

Research and narrative can operate along an axial integration of opposites: liberals, conservatives; east, west; true believer, no believer; democratic, republican; Dodgers, Giants; Mormons, gentiles; FLDS, everybody else. Hawley struggled within a polygamous society of conferred authority while he increasingly yearned for a monogamous culture of patrilineal authority. He would weave those opposites and their data points on the axis into patterns and perspectives both complex and nuanced. I have tried my level best to know John Hawley and what his life was like. I have been sympathetic where sympathy is due, honest about his human failings, and flexible to fit the emerging theme to the data.

John Hawley was an average person who climbed to uncommon heights. Lay persons and scholars of Mormonism are privileged that Hawley, despite his lack of formal schooling, recorded his life and times. He wrote well for a man who was born, raised, and lived on the moving frontier of nineteenth-century America. I have been faithful to his spelling. He began writing his story more than fourteen years after leaving Utah Territory, and at times he was recounting events almost five decades earlier. However, after Hawley joined the Reorganized Church of Jesus Christ of Latter Day Saints (RLDS, now Community of Christ) in 1870, he at times clouded or deliberately falsified issues about Mormon leaders and controversies. I note where I think Hawley purposely confuses these subjects.

Let's compare our trials to Hawley and his companions.

Have any of us as a small child ever been so hungry as to cry tears of joy at finding a rat-gnawed molded rind of bread?

Have any of us traversed by horseback or on foot out under the vaults of Heaven or the vast, rising plains and the rolling hills of Indian Territory and Kansas and Nebraska, or scaled the staggering mountains of the West? Hawley crisscrossed the American interior at least five times.

Some of us have endured the horror of losing a child. Sylvia and John Hawley buried four little ones in nine years in the wild beauty of Pine Valley, Utah Territory. Their losses were not rare, not even uncommon in that time and place.

At what costs have we responded to moral challenges in our lives? Hawley came close to being slain for opposing the horrific events at Mountain Meadows in 1857, while two of his brothers lived the rest of their lives with a memory of their presence on those bloody fields. George Hawley certainly participated, perhaps using John's revolver. John D. Lee's accusation that John Hawley was at the massacre is the only one we have, and it is unsupported by other statements. Uncle Billy Young (a distant Hawley relative by marriage and who had been on or near the killing ground) warned John to be quiet about the massacre, or he would be put out of the way. The facts give Hawley the benefit of the doubt, but new evidence could alter that verdict.

Hawley's story trails the western frontier and backcountry; he was a true believer in search of the right path and legitimate authority of the Mormon restoration. Priscilla Hawley Young, one of John's sisters, wrote in her ninety-third year, bearing witness to her brother's as well as her own struggle: "[A]dmonish both the young and old to study the history of the struggles of the early church to establish the truths of this religion. Such study will give us courage to battle with the problems of today." Priscilla and John's narratives can verify how their struggles gave purpose to their lives and validated for them "the truths of this [their] religion."[1]

Hawley encompasses his encounters with man and nature among the various offshoots of the Mormon diaspora. Diverse expressions of the nineteenth-century Mormon Restoration created the track of Hawley's journey. From 1837 on, he followed its sinuous paths until his death seventy-two years later. Either as an associate or as a member, Hawley affiliated with the Church of Jesus Christ of Latter-day Saints (LDS) until the murder of its founder, Joseph Smith. He then was an associate or supporter of Brigham Young's church in the west (Brighamites); Lyman Wight's in Wisconsin Territory and the Republic then State of Texas (Wightites); as a missionary to and later as a potential convert of James J. Strang's church (Strangites); and, finally, in the end, a member the Reorganized Church of Jesus Christ of Latter Day Saints (RLDS or Josephites), now known as the Community of Christ. I use these various parenthetical terms neutrally for identification, although members of the various denominations have used them derisively at times to refer to the other sects.[2]

---

1. John Hawley, "Autobiography of John Hawley," 13. Priscilla Hawley Young, Statement, 1923.

2. The official name of the Church assigned by Joseph Smith in 1838 was the "Church of Jesus Christ of Latter Day Saints." The hyphenated "Latter-day Saints" was later adopted by those who followed Brigham Young but not by other churches that descended from Joseph Smith such as the "Reorganized Church of Jesus Christ of Latter Day Saints." This writing will prefer the nomenclature

The first two chapters of this biography, from 1826 to 1854, focus on John Hawley's experiences in Illinois, Missouri, Wisconsin, and Texas, with the Restoration as the stage to his story.[3] America's antebellum frontier and backcountry fashioned young Hawley's life from birth in Illinois (1826) onward. John Hawley's parents converted to the LDS Church in 1833 and always followed its founder, prophet, and president: Joseph Smith Jr. They endured the driving of their people in Missouri. There John was baptized and confirmed. The Hawleys later moved to Montrose, Iowa, across the Mississippi River from Nauvoo. The family joined Lyman Wight and the Black Pine Mission in the wilds of Wisconsin Territory (1843); there John Hawley and his brothers learned the logging, milling, and woodworking industries. The Mormon millers rafted the timber down the Mississippi for the Nauvoo Temple and Nauvoo House.

After Joseph Smith's death, Hawley family members developed a dislike and distrust of Brigham Young as he and the Quorum of Twelve Apostles succeeded to the leadership of the major body of Mormonism. The Hawleys and many of their neighbors followed Apostle Lyman Wight's exodus to Texas in 1845, whereas Brigham Young and his fellow apostles fashioned in the Rocky Mountains a theocratic, millenarian, polygamous Kingdom of God as they awaited the imminent coming of Jesus Christ. Some of Wight's colony, including most of the Hawley family, joined the LDS church in Utah Territory.

John Hawley stated that he believed Joseph Smith was the fount and founder of polygamy yet would qualify that statement later that he first became aware of plural marriage among the Wightites. As a young man, he courted a young woman without being aware that she was the plural spouse of another colony member. One of his sisters married Wight as a

---

contemporary to John Hawley: "Church of Jesus Christ of Latter Day Saints," "Latter Day Saint," or "Saint."

3. For a fuller narrative of Wight and his colony, in which Hawley participated as a teenager and as a valued adult member, see Melvin C. Johnson, *Polygamy on the Pedernales: Lyman Wight's Mormon Villages in Antebellum Texas, 1845–1858*; Melvin C. Johnson, "'So We Built a Good Little Temple to Worship In': Mormonism on the Pedernales Texas, 1847–1851"; Melvin C. Johnson, "Wightites in Wisconsin: The Formation of a Dissenting Latter Day Community (1842–1845)"; Melvin C. Johnson, "The Mormon Cowboys of Bandera County and the Texas Hill Country"; Melvin C. Johnson, "Bishop George Miller: A Latter Day High Priest and Prince on the High Plains"; and Melvin C. Johnson, "John Hawley, Mormon Ulysses: His LDS Mission To Iowa And Eventual RLDS Conversion."

plural wife. The Wight colony settled in four western Texas counties and built the villages of Zodiac, Mormon Mill, Medina, and Bandera. John married Harriet Hobart, who later deserted him. Then he married his true love, Sylvia Johnson, a member of the George Miller Company that had trekked to Zodiac from the Missouri River. Hawley traveled to East Texas and along the Missouri River on Wightite missions to other Latter-day Saints and Strangites, guiding new immigrants of the William Smith-Lyman Wight church from Galveston to Zodiac.

The Wightite community at Zodiac, Texas, built the first Latter Day temple west of the Mississippi. John recorded that "Lyman told us we must build a house for to attend to the baptism for the dead and the ordinance of washing of feet and a general endowment in the wilderness. So, we . . . built a good little Temple to worship in."[4] John Hawley received his endowments and was sealed to Sylvia Johnson for time and eternity on the second floor of the large, two-story log building. He also officiated as proxy baptisms for the dead. More than forty years later, in a witness deposition in The Temple Lot case and elsewhere, he compared the Zodiac temple ritual and regalia with the ceremonies of the Endowment House in Salt Lake City. His commentary adds insight about the LDS first and second anointings in territorial Utah.[5]

The Wightite Colony was wracked with schisms in 1853 and 1854, so by the end of the troubles, Patriarch Pierce Hawley, John's father, with most of the family, excepting son Aaron and his family who remained with Wight, moved north of the Red River into the Indian Nations. The Strangite and LDS missionaries in the Territory competed for converts among the former Wightites. Many joined the LDS Church. The Hawley families traveled to Utah Territory in 1856, but Pierce Hawley and his wife would

---

4. Hawley, "Autobiography," 7.

5. Richard E. Bennett, in his Presidential Address at the San Antonio Mormon History Conference (2014), stated that "Melvin C. Johnson in his fine study *Polygamy on the Pedernales* offers convincing evidence that Lyman Wight's Zodiac Community near San Antonio, Texas, completed a two-story log temple in February 1849. Ordinances performed in the Zodiac temple from 1849 to 1851 included baptisms for the dead, washing of feet, a general endowment, adoption, and the marriage sealing of men and women for time and eternity. Wight believed that all ordinances performed in the Nauvoo Temple after Joseph Smith's death were unauthorized and that he, 'not Brigham Young, was the Lord's appointed messenger' and that his temple at Zodiac was the only 'acceptable' place for such ordinances.'" Richard E. Bennett, "'The Upper Room': The Nature and Development of Latter-Day Saint Temple Work, 1846–55," 5.

not join his sons' families. He held his grudge against Brigham Young for taking his property in Lee County, Iowa, and depriving the Wight Colony of the steamer Maid of Iowa. He believed that the sons of Joseph Smith Jr. were the patrilineal leaders of the Restoration church and rejected the conferred authority claims of the LDS Church. When Jacob Croft, the Hawleys' wagon train captain to Utah, wrote and asked the elderly Hawley to reconsider and join them, Pierce Hawley replied that the Utah faction had no authority and that Brigham Young was a pretender and an imposter. Pierce Hawley counseled all to wait "till the Lord raises up the man to lead us to sion [sic]."[6] Hawley died two years later in the Indian nations.

The members of the Croft Company moved out in the last week of June 1856. The Hawleys, without incident, arrived in Salt Lake City and were rebaptized and tithed, deeding over their excess property for consecration. They moved on to Bingham Fort in Weber County but were not destined to stay. Brigham Young, aware that many of the Company had proven frontier experience, called John Hawley, George Hawley, and some of their relatives the next spring to Washington County in southern Utah.

The atrocity of the Mountain Meadows Massacre caught up to John, George, and William Hawley, as well as others of their Texas companions. In September 1857 Mormon militia members, many dressed in feathers and paint, aided by a few local Native American freebooters, destroyed a wagon train a few miles north of Pine Valley. The killers then butchered 120 of the California-bound immigrants, many of whom had surrendered. John Hawley angrily denounced the killings of those who had surrendered to the militia under the protection of local religious and military leaders. Hawley's LDS opponents in Washington Ward wanted to "use him up" and plotted to kill him until an express rider from Brigham Young arrived, too late with instructions to let the wagon train pass unmolested, but in time to save John's life.[7]

The Hawleys and other Texans in 1858 joined Mormon settlers at the lumbering and milling community in Pine Valley, a day's ride west of Cedar City, Utah. John was among the first settlers, served as Presiding Elder, and was a primary mover in that most beautiful location in Utah's Dixie. Pine Valley possesses the oldest standing LDS chapel in Utah and produced

---

6. Pierce Hawley, Letter to Jacob Croft, June 6, 1856; Elsie Hawley Platt and Robert Hawley, *House of Hawley*, 49; Hawley, "Autobiography," 13.

7. Will Bagley, *Blood of the Prophets: Brigham Young and the Massacre at Mountain Meadows*; Juanita Brooks, *The Mountain Meadows Massacre*; Ronald W. Walker, Richard E. Turley Jr., and Glen M. Leonard, *Massacre at Mountain Meadows*.

the major pipes for the magnificent organ of the Salt Lake Tabernacle. The Utah leadership sent John Hawley on a mission in 1868 to Iowa to convert his RLDS relatives, but he ended up eventually a convert to the Reorganization. Before leaving Pine Valley, he wrote to RLDS President Joseph Smith III in June 1870 that he enjoyed defending "the Book of Mormon, and Covenants, and the history of your father, as well as the Bible." He condemned LDS polygamy, being perplexed exceedingly for twenty-five years by it. He also cast aside Brigham Young's Adam-as-God teachings. John and George Hawley's families were baptized members of the RLDS church and left Utah to join friends and relatives in Iowa. This was the last conversion for John Hawley. He remained an active RLDS elder, high priest, and missionary until his death in 1909.

John Hawley's search for the authentic Restoration finally ended with the RLDS Church. The histories of Pine Valley generally ignore the Hawleys, while he and his brothers still figure in their roles at Mountain Meadows. This book of John Hawley's faith odyssey through the American West concentrates primarily on his life to the age of forty-four. He would yet live another thirty-nine years, more than half of his adult life, active in the service of RLDS Mormonism.

The historian Judy Nolte Lensink offers a cautionary note on the importance of heritage: "If we kill off the sound of our ancestors, the major portion of us, all that tis past is . . . lost and we come historically and spiritually thin, a mere shadow of who we were, on the earth."[8] This narrative of John Hawley is an attempt to catch his sound and tone and voice, and to reveal his humanity as he journeys the West in search of an authentic Mormon faith.

---

8. Judy Nolte Lensink and Christine M. Kirkham, "'My Only Confidant' –The Life and Diary of Emily Hawley Gillespie," 289.

CHAPTER 1

On The Borderlands of America

1826 to 1842

"He was without arms but the Lord helped him out and let me bare testimony That he is a sure and true helper in time of need and we always knew help from him."

Millions of Americans in the North American borderlands and backcountry mirrored the lives of John Hawley and his family. Joseph Hawley, an ancestor of John Pierce Hawley, came to North America in 1632 and eventually established his family in Connecticut in 1639. The first two generations became prosperous and well-known landholders, town officers, and members of the legislature from the areas of Stratford and Bridgeport.[1] Several generations later, Major Aaron Hawley (born in 1732), a War of Independence veteran, traveled north on the Hudson River and settled to the east on Long Bay, in Vermont. The land was deeded to Gideon, the Major's son. Gideon Hawley and wife Lavinia Darrough moved to Ferrisburgh Township, Addison County, Vermont. There they raised five sons and three daughters, including the third son, Pierce Hawley, father of John Pierce Hawley.[2]

Pierce Hawley's early history is incomplete. He was born on November 14, 1788, at Vergennes, Addison County, Vermont. Like many Hawley men, he grew "well proportioned" to about six-foot-tall, "with light hair, hazel eyes," and was "energetic and quick in his movements." Pierce and his brother Gideon joined the Free Masons in 1811. Pierce wrote some years later to a granddaughter that in 1845 Lavinia, his mother, and her great-grandmother, died aboard the "Gen Brooks" as the followers of Lyman Wight steamed upriver to Wisconsin Territory for the winter. She was buried in accordance with Masonic rites.[3]

---

1. Laurel Hawley Stubblefield, *Pierce Hawley 1788–1858: A History of His Family and Their Conversion to The Church of Jesus Christ of Latter-Day Saints*, 2–3.
2. Elsie Hawley Platt and Robert Hawley, *House of Hawley*, 26.
3. Stubblefield, *Pierce Hawley*, 4; Platt and Hawley, *House of Hawley*, 40; "Pearce Hawley took Freeman's oath, Mar. 22, 1811," Ferrisburgh Town Clerk's Office, Book No. 1:76.

Major Aaron Hawley and his sons, Isaac and Pierce, a lieutenant and sergeant, respectively, served in the War of 1812 as construction troops in the campaign at Plattsburg in 1814. They dug trenches, built fortifications, and improved firing lines and trajectories. Aaron's father died shortly after the campaign, widowing Lavinia. His death released his sons to seek bounty lands in Illinois, Michigan, and Arkansas awarded to soldiers. Between 1818 and 1820, several of Gideon's sons and two of their sisters with their mother, Lavinia, emigrated to the Illinois frontier with several neighbor families. The Census of 1820 locates Pierce Hawley living near the Wabash River's junction with the Ohio River in White County.[4]

Sarah Schroeder, born in Knox County, Tennessee, on June 3, 1800, married Pierce Hawley on July 4, 1822. Pierce apparently had a daughter named Caroline from an early relationship, whether in marriage or out of wedlock. The child remained with her father. Little is known about Sarah Schroeder Hawley, the family matriarch. In fact, Hawley family lore from women is very limited. Capturing the life and thought of nineteenth-century American women remains problematic for twenty-first-century writers. Such history before the Civil War, particularly in the American West, is difficult to recreate. Although historians and writers continue to unearth a treasure trove of women's diaries of their journeys into the West, the adventures, joys, and sorrows of the Hawley women are viewed distortedly through the prisms of their men's memories and writings. Henry Adams's prescient remark, recorded by Judy Lensink in a biography of a nineteenth-century Hawley woman, reminds the reader that "the woman who is known only through a man is known wrong." Sources from Hawley women in this book are admittedly limited. However, even though they seem trapped "in purity, piety, domesticity, and submissiveness," as I report them through the available writings of masculine impressions, one always should remember Lensink's words, "that they were creative actors who defined domestic roles to empower their lives." Such sentiment excellently frames the American Mormon woman and her role in the nineteenth-century West.[5]

Pierce and several of his brothers came to own land near present-day Peoria in Tazewell County. The small Hawley cemetery there, now over-

---

4. Stubblefield, *Pierce Hawley*, 4–5; Platt and Hawley, *House of Hawley*, 29, 33, 37, 39–40; "United States Census, 1820."

5. Emily Hawley Gillespie, *'A Secret to Be Buried': The Diary and Life of Emily Hawley Gillespie, 1858–1888*, quoted from Henry Adams, *The Education of Henry Adams*, 353.

grown and vandalized, contains only six graves, including that of Gideon Hawley, a younger brother of Pierce.[6] Gideon operated a hotel and tavern in the village of Pekin using the first liquor license purchased in Tazewell County. Hawleys were living in the Peoria area in 1830 and for many years after. Among Pierce's eleven children, many of his oldest were born in the area. They were described as typically "tall and well formed. . . . Their general color was about the same, black or brown hair, blue or grey eyes. . . . Family ties were said to be strong, the women prolific and love of off-spring apparent."[7] Elsie Hawley Piatt, one of Pierce Hawley's nieces, described Pierce's children as literate, although lacking formal schooling. She believed them to have a "more serious view of life, and to be more religious and more clannish than their cousins." John and his siblings, like many in the backcountry, could have raised the Bible and proudly said, "God taught me how to read and write." John Pierce Hawley modeled his cousin's description of the family members of his generation.[8]

John's autobiography states he was born on March 4, 1826. He was one of the first white children born in Tazewell County, close by the "Fox River." He may have confused the Illinois River for the Fox, or as it is known, "the Little Wabash River" to the south and east of the county. The Native Americans then local to the region were of the Sauk and Fox tribal clans. White settlers were not numerous.[9]

The Hawley family history was associated with first peoples for years. While in Illinois, the Hawleys' "close relationship with the local Indians" benefitted the family in times good and bad. For example, a daughter of Priscilla Hawley Young, John's sister, wrote a letter that indicated the Hawleys were at ease with Native Americans, which seemed a thread knitted throughout Pierce's lifetime. Dora Young, Priscilla's daughter, "recalled hearing grandmother, Sarah, tell how the Indians would always stop by their home, no matter where they were living and often would spread out blankets and spend the night. She said, 'Grandmother said they were often

---

6. Stubblefield, *Pierce Hawley*, 5.

7. Pierce Hawley, citing "1830 United States Federal Census," 303; Platt and Hawley, *House of Hawley*, 4.

8. Stubblefield, *Pierce Hawley*, 8–9.

9. John Hawley, "Autobiography of John Hawley," 1; *The Reorganized Church of Jesus Christ of Latter Day Saints, Complainant, Vs. the Church of Christ at Independence, Missouri: Richard Hill, Trustee; Richard Hill, Mrs. E. Hill, C.A. Hall [and Others] ... as Members of and Doing Business Under the Name of The Church of Christ, at Independence*, 451, hereafter cited as Temple Lot Case.

so thick on her floor that she had to be careful not to tread on them.'"[10] John recorded in his autobiography that the women (he referred to them as "squaws," a term that in 1885 did not always express the depth of opprobrium it does today), often carried him "off to their wigwams" for the day and fed him at the breast. The record of John's adult life, however, reveals no personal or family closeness with Native Americans.[11]

Pierce Hawley had moved his family by 1832 thirty-eight miles west of Chicago in DuPage County. The family subsisted by farming, and Pierce, being an exhorter in the Methodist Church,[12] served as an American Indian missionary. Their Native American friends protected the Hawley family, keeping them "aware of any imminent danger to the homestead or stock" whenever Pierce needed to travel to the mill grain eighty miles away.[13] The Black Hawk War of 1832 led to hardship and tragedy for the Hawley family as well as others in Illinois. Not all the American Indians had considered the Hawleys friendly, thinking the white "strangers" posed a deadly threat. The family "forted with the other citizens" in Chicago for the duration of the short war. Lack of sufficient vegetables and milk caused hardship for the children. John wrote that he came, "near dying for want of milk and vegetables. But I lived there and when we got back to the farm and had plenty of milk and butter, I got well." Pierce Hawley escaped death through the help of friendly American Indians, but his brother Aaron did not survive a skirmish. The rumors abounded: the body was never found, or he was taken as prisoner and was tormented "by fire for three days and then scalped." Aaron's death at their hands is not in question.[14]

The Hawleys during this period were aware of Joseph Smith Jr., who founded the new Latter Day Saint religion based on the visitations of angelic messengers and golden plates that told of Jewish immigration to the Americas about 600 BCE. The family may have heard the preaching of Joseph Smith's followers as early as 1831. Charles C. Rich wrote that Lyman Wight and John Corrill were missionaries active in the area as early

---

10. Dora Young to Elsie Piatt, quoted in Platt and Hawley, *House of Hawley*, 48; Stubblefield, *Pierce Hawley*, 8–9.

11. Hawley, "Autobiography," 1.

12. For the relationship and parallels of Mormonism and Methodism during the era, see Christopher C. Jones, "The Power and Form of Godliness: Methodist Conversion Narratives and Joseph Smith's First Vision," 88–114.

13. Hawley, "Autobiography," 1; Stubblefield, *Pierce Hawley*, 9.

14. Platt and Hawley, *House of Hawley,* 51–52; Hawley, "Autobiography," 1; Stubblefield, *Pierce Hawley*, 9.

as that year. Others in the area included the families of Morris Phelps, William O. Clark, Hosea Stout, and Charles C. Rich.[15] Pierce Hawley was baptized by Elder James Emmett in the winter of 1833–1834. According to John Hawley, Mother Sarah thought that Pierce "had almost committed the unpardonable sin in leaving the Methodist Church and joining the Mormon Church, as they was both good Methodist members." Within a short time "Mother soon got over this bad feeling and united with the same church and was one with her husband in faith and doctrine." Pierce and Sarah would be courted by various sects of the Restoration over the years and put their faith in the Book of Mormon and the prophetic calling of Joseph Smith Jr. for the remainder of their lives.[16]

One Detroit newspaper many years later could still capture the colorful spirit and thunder of those who were caught up in the early Latter Day Restoration: In part, it read,

> When in 1830 Joseph Smith appeared with his revelations this country was awaiting religious conquest. It was at once hungry and skeptical. The soil was virgin. Joseph Smith appeared to the waiting people with a magic sword for spiritual conquest. He had the records of an early people of God who had ruled upon this continent, and had shared the enlightenments and covenants of Israel. He preached the doctrines of the orthodox faith, and with them went a dream of reconstructing a church of the apostolic age. He broadened the horizon and gave hope and comfort. But for the untimely death of the founder the Mormon church might have become greater.[17]

The wife of William C. Hawley, a cousin to John, wrote that her husband thought Pierce was obsessively dedicated to Latter-day Saint doctrines. According William, Pierce was so caught up in the faith that even after failing "all night trying to persuade" his brothers and their families to join the Latter Day Saint cause, he persisted by sending letters "in the same vein" to his brother Gideon.[18]

The Hawley family wanted to join with their co-religionists in Jackson County, Missouri. After selling the farm and starting the move, Pierce received reports that the Saints were being driven by the southern "old settlers" out of Jackson County, Missouri. He stopped in Sangamon County, Illinois, and bought a farm to wait for more friendly events.[19] The Saints

---

15. Stubblefield, *Pierce Hawley*, 10.
16. Hawley, "Autobiography," 2.
17. Quoted in Platt and Hawley, *House of Hawley*, 41.
18. Mrs. Wm. C. Hawley, quoted in Platt and Hawley, *House of Hawley*, 46.
19. Hawley, "Autobiography," 2.

had been quarreling with their Missouri neighbors for two years, and, at times, violence erupted. The Latter Day Saint printing press was wrecked, and homes burned in Jackson County as zealous Saints fought with equally staunch Missourians who contended against "the Lord's favored people," as many Latter Day Saint homesteaders thought of themselves. The Saints' lack of numbers and their weakness in weaponry resulted in their religious cleansing and removal from Jackson County into Caldwell County.

Once matters seemed to have quieted, the Hawley family moved to Missouri in 1836. There they would have heard the folk stories of the warrior high priest, Lyman Wight, who never forgot being forced to give up his own and his friends' properties. The Hawleys would discover firsthand why one Church newspaper decades later described this indomitable warrior chieftain as "a dread to his enemies and a terror to evil doers." The Hawleys would follow Lyman Wight's leadership in Wisconsin Territory and Texas for ten years.[20]

The Hawleys rented a farm. During 1836, the two older children, Mary and George, were baptized into the Church by Morris Phelps. The next year, William O. Clark baptized John, Aaron, and William in Sugar Creek. Almost fifty years later, John wrote: "Here I became a member of the kingdom of God and . . . covenanted with the church and had to keep the commandments of heaven and live to the best of my ability and understanding of the doctrine of Christ and then I bowed before God in secret with more faith than before to ask for blessings at his hand. Let me say right here, I found great help and was comforted many times."[21] John, retrospectively, was describing the keys for determining religious truth that would shape him as a Latter Day Saint in the coming decades.

First, to covenant with the church.
Second, to keep heaven's commandments.
Third, to live as a good person.
Fourth, to understand Christ's doctrines.
Five, to bow secretly to God in faith and ask for blessings.

In the latter part of 1838, incremental violence blazed in northwest Missouri. Ferocity characterized the behavior of both sides. According to

---

20. Hawley, 2; Orange Lysander Wight, "Recollections of Orange L. Wight, Son of Lyman Wight," 7; Nathan Tanner Porter, "Reminiscences," 69; *Latter-Day Saints' Millennial Star*, July 22, 1865, 455; Kenneth H. Winn, *Exiles in a Land of Liberty: Mormons in America, 1830–1846*, 91–92; Melvin C. Johnson, *Polygamy on the Pedernales*, 11–12.

21. Hawley, "Autobiography," 2.

noted historian Stephen C. Lesueur,[22] each side deserved culpability for the war. Latter Day Saint and "old settler" local militia units mobilized, claiming legitimacy to restore order and liberty while framing their enemies as guerillas and vigilantes. Early Saint victories were followed by defeats. The Latter Day Saints were eventually driven from the state. Two days after Lieutenant Governor Lilburn W. Boggs issued a declaration ordering the Saints to flee the state or be "exterminated," Missouri militia units overran the Latter Day Saint hamlet of Haun's Mill: more than a dozen children and women were wounded while eighteen men and boys were systematically slaughtered and then mutilated, two of whom were no older than ten.[23]

The Latter Day Saint leadership surrendered to the state militia units led by General Samuel D. Lucas. Initially, that seemed a disastrous decision, because the general issued orders for the summary execution of Joseph Smith and others, including Lyman Wight. Offered the chance to save his life if he turned evidence against the Smiths over to the state, Wight supposedly ripped his shirt and baring his breast snarled, "Shoot and be damned." The officer in charge of the prisoners, General Alexander Doniphan, refused to carry out orders he believed to be a war crime. Doniphan's commanding officer, considering Doniphan's threats to hold him accountable for summary executions, backed down. Joseph Smith and six others were jailed for some time before escaping the following year to rejoin the Saints in Illinois.[24]

---

22. For the events of the civil war in Missouri during 1838–1839, see Stephen C. LeSueur, *The 1838 Mormon War in Missouri*; John Portineu Greene, *Facts Relative to the Expulsion of the Mormons*, 20–21; Linda King Newell and Valeen Tippets Avery, *Mormon Enigma: Emma Hale Smith, 2nd ed.*, 73; Sampson Avard, Testimony of Samson, Avard; Stephen C. LeSueur, "The Danites Reconsidered: Were They Vigilantes or Just the Mormons' Version of the Elks Club?" 48, 50; Dean C. Jessee and David J. Whittaker, "The Last Months of Mormonism in Missouri: The Albert Perry Rockwood Journal," 5–41. For a recent perspective of the original Twelve Apostles and their roles in the war crisis and aftermath, see William Shepard and H. Michael Marquardt, *Lost Apostles: Forgotten Members of Mormonism's Original Quorum of Twelve*.

23. See John Doyle Lee, *Confessions of John D. Lee*; John Corrill, *A Brief History of the Church of Christ of Latter-Day Saints (Commonly Called Mormons)*, 27–29; William Swartzell, *Mormonism Exposed, Being a Journal of Residence in Missouri from the 28th of May to the 20th of August, 1838*, 13, 17, 32.

24. Quoted in D. Michael Quinn, *The Mormon Hierarchy: Origins of Power*, 99; Roger D. Launius, *Alexander William Doniphan: Portrait of a Missouri Moderate*, 63–64; *Latter-Day Saints' Millennial Star*, July 29, 1865, 471; Joseph

The Hawley family was tossed back and forth in the Missouri conflict as were thousands of their co-religionists. Pierce Hawley, while living in Ray County, had purchased land to the east in DeWitt, Carroll County. He fled for his life into Caldwell County,[25] telling his loved ones, "I have got to go or I am likely to be killed." Local Missourians attended a meeting in DeWitt in the latter part of July, giving the religionists until August 7, 1838, to leave the county. Pierce fell into the hands of his enemies on at least two occasions, and he had to hide out often in fear for his life. On August 19, Pierce was sent by the Missourians, according to John Murdock, "to Dewitt apparently frightened & said he had been a prisoner all night by a mob of 60 or 70 who were within 4 miles of town & would be upon us in two hours & his orders was to be out of town in two hours."[26]

Later that fall, Pierce Hawley tried to reach Far West. Avoiding a Missouri bivouac at Crooked River, he forded seven miles upstream. He was discovered, however, by a militia patrol, and putting "spurs to his horse . . . landed safe in Far West." John Hawley wrote that members of the mob told him and other family members they shot inaccurately at Pierce because their arms trembled. John believed that "the Lord fought his battle and by the power of God he was rescued from his enemies. He was without arms but the Lord helped him out and let me bare testimony that he is a sure and true helper in time of need and we always knew help from him."[27]

The Hawley children had to carry burdens that would have tormented adults. The Missourians continued to trouble the family in their father's absence. The older sister, Mary, despite "being very athletic and of a masculine nature and resolute in spirit," was unable to prevent two men from driving off the sheep. The children conspired to save the family cattle by trailing them about sixty miles to Alpheus Cutler's place in Ray County. Hawley believed Cutler had saved his property by standing neutral in the struggles and considered him a poor Latter Day Saint for doing so.[28] Missouri out-

---

Smith III, *Saints' Herald (True Latter Day Saints' Herald)*, July 15, 1879; also in Joseph Smith III, "Statements of Joseph Smith," 414, 418.

25. Stubblefield, *Pierce Hawley*, 16.

26. Clark V. Johnson, ed., *Mormon Redress Petitions: Documents of the 1833–1838 Missouri Conflict*, 211–305; Stubblefield, *Pierce Hawley*, 16.

27. Hawley, "Autobiography," 2.

28. Hawley's later memories of these events were influenced by age and the hardships inflicted on a twelve-year-old boy. Alpheus Cutler was then and later a noted Latter-day Saint of good standing. Although the Cutler families were neither Danites nor in the Mormon militias serving at Far West, they

riders caught up with George, John, and Aaron Hawley, ages about fourteen to eleven, along with the cattle several miles from Richmond. George and John lied and said they were not Mormons when threatened. Young Aaron was so scared that he told the truth. The Missourians, heading away from Richmond, tried to send word to not let the cattle through town. Dusk had fallen by then, and the cattle had scattered in the woods. The boys managed to gather their herd, move the cattle around the town during the night and trailed on. When stopped later by a militia unit, John wrote, "We had no trouble when we told the truth and let me now say that [earlier] was the first time in my life that I denied being a Mormon and unto date the last time." The boys made it safely to Cutler's farm, but by the time they returned home they had only five cows left.[29]

The attacks continued. Enemies kept the Hawley farm in Ray County under watch, hoping to kill Pierce Hawley if he visited his family. John wrote that his mother's prayers and his father's good sense "in not coming home even after peace was declared saved his life." The family still lost the sheep, the hogs, a wagon, and a carriage with the harness. They possessed some cattle and their clothes.[30] The family moved out of Ray County to Log Creek in Caldwell County. The troubles in Missouri fused the sacred with the temporal in John's mind. This was reinforced during a time of illness after the family arrived in Caldwell County. He wrote that he "was taken very sick and the ordinance of laying on of hands was attended to by William O. Clark and I was healed immediately. Mother says I was the first one of the family that was administered to for being sick."[31] At

---

did not escape loss. In October 1838, Missourians occupied the Cutler farm, appropriated hay for their horses, killed cattle for food, forced the Cutler women to cook for the officers, and shot up the mill. Sylvia Cutler Webb, quoted in Rupert J. Fletcher and Daisy Whiting Fletcher, *Alpheus Cutler and the Church of Jesus Christ*, 24. Some of the Cutlers were accosted by the Missourians after the Battle of Crooked River. Their wagons were ransacked. The Missouri leaders told the women they would not be touched but would not vouch for the men's safety, as noted in Emma L. Anderson, "An Incident of the Past," 315–16. Danny L. Jorgensen, in his forthcoming biography on Alpheus Cutler, informed me that the "Cutler families fled Missouri with other Saints; and, as is well known, Cutler later returned with the apostles to Far West where he blessed the temple site—marking his ascendancy to the top of the Nauvoo Mormon hierarchy." Danny L. Jorgensen email, February 21, 2018.

29. Hawley, "Autobiography," 2–3.
30. Hawley, 3–4.
31. Hawley, 3–4.

various times, John would rely on the laying of hands and baptism for the restoration of health.

The time for harvest had come, but the family corn was in Ray County, and Pierce Hawley could not go without jeopardizing his life. Yet again, George and John shouldered adult responsibility and went with a hired man to gather the corn. Enemies of the Latter Day Saints took the three prisoners at the farm, and although the hired man and the boys truthfully told their captors the man was not a Mormon,

> They swore he was and for us to shut up or they would whip us. With all our pleading it made them the more fierce. They tied his hands together and then they welted his back. When they would strike twice in one place, the blood would fly and they whipped him unmercifully and they would not let up till they saw he was about to faint away for loss of blood and then left the field. George and I got him on a load of corn and we had to drive about 6 miles before we dare stop to have his wounds dressed.

The man nearly died and took an oath to avenge his wounds on his enemies. Very little of the harvest was taken to Caldwell County.[32]

The remainder of their time in Missouri played out at the end and beginning of 1838–1839 as the Saints were driven from pillar to post and then, finally, from the state. John recorded that the "treaty of peace had to be complied with and that was to leave the state or be exterminated, this being the governor's orders."[33] By the beginning of January 1839, the Saints understood they had no choice but to leave. Joseph Smith and other leaders were still in jail. A meeting of Church leaders on January 26 ended with a proposal drafted to direct the exodus from Missouri. More than two hundred men and women alike, including Pierce Hawley, agreed to aid one another in the removal, vowing not to abandon the worthy poor. They gave permission to dispose of their property for "moving the poor and destitute." Those Saints, already safely in Illinois, continued their effort to bring their poor and lame and ill out of the land of their enemies to a place of refuge.[34]

Several months later, Pierce Hawley swore a declaration of facts before C. M. Woods in Adams County, Illinois, which listed his losses.[35] No evidence exists that he received compensation. "Pierce Hawley left

---

32. Hawley, 4.
33. Hawley, 4.
34. Stubblefield, *Pierce Hawley*, 18.
35. Sworn to before C. M. Woods, quoted in Stubblefield, 16–17.

Sangamon County Illinois to go to the State of Missouri on the 4 of Sept 1837 giving oath [in his own hand] that,

i left I went with 34 head of cattle 69 head of Sheap 6 hosses 3 waggons arived in colwell county on the 20 of November to high wal expences	$255.50
purchesed 30 acros of land and lost of laber and land	250.00
Moved to ray county to rent a farm the loss of the crop by being drove from the same	425.00
one man was whiped that i sent to gether my grane Sept 1838 i baught a lot in Duett for to move there but was prevented by the mob i was take a prisner and forced to moove then on the penalty of my life and had to loose my lot for i could not sel it the lot cost	100.00
Damage Sustained	100.00
Driven from ray county on the 24 of octtober by the mob to colwell count Damag for beng driveen with my wife and nine children	300.00
then haveing to leave the S[t]ate with my famaly in the wintir and the lose of propperty by suirepise by being compeld to sel my property at a redused prise	1,000.00
the mob stole 2 ho[r]ses one 3 hogs which was worth	350.00
the lose of time from the first of October 1838 to the first of may 1839 with my self and famaly	500.00
	$3280.5

The Hawleys and their neighbors trailed east in January 1839 across Missouri to a point on the western bank of the Mississippi River facing Quincy in Illinois. Ice flows prevented crossing. "The River was lined with Saints, all hungry," John Hawley remembered, and "the Lord sent a lazy catfish ashore by the ice. Father helped and I remember old Father Gifford and his large family of 14 children got the head for his share. It made a good soup for all the family." John remembered those times of forced flight when the Latter Day Saints "all lived on one another and would willingly divide all we had." The trials of Missouri and persecution emotionally bound the fleeing religionists, John thought, "together in love for one another" as well as a "gospel or the rock, whichever we choose to call it, either suits me." He wrote at Dow City, Iowa, more than fifty years later, "I wish the rock bound us as close together now as it did then. Now every man and woman must stand or fall for themselves."[36] The Hawleys crossed over the icy Mississippi River in January 1839. They worked for a couple of weeks in the small village of Tipton. Needing the company of their co-religionists, Pierce apprenticed John to a "taylor" and moved the family back to Quincy. John, not yet thirteen, was homesick and "the anxiety of seeing" his mother, even though the tailor held John's wages, drove him to walk the forty miles in search of his family. Slightly more than a week later, John showed up at the Methodist campgrounds where his relatives with other Latter Day Saint families had sought shelter as refugees. The family farmed, probably as laborers, the rest of the year several miles from Quincy.

The family settled across the river from Nauvoo, about four miles west of Montrose, in Iowa Territory. Since Pierce Hawley was the first settler, the little outpost was called Hawley's Grove, later Ambrosia. The family continued farming for the next two years, then Pierce bought land closer to Montrose in a small hamlet named Zarahemla. Pierce and Sarah Hawley continued in their walk as faithful Latter Day Saints. They performed the ordinance of baptism for the family's dead relatives in the river. John Hawley, at Nauvoo, was rebaptized by Joseph Smith in the summer of 1842, and was ordained to the office of teacher by the prophet's uncle, John Smith, later that year at Ambrosia.[37]

The quiet hiatus was ending, though. John Hawley's religious strength and physical endurance would be tested during the coming thirteen years along the face of America's borderland, from the wilderness forests of Wisconsin Territory to the frontier of the Texas Hill Country to the Indian Nations north of the Red River.[38]

---

36. Johnson, *Polygamy on the Pedernales*, 19; Hawley, "Autobiography," 4.
37. Temple Lot Case, 451.
38. Hawley, "Autobiography," 5–6.

CHAPTER 2

Wisconsin Territory to the Republic of Texas

1843 to 1851

"A GRAND CONSPIRACY IS ABOUT BEING ENTERED INTO BETWEEN THE MORMONS AND INDIANS TO DESTROY ALL THE WHITE SETTLEMENTS ON THE FRONTIER."

John Hawley wrote only a few paragraphs about the family's brief stay in Wisconsin Territory. In his seventeenth and eighteenth years, he learned the arduous trades of logging and dressing timber, piloting lumber rafts down rivers, and, foreshadowing his later years, in woodworking and mill operations. The Black River mill village and logging fronts that were overseen by Lyman Wight covenanted to proselytize the indigenous peoples "till they was hunted from every nook and corner of the earth and we had preached the gospel to them." No records of successful conversion of any local American Indians exist. The Hawleys worked in Wisconsin from 1843 to the late spring of 1844 and then came down the Mississippi River to Nauvoo after news reached them of the death of Joseph Smith. Late in the summer of 1844, they returned to winter in Wisconsin as they prepared for a colony mission to the Republic of Texas.

The Hawley clan would follow Lyman Wight's leadership for a decade. The junior member of the Twelve, Wight had become a church member in 1831. After demonstrating gallant heroism in the Missouri-Mormon war and absolute loyalty to Joseph Smith, the religious warrior became a member of the Twelve (1841) and the Council of Fifty[1] (1844). Joseph Smith secretly directed the Fifty to locate a new place and remove the church membership beyond the borders of the United States. The Fifty were to secure a setting where the Saints could build Zion without inter-

---

1. For more on the Council of Fifty see Jedediah S. Rogers, ed., *The Council of Fifty: A Documentary History*; and Matthew J. Grow, Ronald K. Esplin, Mark Ashurst-McGee, Gerrit J. Dirkmaat, and Jeffrey D. Mahas, eds., *Council of Fifty, Minutes, March 1844–January 1846*.

ference from secular governments and await the anticipated coming of Jesus Christ.²

A dominant and proud personality, Wight was charismatic and inspirational. He had addiction problems in his adult life with excesses in alcohol in Wisconsin and opium later in Texas. Yet he inspired Latter Day Saint followers for more than twenty-five years—from Ohio to Missouri to Illinois to Wisconsin to Texas. I have elsewhere written, "To understand Wight is to understand that his *persona* characterized the dedication, the strength, and the personality of early Mormonism and its converts." Wight never wavered from his absolute belief that Joseph Smith was God's chosen messianic champion of the Latter Day Restoration. Wight believed in Smith's vision of Zion, a gathering place for the saved Latter Day believers in America where they would prepare for the quick arrival of Jesus Christ to reign in the final days.

Wight, known as "The Wild Ram of the Mountains,"³ believed in apostolic New Testament economic primitivism and tried to follow such in his communities. He and colleague Bishop George Miller organized a priesthood-directed common-stock economic order in the Black River Pine Company on the lines of earlier Rigdonite communities in Ohio, where all belongings and materials were held in common and at the direction of the elders. The antecedents can be traced to a group called "The Family" near Kirtland, Ohio. That communitarian group was informally part of Sydney Rigdon's religious offshoot of Campbellism.⁴

Alexander Campbell was the first major American religious leader to denounce as heterodoxy Joseph Smith and his new religion, polygamy,

---

2. John Hawley, "Autobiography of John Hawley," 5–6; Dennis Rowley, "The Mormon Experience in the Wisconsin Pineries, 1841–1845," 119–48; Melvin C. Johnson, *Polygamy on the Pedernales*, 22–38; David L. Clark, "Mormons of the Wisconsin Territory: 1835–1848," 57–85. Also see Melvin C. Johnson, "Wightites in Wisconsin," which narrates a history of LDS Apostle Lyman Wight and his lumber mission colony in Wisconsin that transformed into a dissident organization opposed to Brigham Young and the Twelve. The core of the Texas colony originated in this common-stock community at Mormon Coulee.

3. *New York Sun* (August 1845), in LDS Journal History of the Church, 45:6.

4. See Richard S. Van Wagoner, *Sidney Rigdon: A Portrait of Religious Excess*. Lyman Wight, George Miller, James Emmett, and Alpheus Cutler would organize such communities in what is now Wisconsin, Texas, South Dakota, Nebraska, Iowa, and Minnesota.

and religious common stock economic systems.⁵ Campbell's essay in his monthly *Millennial Harbinger*, published on February 7, 1831, chastised what he considered the heresies "that all christians should put their possessions into one common stock, and live together in that state of equality, which becomes members of the same family, and that polygamy was not incompatible with either the Old or New Testament." Campbell said nothing at the time about "The Family" in Ohio and its common-stock program because he did not know the members were being baptized into the Latter Day Saint church until it was too late.⁶

Historian Richard Van Wagoner has noted that Joseph Smith, in the same week that Campbell published his criticisms, had instructed his flock including the Rigdonites in "the more perfect law of the Lord" that was replacing the abandoned common-stock principles of "The Family."

> A week later, on 9 February 1831, Smith announced God's revealed 'Law of Consecration and Stewardship.' Members were advised that 'all things belong to the Lord' and were directed to deed all personal property to the bishop of the Church. The bishop then returned a 'stewardship' to each head of a household, who was expected to turn over any accrued surplus to the Church. Known as the 'Order of Enoch,' 'The Lord's Law,' and the 'United Order,' the Mormon Order of Stewardship was intended as a pattern of social and economic reorganization for all mankind.⁷

Wight and rest of "the Family" accepted Smith's changes. For whatever reasons, the Latter Day prophet had utterly precluded common stock principles from 1831 in Ohio as well as during the Missouri and the Nauvoo years. In one sermon in Nauvoo, he spent an hour preaching the common stock system was "folly [and that] each individual is his own steward over his property."⁸

---

5. See comparisons of LDS and Anabaptist theologies in Suzanne Heninger, "Building a New Jerusalem: Comparison of the Anabaptists in Münster with the Latter Day Saints in Missouri & Nauvoo."

6. Alexander Campbell, "Delusions," 86.

7. Richard S. Van Wagoner, "Mormon Polyandry in Nauvoo," 68; Joseph Smith et al., *History of the Church of Jesus Christ of Latter-day Saints*, 1:146–47, 6:37–38; Glen M. Leonard, *Nauvoo: A Place of Peace, A People of Promise*, 143. Leonard's is a generalized social examination of the development and communal story of the LDS Church at the LDS center place in the 1840s.

8. B. H. Roberts, *A Comprehensive History of the Church of Jesus Christ of Latter-day Saints: Century*, 1:146–47, 6:37–38.

Wight believed that the common-stock philosophy would sanctify his followers to become consecrated individuals and communal creations in the temporal Kingdom of God.[9] At the direction of Joseph Smith, Lyman Wight, George Miller, Peter Haws, and Alpheus Cutler had bought and begun operating sawmills in Wisconsin Territory in 1841. They overcame ongoing business problems and recouping initial losses while recruiting a dedicated community of workers and their families. Henry W. Miller (no relation to George Miller) was brought in to successfully direct the actual logging, milling, and rafting operations. Apostle Wight and Bishop George Miller[10] integrated the faith community of dispersed logging fronts and a small mill town into a devout common-stock wilderness community.

A record of the property of all families were drawn up so that "a general distrabution" could be made, wrote Allen Stout. Excess provisions, in theory, would be available from the community commissary for individual and family needs. Stout clearly approved of the system:

> We have gon in to the whole law of God on Black River that is every man has given a scedule of his property to the bishop and we have all things common according to the law in the book of covenants. . . . Every man his own goods to do what he pleases with. . . . The thing is we are all on an equality eve man fars alike labours alike eats drinks ware alike but at the same time he lives to himself and what he has he has to himself and at his own controll. . . . I have bin thus perticular because of the man falce reports gon out.

Stout encouraged volunteers to come to Black River if "they can go the caper of concecration and equality we wish you to come by all means." No slackers were welcome. "The law of black river is that he will not work shal not eat," Stout wrote.[11]

---

9. Johnson, *Polygamy on the Pedernales*, 3. For the development of the concept of an LDS nation, see David L. Bigler, *Forgotten Kingdom: The Mormon Theocracy in the American West, 1847–1896*.

10. For Miller's excellent first-hand (often self-laudatory) account of the impact of terrain and climate in the Wisconsin frontier pineries, see George Miller, "Correspondence of Bishop George Miller with the Northern Islander," 7–20.

11. Johnson, *Polygamy on the Pedernales*, 138. To understand the difficulty with which the millers and settlers created a community in a remote and forbidding environment, see Rowley, "The Mormon Experience in the Wisconsin Pineries," 133–34, 138–39; George Montague, "Reminiscences," 388–89; H. W. Mills, "De Tal Palo Astilla," 88–156; Johnson, *Polygamy on the Pedernales*, 27–28.

Black River and then Mormon Coulee's primitive living conditions in the terrible winters from 1842 to 1844–45 weeded the weak from the strong, presenting Wight with a dedicated group colony whose members by the end had little use for Brigham Young after the death of Joseph Smith. They believed Brigham Young had withheld their properties from them, including the steamship Maid of Iowa, when in fact Joseph Smith and George Miller were responsible for its sale.[12] Pierce Hawley and Phineas Bird became counselors to Bishop George Miller in Wisconsin, and all three would be leading members of the Texas colony. Other families included those of Spencer C. Smith and John F. Miller, a son of George Miller; both of whom had married daughters of Lyman Wight. Other families that went to Texas were the Gaylords, Curtises, Jenkins, and Monseers (Moncurs).[13]

Wisconsin years were tough for the settlers. Elmira Pond Miller (Henry Miller's spouse) was worried one winter when "the provisions gave out and we had only potatoes and salt for several weeks. . . . The baby was only fourteen months old, but when the flour came he could not wait for it to be baked, but wanted a piece of dough." A small boy, in another shanty, had been without bread for weeks and then joyfully discovered a biscuit in a rat's nest. He happily showed it to his mother. When she discovered its origin, she forbade him to eat it but then his flood of pitiful tears broke her resolve. Another man was spared from cooking putrid ox meat, dead several weeks, with the arrival of critically required provisions.[14]

Joseph Smith's approval for Wight's Texas colony arose from a quarrel between his buyers of indigenous timber with federal agents. Despite the terrible winter of 1843–44, northern mill operations had been productive. Then federal agents for Indian affairs obstructed Mormon negotiation for timber on native lands.[15] Communications within the Office of Indian Affairs, Iowa Superintendency, in the summer of 1843 disclosed

---

12. Donald L. Enders, "The Steamboat Maid of Iowa: Mormon Mistress of the Mississippi," 320–36.

13. Johnson, *Polygamy on the Pedernales*, 24–27; Susan Easton Black, comp., *Early Members of the Reorganized Church of Jesus Christ of Latter Day Saints*, 6:235; Toni R. Turk, "Mormons in Texas: The Lyman Wight Colony," 28–29, 76, 81; Rowley, "The Mormon Experience," 138.

14. Levi Lamoni Wight, "Autobiography of Levi Lamoni Wight," 259–99; Elmira Pond and Allen Stout, quoted in Rowley, "The Mormon Experience," 132–33, 139.

15. Johnson, *Polygamy on the Pedernales*, 28.

concerns of federal officers that Latter Day Saint influence on the Native Americans might lead to skullduggery against other whites on the frontier. Henry King had notified John Chambers in the OIA Iowa office that Joseph Smith and some indigenous leaders had met together in April. King wrote:

> What the result of this meeting has been I am unable to say, but it seems evident, from all I can learn, from leading men among the Mormons and from various other sources that a grand conspiracy is about being entered into between the Mormons and Indians to destroy all the white settlements on the frontier. The time fixed to carry this nefarious plot into execution is about the ripening of Indian corn – This may all be rumour, but I have deemed it too serious a rumour to be trifled with, and have therefore taken the liberty of troubling you with a statement of facts, that in the event of an outbreak we may not be wholly unprepared.[16]

The federal interference with the negotiations for native peoples' timber spurred the Black River leadership to action.

Lyman Wight, George Miller with his counselors Phineas Bird and Pierce Hawley, and clerk John Young petitioned Joseph Smith to remove their colony to the Republic of Texas. They pointed out as reasons to Smith the completion of the Black River Pine Mission and the latest federal interference. There, they wrote, the American government could not interfere "with a gathering place for their people."[17] The petition stirred Joseph Smith to move forward his plan to remove his people and the Church's theocratic rule beyond the reach of the United States. Smith's hopes for an autonomous religious nation frightened Illinois leaders and citizens as they had watched Smith fuse secular and ecclesiastical control at Nauvoo and, at the same time, repress legal opposition and subdue resistance. As other rumors swirled, including those about polygamy, Smith knew the Church had to move. Was Texas the answer?[18]

---

16. Henry King, letter to John Chambers, July 14, 1843.

17. Hawley, "Autobiography," 5; Mills, "De Tal Palo Astilla," 125–26, 129–30; Smith et al., *History of the Church*, 6:255–60; Johnson, *Polygamy on the Pedernales*, 28; Lyman Wight, *An Address by Way of an Abridged Account and Journal of My Life from February 1844 up to April 1848, with an Appeal to the Latter Day Saints*.

18. For political pressures on Smith and his responses, see Michael Van Wagenen, *The Texas Republic and the Mormon Kingdom of God*; Kenneth H. Winn, *Exiles in a Land of Liberty: Mormons in America, 1830–1846*; and Klaus J. Hansen, *Quest for Empire: The Political Kingdom of God and the Council of Fifty in Mormon History*.

Smith saw several opportunities in the Republic of Texas. If his presidential election campaign failed in 1844, the Saints could, as Smith proposed to Congress, raise an army to protect a Texas acquisition, or negotiate for the removal of the Church to Texas. Smith may have been considering the possibility of later overthrowing Texas power, creating a new nation, and negotiating with the Republic of Mexico. In March, the Fifty sent Lucien Woodworth to negotiate with President Sam Houston for moving the church membership to Texas. Woodworth returned on May 2 with the news that Houston was favorable but had to wait on the Congress of the Texas Republic to assemble that fall. Woodworth was ordered shortly after to return and conclude consultations with President Houston. Wight and Miller, still in Wisconsin, were unaware until the April Conference that their Wisconsin timber community was under serious consideration for assignment as the first group to go to Texas.[19]

Wight and Miller met with the Fifty when they came to Nauvoo for the April General Conference in 1844. President Smith instructed Wight on his duties in Texas. The colony would move as soon as the lumber season was over in Wisconsin, and Woodworth produced Houston's bona fides that he supported the move but needed to convince the Texas legislature that December. In the meantime, Wight and Miller went on short missions to the east and south. Wight stated that before he left on his mission, Joseph Smith set him apart as if Wight were to be like unto Moses, commanding "the armies of Israel to Zion . . . [to] lead the children of Israel out of Egypt" and presented "a white seer stone" to guide him. In a final meeting with Wight in the presence of Heber C. Kimball, President Smith gave "final instructions" to Wight. That was "the last time I ever saw [Joseph Smith's] face in the flesh. . . . I shook hands with him and bid him good bye," Wight later wrote. Smith's commission guided him to direct the Texas mission until the day he died almost fourteen years later.[20]

---

19. Miller, "Correspondence," 20; Meacham Curtis, letter to Joseph [Smith] III, September 15, 1884; Joseph Smith III and Heman C. Smith, eds., *The History of the Reorganized Church of Jesus Christ of Latter Day Saints*, 4:463; D. Michael Quinn, *The Mormon Hierarchy: Origins of Power*, 132–34; LDS Journal History of the Church (May 1840): 402; (May 1844): 1.

20. For more detail about the Wightites and the events of their last winter in Wisconsin, see Johnson, *Polygamy on the Pedernales*, 32–53; George Montague, "Reminiscences no. 2," 73; Smith et al., *History of the Church*, 1:176n; 3:289–90, 315, 420, 445–49; 4:341; 6:255–57, 260–62, 356, 377; Willard Richards diary, May 14, 1844; Lyman Wight, unpublished letter to the editors of *Northern Islander*,

John Hawley remembered that the Wisconsin company came to Nauvoo after the deaths "of [the] Prophet and Patriarch" expecting to receive a small Church-owned steamship (the Maid of Iowa) in return for the acre-large lumber raft they had steered down the river. Soon after that, without either boat or timber, the Wightite Company returned to Wisconsin. Persuaded by Wight, the community believed that Brigham Young had cheated them of the lumber and the steamboat.[21] The colony wintered south of present-day Lacrosse at a spot called Mormon Coulee just east of the Mississippi River. The members were once again baptized to remit their sins and covenanted to proselytize the natives. That winter was spent in the Wight-named "Valley of Lamoni." According to Hawley, the Wightites had a difficult time working for local businessmen "on short rations, which gave us a good appetite [sic] and this lasted a long time but we lived thru it all." Once again, the Wightites entered a common-stock covenant in which all goods were held in common. Wight told them that the arrangement was "the orders of God," and Hawley remembered those were "days of order to do as we was told and in this we was well schooled." In the spring of 1845, the community embarked on a fourteen-month journey south along the American borderlands to the Republic of Texas. They traveled by boat to Davenport, Iowa.[22]

Lyman Wight became a practitioner of polygamy in the colony during that first part of the journey, if not before. An older sister of John Hawley, Mary Hawley, was one of his three plural wives. Orange Wight, Lyman's son, married Sarah Hadfield as a plural wife as well. But the reality of it was driven home at Davenport when John found that a teenage girl he had been courting, probably Patience Curtis, was, in fact, a plural and sister wife to Joel S. and Delilia Miles. Wight had performed the cer-

---

July 1855; Wight, *An Address*, 3–4, 5–6; Lyman Wight, letter to William Smith, July 26, 1849, 2.

21. The steamship, in fact, had been sold by Joseph Smith, not Brigham Young. "Agreement with Arthur Morrison and Others, 15 June 1844," 1.

22. Asher Gressman and Effelinda [Essilinda] Gressman, letter to Levi Moffet, November 6, 1844. Hawley, "Autobiography," 5–6; Johnson, *Polygamy on the Pedernales*, 54–69. "That Lyman Wight go to Texas, if he chooses, with his company, also George Miller and Lucien Woodworth, if they desire to go." Smith, et al., *History of the Church*, 7:249. Woodworth explains the delay in negotiations because of the turmoil resulting from the murders of Joseph and Hyrum Smith. On the discussion in the council about relocating the main body of the Church to Texas, see Grow, et al., *Council of Fifty, Minutes*, 1:115–16, 127–28; Hawley, "Autobiography," 12–13.

emony for Joel S. and Patience shortly before they left Mormon Coulee. John admitted that he had "dropped her mighty quick." He also claimed later this marriage was the first plural marriage that came to his attention. He averred that he had not known that polygamy existed before this incident. His veracity can be questioned. John must have known that Mary was Wight's plural wife, yet he failed to offer that fact (or that his brother George had three wives in Utah Territory) when deposed in 1892 in the Temple Lot Case.[23]

The pioneers struck on foot across the country from Davenport with limited transport. Hawley remembers that when the company reached the Missouri River, he was struck down with fever. His father baptized him for health, and John "was healed immediately." The community worked to procure more livestock and wheeled conveyances to carry the little children and the oldest members. The "150 souls or there abouts" reached the Red River that November 1844 and wintered over until the following year. That winter and spring the colonists labored for Texans and Cherokees, and they did well enough to procure more teams and provisions. By May, they had reached Austin and built a small grist/saw mill village about four miles from the capitol, near the junction of Bee Creek with the Colorado River across from the foot of Mount Bonnell. After having been flooded four times during the winter, the mill site was sold, and the colony moved to Fredericksburg.[24]

Lyman Wight ordained Pierce Hawley to the office of a Patriarch. John Hawley wrote that the colonists needed to know "what our lineage and blessing was, for Lyman had taught us in selecting a wife we should get one of our own tribe and lineage" of Israel. All members received Patriarchal Blessings. John's father pronounced that John "was of the tribe of Ephraim

---

23. Temple Lot Case, 452; Johnson, *Polygamy on the Pedernales*, 57.

24. Hawley, "Autobiography," 5–6; Johnson, *Polygamy on the Pedernales*, 54–69; Millie Davis Williams conversations with the author, May 8, 2016, and September 13, 2016. Millie Davis Williams, the senior archivist at Fort Croghan Museum, Burnet, Texas, is the great-granddaughter of the man who bought Wight's Austin mill. "My g-g-g-grandfather Rev. Jonas Dancer, Methodist minister, bought mill from Mormons in 1847 one-half mile from Mt. Bonnell where Bee Creek runs into Colorado River. Mormons were flooded out four times then Dancer two times. So Dancer moved to Llano County to pursue his interest in minerals and had 40 member congregation in Riley Mountains. Was killed by Indians May 23, 1859, there above Blue Hole while building road from Llano to Austin. Buried on bluff near where killed."

and of the royal blood and lineage of Joseph that was sold into Egypt. This lineage and tribe which was pronounced upon my head, Lyman told the company, was the highest lineage." According to Wight, John's royal descent from Joseph "could save any woman whether they are of this tribe or not, for said Lyman." John was sanctioned to take a wife from any of the tribes of Israel. After the resurrection, she would have to return to live with her own tribe, but John could visit his wife in the afterlife.

The three couples were married at Austin on July 4, 1846, and began a life of "Patriarchal orders."[25] John would have performed those patriarchal rites for a woman as did all Wightite men, ordaining them as "kings" for their wives: kneeling and washing the woman's feet, anointing the woman's head with oil, and then the man ordaining his mate a queen. The Wightites considered their religious rites by the power of the priesthood superior to civil forms of marriage. The couples would be bound as mates for mortal time and all eternity, breaking the power of death forever. Hawley testified in the Temple Lot Case in 1892 that Wight performed the sealing/marriage, and Pierce Hawley, as Patriarch of the Wightites and an LDS high priest in the Nauvoo church, once again washed the couple's feet and anointed their heads.[26]

John Pierce Hawley reached full maturity in the years of 1847 to 1850. In 1847, the settlers moved to Zodiac, about three miles east of the German colony Fredericksburg on the Pedernales River. He chose the vocation of "a carpenter and joiner." Wight wanted to build a temple in the wilderness to ensure the colony members could "attend to the baptism for the dead and also the ordinance of washing of feet and a general endowment in the wilderness. So we went to work and built a good little Temple to worship in."[27]

John Hawley, ordained as an elder, commenced his first missionary trip in 1848, which would result in some difficulties. Paired with Joel Miles, the two went without purse or script "down to the eastern part of

---

25. Hawley, "Autobiography," 6–7.

26. Johnson, *Polygamy on the Pedernales*, 142; Temple Lot Case, 452, 454; Hawley, "Autobiography," 6–7, 10–11.

27. Van Wagenen, *The Texas Republic*, ix–xi. For more on the first Mormon temple west of the Mississippi River, see Melvin C. Johnson, "'So We Built a Good Little Temple to Worship In': Mormonism in the Pedernales—Texas, 1847–1851," 89–98. The article describes the Wightite temple in Zodiac, Texas, as the first Mormon (as opposed to LDS) temple west of the Mississippi, with typical Mormon rituals performed there.

state," probably from Houston to present-day Tyler to the north. They were quite "successful in making converts and all was required to sell out and move to our gathering place . . . on the Pedernales River." One of their converts was a man by the name of Henry Bayse. There is no evidence that John or the other Wightites knew that Bayse had, surprisingly enough, served in the Missouri Militia as a corporal in the company of Captain James W. Sanders during the Missouri-Mormon War of 1838. Apparently, the newcomers' reaction to Zodiac's common stock requirements as well as the plural wife doctrine led to "quite a panic" and to the departure of what Hawley called "the breakup crowd." He identified only his own wife, Harriet, as one of those who left the colony at that time.[28]

Hawley and Miles undertook another mission into East Texas, a heavily forested area the size of Indiana. Few roads, unstable rivers, and suspicious locals charged this task with adventure and danger. Lyman Wight had advised the missionaries to remain in harmony with one another. In part, they were returning for Henry Bayse and his family, whose neighbors were unhappy with him for becoming a Latter Day Saint. Wight said all would turn out right for the Bayse family. Hawley wrote that "a mob gathered to drive us out of the county because they said we was Mormons and they were not very friendly toward Henry Bayse. They knew we had come with him or he with us." Hawley was seized by members of the mob and held for some hours. He willingly preached when ordered to do so. He wrote, "And let me say right here, the Lord softened their hearts and they said 'Let us release this man, he is innocent.'" He was ordered "out of the neighborhood" by four o'clock or he could expect a "blackjacking." By six o'clock, the small encampment had moved about a mile where they stayed for four days. Mrs. Bayse had been in her final days of pregnancy and was unable to move. Hawley reported that Wight's earlier prophesy came true as Bayse' "worst enemies" became his best friends by the time the small party departed for Zodiac.[29]

On the trip to Zodiac, Joel S. Miles and John Hawley had a falling out. The issue, although not identified, may have begun with John's courtship of Patience Curtis, the secret plural wife of Joel.[30] Wight had instructed them "never to fall out," yet Miles and Hawley quarreled and would not talk to each other for three days. One night, however, a convert

---

28. Hawley, "Autobiography," 7; Henry Bayse, Record of Service Card, Mormon War, 1838.
29. Hawley, "Autobiography," 8–9.
30. Johnson, *Polygamy on the Pedernales*, 137.

member, Sister Garberry, suffered "evil spirts" and had a severe nightmare. Joel thought that their disagreement had let a devil into the sister "because of our transgression." John believed the devil was in them and they should get rid of it first. She quieted down that night, and then the two elders continued avoiding each other for another two days.

John was very dissatisfied with the tension with Joel. On the third day, the travelers came to a small body of water. John thought the lake big "enough for Joel to baptize me for the remission of my sins." The two men confessed to each other they both were unhappy and talked to each other in the morning. Unbaptized but content, they went to sleep. However, the night was not yet finished, for each had a vision and related it to the other. John wrote:

> I saw a large tree just 60 feet high and on one side there was a large snake covering half the tree and the other side was covered with small ones. When I saw this I turned to Joel and he turned to me at the same time. I told him what I saw and he said just as he turned from me he saw a bed-stead sitting before him with a good bed upon it but no one on it. This ended our night's talk and we was carefull after this to not disagree and we arrived home all well in body and mind.[31]

Miles, Hawley, and the others reached Zodiac safely on May 9, 1848. Once again, most of the new converts stayed at Zodiac for "but a short time and left." Hawley indicated that polygamy may have been the reason for the latest departures from the colony. The common stock property requirements may have also influenced the dissenters. More importantly for him, Harriet, his wife, had left with the others earlier in 1848. John was gracious yet patronizing to her memory when he wrote, "But let me say she was of a quiet disposition and made me a good housekeeper." Wight informed John there was no need for legal action, and that he was divorced from Harriet.[32]

John decided "to do my own sparking for the next wife and right here Lyman wished me to marry a girl by the name of Lyzia Salona" (actually named Eliza Leyland) who would later marry one of Wight's sons in 1853. Wight then discovered that John and Sylvia Johnson had exchanged personal vows "to be married." Sylvia was a daughter in one of the families that the Hawleys had known for a decade, that of Eber (also Heber) and Sally Johnson. She had come to Zodiac with her family in 1848 in

---

31. Hawley, "Autobiography," 8–9.

32. Heman C. Smith, "The Truth Defended, or, A Reply to Elder D. H. Bays' Doctrines and Dogmas of Mormonism," 33; Hawley, "Autobiography," 8–9.

the George Miller Company.³³ Wight told John that "Lyzia was a good girl" but thought Sylvia should become the plural wife of his son-in-law, Spencer Smith. John showed the steadfastness of intent that characterized his adult life. He assured Lyman, "I was satisfied she (Lyzia) was good enough for any man but I did not propose to violate my covenant with the one I was engaged. As Lyman could not prevail in having me break my covenant, he concluded to torment us by not attending to the marriage ceremony." The fifteen-year-old Sylvia and John, eight years older, balked and waited Wight out until he gave his permission.

Hawley wrote that

> we was to gritty and in about a year after, 22nd of October 1849, he performed the marriage ceremony to us. We was pronounced man and wife according to the laws of the State of Texas. Here let me say my wife was satisfied. I was to be her husband before we had said anything about marriage and it was predicted upon her head by Patriarch Father John Smith in Nauvoo that she should have a companion which would be of a quiet and good disposition and to let me tell it she got just such a man when she got me. It was further predicted by the Patriarch that she should live a long life with him and in the resurrection she would join him again and a part of this has been literally fulfilled and we expect the balance to be.³⁴

John's marriage to Sylvia was held in the Zodiac Temple. Officiators included Wight, Pierce Hawley, and Otis Hobart, John's former father-in-law. The rites included an ordination to be "a King and a Priest[.] Under there hands I was considered worthy to be and was ordained a King and a Priest and annointed with oil after feet washing." John then washed his wife's feet and anointed "her a Queen to me." Lyman Wight "then sealed for time and eternity" the new King and Queen in Zion. Hawley then observed that the colony and its members thought of themselves as the house of ancient Israel. They had "adopted a portion of the Law of Moses, that portion of cleanliness respecting woman when their blood of impurification was upon them." The men had to leave their conjugal beds for eight straight days. If a child was a boy, the husband had "to absent her bed 33 days and if a daughter," the separation was required to be sixty-six

---

33. For more about Bishop Miller, see Melvin C. Johnson, "Bishop George Miller: A Latter Day High Priest and Prince on the High Plains," 84–106.

34. "Eliza Leyland to Lyman Lehi Wight," Table 2: Lyman Wight Colony Marriages and Plural Relationships 1844 to 1858, in Johnson, *Polygamy on the Pedernales*, 80; Hawley, "Autobiography," 9–10.

days. This "law of Moses correct and revised" by Lyman Wight "was not so awful bad to observe this clean law either," Hawley thought.[35]

The endowment ceremony in Texas was entirely concerned with the sealing (marrying) of man and wife or wives beyond mortality into eternity. The difference between secular marriage and sealing, John stated, was that the former was done by the power of secular law while spiritual authority sealed a man and spouse together forever. John and Sylvia would experience a far more complicated endowment ceremony, sealings, and other rituals in 1857 in Salt Lake City than in the Zodiac Temple. They remained husband and wife for fifty-eight years.[36]

More than forty years later, Hawley probably gave a misleading deposition on the roles of temples and endowments in The Temple Lot case. John deposed that Lyman Wight had first introduced the idea of endowments in Texas as he had polygamy in Wisconsin. According to Hawley, neither doctrine so distinctive in the Joseph Smith years was taught or known in Nauvoo. John stated he would have known because his father was a leading figure in Mormonism and his father had not told him. Lyman Wight, as John probably knew, along with the rest of the Twelve had been instructed by Joseph Smith at Nauvoo in plural marriage and temple ritual. The Twelve took plural wives, including Wight and his three new wives in Wisconsin in 1844 and 1845. In Texas, Wight, remembering the ceremonies of the Kirtland and Nauvoo endowments, created "his own . . . endowment, washings, anointings, sealings, and baptism for time and eternity." Hawley undoubtedly testified for denominational reasons having been a member of the RLDS Church for twenty-two years before testifying in the Temple Lot.[37]

In 1850, Hawley, with William Curtis and Andrew Huffman, were sent on yet another mission to meet, greet, and escort a contingent of

---

35. Hawley, "Autobiography," 10.

36. Temple Lot Case, 452; Hawley, "Autobiography," 7–10; Johnson, *Polygamy on the Pedernales*, 130, 142. Typically, John did not record in his autobiography Wight's attempt to marry Sylvia as a plural wife to Spencer Smith, a son-in-law. Wight's grandson and great-grandson, the RLDS historians and authorities Heman C. Smith and Heman H. Smith, ignored almost all such items about polygamous Wightite activities in their writings.

37. "History of Lyman Wight," 456; Joseph Smith, blessing given by Joseph Smith Jr. to Lyman Wight, Kirtland, Ohio, December 29, 1835; Quinn, *The Mormon Hierarchy*, 66; B. Young, April 6, 1853, *Journal of Discourses*, 2:31; Johnson, *Polygamy on the Pedernales*, 13.

church members from Joseph Smith's youngest brother, William Smith, in Kentucky. The newcomers who were joining the Wightites in Texas to "receive 'endowments and blessings' in the Zodiac Temple." By 1851, the merger had failed, and the Smithites caused yet another serious schism at Zodiac.[38]

Hawley recounted that Lyman Wight had ordered them "not to drink any liquor while on our mission and we should be blessed." However, temptation came in the form of helping one's neighbor. On the trail, the missionaries came upon a man whose outfit was trapped in the mire. After helping the wayfarer, "nothing would do but we must drink." Hawley told his companions and the Smith party that on the return to Zodiac consequences might arise for disobeying Wight's orders. The party soon encountered a Comanche hunting party. Although John knew several of the tribe, he did not recognize any of this group. The band threatened Hawley's traveling party from a distance. Hawley recalled:

> After camping at night, I called the family together, as the other comrades of mine wished me to act as I thought best in our periless condition, and told them we had violated Lyman's order and all we could now do was to ask God to forgive the past. We all knelt down and I was mouth in prayer. After we rose from prayer the spirit of prophesy rested upon me and I prophesied all would be well and we should not be hurt nor disturbed. So we lay down to rest for the night.
>
> About 12 o'clock we heard horses feet running in the distance and the women and children was frightened at the earth shaking fiercly, for about 50 Indians was coming under a dead run. I remember well what I told them, Be quiet, there is no danger. When the Indians rode up they was all painted and without arms. We knew the Lord overruled for our safety and after smoking the pipe of peace, they mounted their horses and rode home or to their camping place.

The Comanche bothered them no more, and they journeyed safely on to Zodiac.[39]

The remainder of 1850 and into early 1851 witnessed chills, fevers, and the three-day ague, the latter affecting nearly every member of the colony, according to John. A series of problems plagued the colonists. Election troubles had developed with their Texas German neighbors in

---

38. Johnson, *Polygamy on the Pedernales*, 137; Hawley, "Autobiography," 7; Isaac Sheen, ed., "A Revelation, given March 20, 1850, in Covington, Kentucky," 1. Hawley misdated the mission to the coast as 1848 instead of 1850.

39. Johnson, *Polygamy on the Pedernales*, 130; Hawley, "Autobiography," 7–8.

the county, a terrible flood washed away the arable land, and then rumors abounded in the area that the Mormons were practicing polygamy. John may have been exaggerating the latter when he wrote, "To escape the courts of justice we moved over to another county called Burnet on the Colorado River." On the beautiful Hamilton Creek in Burnet County, the Wights and the Hawleys came to disagreement and separation of ways.[40]

---

40. Hawley, "Autobiography," 10.

CHAPTER 3

Mormon Mills, Texas, to the Indian Nations

1851 to 1856

"But the Lord, through the firearms we had, persuaded them to let us Pass on our way Quietly."

The Wightites moved in 1851 some fifty miles to the northeast from Zodiac to build a new grist and sawmill in Hamilton Valley in Burnet County at what became Mormon Mill. The year sped by. John became ill on Hamilton Creek that year, possibly from the ague, and it "brought [him] upon a bed of affliction and all the administering ordinances did not seem to effect any cure, so I besought the Lord to know the reason." A "messenger" in a night dream came to John to tell him death would flee from him, and he would recover. John began mending quickly and soon was healthy in both body and mind.

Sylvia and John gave birth to their first two children at Hamilton Valley: Abinadi, October 24, 1851; and Alma, March 5, 1853. Sylvia and John named Abinadi after the great Book of Mormon prophet. They named Alma after another important Book of Mormon character who followed Abinadi's teachings (Mosiah 17).[1] The choosing of their names would rupture the harmony in their community and eventually cause the Hawleys, excepting Aaron Hawley and his family, to leave Lyman Wight. John and Sylvia Hawley would have a total of twelve children: their first two at Mormon Mill, one in the Cherokee Nation, seven in Pine Valley, Utah (of whom four died young), and two in Iowa. All the surviving children would become members of the RLDS Church.

The young father cryptically wrote that his father, Pierce Hawley, was displeased with several of Wight's decisions. A quarrel ensued between the two old men about the naming of John's sons. Custom required that a baby was brought before Wight to be given a spiritual name. John at-

---

1. John Hawley, "Autobiography of John Hawley," 9–10.

> CHILDREN
>
> Abinadi Hawley b: Oct 24, 1851, in Hamilton Creek, Burnet, Texas
> Alma Hawley b: Mar 5, 1853, in Hamilton Creek, Burnet, Texas
> Sarah Hawley b: Jan 20, 1856, in Cherokee Nation, Arkansas
> *John Hawley* b: Jun 5, 1858, in Pine Valley, Utah
> Eber Pierce Hawley b: Apr 18, 1860, in Pine Valley, Utah
> *Sylvia Amelia Hawley* b: Mar 9, 1862, in Pine Valley, Utah
> *William Nephi Hawley* b: Jan 7, 1864, in Pine Valley, Utah
> Isaac Zimri Hawley b: Jan 8, 1866, in Pine Valley, Utah
> *Gazelam Hawley* b: Jan 31, 1868, in Pine Valley, Utah
> Lucy Lovina Hawley b: Apr 1869, in Pine Valley, Utah
> Mary Caroline Carrie Hawley b: Jun 22, 1873, in Gallands Grove, Iowa
> Francis Aaron Frank Hawley b: Jun 12, 1875, in Gallands Grove, Iowa
>
> **Italicized*: interred in Pine Valley, Washington County, Utah

tempted a compromise, taking his boys to Wight, who then resentfully agreed the names were correct.

Other matters compounded the tension. One was the death of Mary Hawley Wight in 1852, Lyman's fourth wife, more than twenty-five years younger than her husband. She was buried in the Mormon Mill Cemetery, the only surviving Wightite material artifact of significance. Another major issue, John wrote, was a revelation that Wight claimed gave him authority to move the colony to Mexico. John "thought this was not his mission . . . to govern the church" and change the Texas Mission to a Mexican Mission. In other words, John, a believer in conferred authority, had reached the conclusion that Wight had the authority to follow Joseph's call to take the colony as far as Texas but no further.[2]

The patriarch refused to defer to the apostle and left the colony. Some of the Hawley familial and marital relations followed Pierce Hawley and his wife to Indian Territory northeast of the Red River. John Young, his son-in-law, with his wife Priscilla (Hawley) went with her parents. George Hawley also went. He had his own reasons to follow his father: he had taken Sarah Hadfield Wight to wife, sister to his legal wife, Ann. Sarah had been a plural spouse of Orange Lysander Wight.[3]

---

2. Hawley, 9–10.

3. Hawley, 11; Elsie Hawley Platt and Robert Hawley, *House of Hawley*. Harriet Martenisia Wight, Sarah Hadfield Wight Hawley's daughter by Orange Wight,

John did not immediately follow his father, but eventually gave up Wight as his religious leader. He told Wight he would remain at the Hamilton Valley mill after Noah Smithwick's purchase of it in 1853. Hawley continued to work at the mill with several other dissident Mormon families, telling Wight that if his father returned, he would rejoin the colony as well.[4] Hawley knew that if he left the common stock community, he would forfeit the Wightite cows, wagons, and tools at the mill. Hawley knew and had agreed that the property "in my possession was at [Wight's] disposal. For this was the covenant we entered into while in Wisconsin that if any got disaffected and wished to leave the company they must do so nothing [with] but the cloths on their backs." Hawley asked Wight for the continued use of the property, which the old apostle refused: "So in a day or so Lyman sent over and drove off the cows and took what company property was in my charge."[5] John later estimated that after "about a year" no one in Wight's colony was worth more than him "if the property had been equally divided." John and Sylvia pulled up stakes and, "desiring to get a little near the Center Stake of Zion," joined the Hawley family in the Indian Nations to be near to his father as well as the families of his brother George and sister Priscilla Young. Their brother Aaron and his family remained with the Wightites.[6]

---

remained in her mother's home with George Hawley in Indian Territory and Pine Valley, Washington County, Utah Territory. Her mother and her infant half-sister by her mother's new husband from the Earl family died at Pine Valley in 1863 and 1864, respectively. Wesley W. Craig, Old Pine Valley Cemetery, Cemetery Indexes for Washington County, Utah (1852-1996).

4. Marvin J. Hunter, *The Lyman Wight Colony in Texas, Came to Bandera in 1854*, 36; J. Hawley, letter to Lyman Wight, August 28, 1853; Population Schedule, Census of 1860, Burnet County, Texas; Noah Smithwick, *Evolution of a State; or, Recollections of Old Texas Days*, 228; Melvin C. Johnson, *Polygamy on the Pedernales: Lyman Wight's Mormon Villages in Antebellum Texas, 1845-1858*, 93.

5. John Hawley, letter to Lyman Wight, August 28, 1853; Hawley, "Autobiography," 12.

6. Hawley, "Autobiography," 12. For more on the integration of the former Wightites into the Texas Hill Country culture, see Melvin C. Johnson, "The Mormon Cowboys of Bandera County and the Texas Hill Country," 159–77. This article narrates the history of the Wightites in Bandera and Medina counties with a particular focus of the Latter Day Saint influence on the early and later development of Bandera, Texas. After the Civil War, an RLDS religious revival converted the remaining former Wightites in the area, which introduced a continuing presence of the Reorganized Church of Jesus Christ of Latter Day Saints in Central Texas.

That first winter in the Indian Nations, Hawley built a log house and a frame building for a man named "Rogers" who cheated him and paid nothing, despite John having received a "permit from the Chief of the Nation." The man may have been Lewis Rogers with whom some of the Latter-day Saints later would have continuing problems. Feeling cheated by Native American law, John Hawley and John Young ranged as "far north as Fort Scott" in Kansas Territory casting for a home, but all the forested land was infested with squatters. On returning to their families, John Hawley, Joseph D. "Choosdale" [Goodale], John Young, and Pierce Hawley settled near Spavinaw Creek some miles east of present-day Tulsa, renting "a salt works" on the creek and "labored at the business and cleared nothing but a living."[7]

The Hawleys clan was not the first organized Latter Day Saint group or individuals to settle in Indian Territory.

The Latter Day Saints had been west of the Missouri in the Indian Territory as early as 1831 with Oliver Cowdery's Lamanite Mission. The Lyman Wight colony had traveled through the Indian Nations in the summer and fall of 1845, wintering just south of the Red River while woodworking and milling on Native American contracts.[8] Bishop George Miller, their former companion in Wisconsin and in Texas, had quarreled with Brigham Young and left the main body's westward trek in 1847 to join his son at Zodiac. The Daniel Newell Drake clan was another of several families in that small Miller Company. Drake's wife, Cynthia Parker Johnson, was a daughter of the Johnson family at Zodiac. So was Cynthia's fourteen-year-old sister, Sylvia, who later became John Hawley's wife. Miller's company stayed near the Cherokee capital of Tahlequah from July to December of 1847 and then moved on to Zodiac. The shortness of the stay may have been, according to a comment in the *Chronicles of Oklahoma*, because the local citizens did not like Mormon preaching.[9]

Richard Hewitt, who knew the Hawleys, later traveled part of the way with Miller's company from Zodiac to the Strang colony at Beaver Island

---

7. Hawley, "Autobiography," 12.

8. Hawley, 5–6; Johnson, *Polygamy on the Pedernales*, 54–69.

9. Andrew Jenson, quoted in Heman H. Smith, "George Miller," 229; Vida E. Smith, "Two Widows of the Brick Row," 208; H. W. Mills, "De Tal Palo Astillo," 111, 143, 145; George Miller, "Correspondence of Bishop George Miller," 34–36; Grant Foreman, "Missionaries of the Latter Day Saints in Indian Territory," 196–213; Johnson, *Polygamy on the Pedernales*, 93; WPA, *Oklahoma: A Guide to the Sooner State*, 259.

in Michigan. Hewett stopped, however, in the Indian Nations. He had detested the plural wife system ever since the Nauvoo days and had trouble with it in Wight's Texas colony as well as in the Miller Company.[10] Hewitt died on September 25, 1853, at McCoy's Prairie, Cherokee Nation, and was buried at Tahlequah, Cherokee County. Before his death, according to a family member, he had a dream "about hords of people coming into Oklahoma. Hewitt told his wife to get out of Oklahoma. He also said he had never left the church. He was an Elder." Mary Jane, his daughter, would later marry Stephen Molloy [Maloney], and both would rejoin the Utah Church as converts and move on to Utah Territory during Henry W. Miller's presidency in the Cherokee Nation. There the Maloneys joined the RLDS Church during the Josephite missions of the 1860s and would send RLDS literature to then-Latter-day Saint presiding elder, John Hawley, in Pine Valley, Utah Territory.[11]

While the Hawleys had known Hewitt earlier in Texas, they met many new Latter-day Saints who had moved from Texas to Indian Territory. William Rufus Slade and his family had settled in the same area as the Hawleys. The little shanties and the old mill allowed them to discover others and seek both communal and religious refuge. "Dorinda" Moody Slade, William's wife, "set up a quilting frame in the old mill and spent her spare time quilting. She called . . . one 'The Rising Sun.' She also worked on a bed spread and when it was finished she gave it to a young girl, Melissa Meeks." The women of the hamlets found comfort and companionship in each other's company.

Another Latter-day Saint family was that of the Harris County sawmiller, Jacob Croft, a man of some prominence in the Houston, Texas,

---

10. Miller, "Correspondence," 45; George Miller, letter to James J. Strang, June 12, 1849, with an addendum by Richard Hewitt, quoted in Smith, "George Miller," 230–32.

11. John Hawley, "Experiences of John Hawley," 223. Hewitt had queried Hyrum Smith at Nauvoo about polygamy: "Whereas brother Richard Hewitt has called on me to-day, to know my views concerning some doctrines that are preached in your place, and states to me that some of your elders say, that a man having a certain priesthood, may have as many wives as he pleases, and that doctrine is taught here: I say unto you that that man teaches false doctrine, for there is no such doctrine taught here. And any man that is found teaching privately or publicly any such doctrine, is culpable, and will stand a chance to be brought before the High Council, and lose his license and membership also: therefore he had better beware what he is about." Hyrum Smith, *Times and Seasons*, March 15, 1844, 474.

area, and a slave owner. The Houston *Morning Star* reported in 1840 that "Messers Croft & James have erected a water-powered saw and grist mill on Spring Creek, Harris County." Croft's mills are examples of the necessity of economic mechanization in creating sustainable communities as the pioneers moved forward on the frontier. The *Democratic Telegraph & Texas Register* in 1848 noted that Croft was located a mile above Houston and that the mill employed a Hotchkiss water wheel. According to census records for the farming year ending June 1, 1850, Jacob Croft's water-powered sawmill and grist mill produced 600,000 feet of lumber and 1,200 bushels of corn meal during the census year. Raw materials included 600 logs at $1,800 and 1,000 bushels of corn at $1,000. Croft employed four men, each averaging $25 monthly during that time, and estimated the mill's value at $3,000. The dollar value of the lumber produced was $9,000, and the value of the meal was $1,500.[12] The sums and amounts were substantial for frontier Texas. Such enterprises were encouraged across the West.

Mrs. Sebrina Cropper, a widow, had converted to the Latter-day Saint Church in 1851. She joined an emigrant company of converts to Utah Territory organized by Elder Preston Thomas in 1853. Traveling north on the Military Road, the Preston Thomas Company reached the Cherokee Nation near the Verdigris River. Jacob Croft also had left Texas and went to the Cherokee Nation that fall of 1853. He financed his move by selling off slaves "or traded them for cattle and other things."[13] In the Indian Nations, some of the Preston Thomas Company apparently heard for the first time about polygamous wives in Utah and elected to stay in the Cherokee Nation for the winter before moving on to Utah Territory. On September 12, 1853, the members camped along the Verdigris River, where they would winter. After speaking with Sister Cropper that afternoon, Elder Thomas held a meeting at which "most of the brethren were present. I spoke to them at length upon their duties and obligation to God and to one another." He then organized the Texas Branch of the Church of Jesus Christ of Latter-Day Saints. The following were chosen to fill various offices: Alexander Barron, president; Bro. William Slack [Slade], priest; Robert Loyd,[14] teacher; and John Richards, deacon. William Coats was authorized to go to Texas "on business for the saints, who are here, and to visit those who are there and gather them out as many as will

---

12. Theda Perdue, *Slavery and the Evolution of Cherokee Society, 1540–1866*, 108.
13. Thomas Waters Cropper, quoted in the *Millard County Chronicle*, July 31, 1930.
14. Also spelled "Lloyd."

come with him." Coats was to bring the Texas members to the colony on the Verdegris (Verdigris) River. Together the combined companies would journey on to Utah Territory.[15]

Tom Cropper, many years later, wrote that "[d]uring the winter mother [Sebrina Cropper] married Mr. Croft, and his children came to live with us. Croft was a mill-wright and did not belong to the Church at that time."[16] Croft was disillusioned by the local events involving his new family's religion. He accepted the offer of Joseph Lynch Martin, a Cherokee cattle owner (and like Croft, a slave owner), to restore the mill in the Greenbriar area, about sixty miles from the Latter Day Saint settlement.[17] Martin had a one hundred thousand-acre lease, stretching "from Salina through . . . Spavinaw to include Big Cabin where he owned a second spacious home. Before the Civil War Martin owned a general store, a blacksmith shop, and the mill in Spavinaw." Some of the Latter-day Saints would stay in the Spavinaw area for some time before continuing their journey to Utah and Salt Lake City in 1856. After the mills were repaired in the winter of 1853 and 1854, Croft took some of the wheat tolls, bought and traded slaves and cattle, and moved his family north to the Greenbriar area.[18]

Croft and his stepson Thomas Cropper recorded that the first mill did not bring in much money during the winter of 1853 and 1854. Croft took in some extra work doing "repairs." When he contracted to erect another mill along the Spavinaw River in 1854, he employed all four Hawley brothers (John, George, William, and Isaac), newly arrived from Texas, to build "a sawmill and a grist mill with a turning lathe added."[19] By November 1855, "Bro Croft was Building a Large Flouring and Sawmill Mill. Others were Engaged in Cutting Logs for Sawing" and "others hauled Logs to the saw Mill." Salt manufacturing was, because of "the Salt Spgs that abounded in that" region, a growing concern. The salt product was sold as far east as Arkansas. And the farming "settlement Looked quite Mormon Like."[20]

---

15. Daniel H. Thomas, *Preston Thomas, 1814–1877, a biography*, 34.
16. Thomas Waters Cropper, "The History of Thomas Waters Cropper," quoted in *The Robert L. Ashby and Hannah Cropper Family Book of their Descendants and Ancestors*, 659, 662.
17. Cropper, *Millard County Chronicle*, July 31, 1930; Cropper, "History," 662.
18. Cropper, *Millard County Chronicle*, July 31, 1930.
19. Cropper, "History," 666.
20. George B. Higginson, letter to Andrew Kimball Esq., March 1892.

President Brigham Young had been planning to secure access to his Rocky Mountain kingdom. At General Conference in April 1855, the Indian Mission was established, and missionaries were called to serve from the Missouri River west to the Sandwich Islands of the Pacific Ocean. The strategy planned the creation or expansion of the Nevada colonies in the Carson Valley, at Las Vegas Springs in southern Nevada, and an exploring expedition for a settlement in the White Mountains; in Idaho, on the Salmon River; and in Wyoming at Fort Supply and Fort Bridger. A total of forty-one missionaries also were called to the Elk Mountain Mission in southeastern Utah on the Colorado River crossing at present-day Moab.[21]

Henry W. Miller was called to be the mission president in the Cherokee Nation, where he knew several of the Mormons in the Nations, including the Hawleys. The longtime sawmiller and businessman, who had been a fellow colonist of the Black River Pine Company in Wisconsin, brought fellow missionaries R. C. Petty, John A. Richards, and William Richey. Blessed by apostles Wilford Woodruff and E. T. Benson,[22] the missionaries traveled east with another company of missionaries going to the British Isles. The Miller Company was organized with Hector C. Haight as Captain, Miller as Captain of the Guard, and Robert C. Petty as chaplain. The missionaries departed from Salt Lake City on May 7, 1855, traveling by way of Fort Laramie and Fort Scott, arriving in St. Louis, Missouri, on June 25, 1855.[23]

Miller and his missionaries reached S. A. Duggins' homestead near Spring River on July 2, and on July 4 arrived at "Captain Jacob Crofts" and suppered with the family.[24] Henry Eyring, who arrived with additional St. Louis missionaries later in November, wrote "that Bro J. Croft and Family, in connexion with the Lyman Wightites, were the Main Support to the Mission to commence with, and are Entitled to Much consideration in connexion therewith, for their Liberality to the 'Elders.'" The next week was spent teaching and trying to convert the Hawleys and others who had been earlier associated with the Saints. Missionaries from James J. Strang's

---

21. Minutes of Missionary Meeting, April 8, 1855. Early narratives include Andrew Jenson, "The Elk Mountain Mission," 188–200.

22. Henry W. Miller and Elmira Pond Miller, Journal of Henry W. Miller and Elmira Pond Miller, Cherokee Indian Mission, 1855 April–1862 October.

23. LDS Journal History of the Church, May 9, 1855; Grant Foreman, "Missionaries of the Latter Day Saints Church in Indian Territory," 196.

24. Miller and Miller, Journal, 6.

sect in the upper Midwest also were gleaning among the Restoration fields for converts and apostates.

The Strang evangelists had apparently "told all sorts of stories about conditions in the valleys of Utah." Miller noted in his diary that the Strangites believed Croft and his family had become "dissatisfied and had stopped herein the Cherokee Nation."[25] Anson Prindle and James C. Hutchins were on assignment in Texas to locate a home for the Strangite church "near the new boarder" of the Rio Grande River. John Hawley listened to both the Strangite and the Utah "Brighamite" missionaries as they proselytized in the Indian Nations. The *Northern Islander*, the Strangite newspaper, reported that A. W. (Anson) and L. T. (Luther) Prindle returned from their "mission to the Indian Country" on May 9, 1856.[26] Several weeks earlier the *Northern Islander* had reported the lack of success of the Strangite missionary effort among the Indian Nations, noting that a high priest named A. J. Porter had returned from the mission to the Indian country, beyond Arkansas. The mission succeeded in turning over "most of the Brighamites and scattered Mormons, who have gone into the Indian country." But "one family only will come up, as they did not advise gathering from there." The newspaper celebrated that the missionaries were "kindly received, and preached at [Tahlequah], and many of the principal settlements" and that the Brighamites were having trouble with the Indian Nation leadership.[27]

The Croft family took some powerful preaching to get them to affiliate with the Utah church. In a letter on August 8, 1855, Croft told George A. Smith that he would have started for the valley two years earlier, but "his wife & Dauters had bin batitered [battered] in Texas they had all got Disputed & rather go eney whare else than to the valley." A letter published in *The Latter-Day Saints Millennial Star* from President Miller described the outcome. Duggins and Slade "had gone over to Strang; but since we got here we have baptized Mr. Croft and family, Mr Slade and wife, Mr. Duggins and wife." Elder Cooper baptized the Duggins on the 8th, and on the 10th Elder Moody baptized and confirmed "eight members of Croft's family, along with Jacob." Joseph Hadfield, Sarah Wight, and her daughter (George Hawley's plural wife and his stepdaughter, Harriet Martenisia Wight, Orange Lyman Wight's daughter), were baptized on the 14th. The

---

25. Foreman, "Missionaries," 197; Henry W. Miller, Diary, April 1855–October 6, 1862, 6; The Journal of Henry Eyring, 1835–1902.

26. "The Lady Brings A.W." 4.

27. "Report of the Returned Elders," 2.

next day, Sunday, President Miller preached through an interpreter to a congregation of four hundred. On the 17th, the Cherokee Branch was organized by President Miller and his missionaries. William Slade was set apart as the presiding elder. George Hawley and his first wife, Ann (Sarah Wight's sister); his brother, William Hawley; and George Crouch were baptized. The missionaries ordained a total of "four elders and two teachers."[28] John Hawley and his family were holdouts.

The missionaries continued to visit and exhort that summer and early fall throughout the Indian Nations. Elders Cooper and Moody continued to their Texas Mission. Elder Petty did not get better but remained ill. Henry Miller and William Slade visited with Chief John Ross of the Cherokee Nation at Tahlequah. Miller gave Ross his letter of introduction from Brigham Young. The federal Indian Agent was friendly to them. On August 15, Elders John H. Richards and Washington N. Cook reported to President Miller that the Delaware tribe would not permit them to preach. During those months, Miller must not have forgotten the remainder of the Hawleys who remained unconverted,[29] for, on September 19, 1855, he baptized John and Sylvia Hawley; Sylvia's father, Eber Johnson; family members William and Sarey Jane Johnson, Saminay Drake, Abraham March, and Frances Croft. Only John's father and mother, Pierce and Sarah Hawley still held aloof.

Joseph Goodale, Hawley later wrote, did not let President Miller baptize him because of the mission president's addiction to tobacco. Miller ordained John Hawley to the office of elder so that the latter could baptize Goodale. Hawley believed, "if my memory serves me correct," that Goodale was in the church about eight hours. After being confirmed a member of the church, he "knelt in prayer and asked for a witness whether Brigham was the lawful successor of Joseph. God did not tell him. Because he got no witness, he told the church they could erase his name from the record which we did . . . [and] his wife's name also." The final Hawley family member to be baptized and confirmed by President Miller was Isaac Hawley on October 3, 1855.[30]

---

28. A. W. Miller, "The Cherokee Nation," 637–38; Foreman, "Missionaries," 197–98; Miller and Miller, Journal, 8; Henry W. Miller, letter to George A. Smith, August 8, 1855.

29. Foreman, "Missionaries," 198–200; Miller and Miller, Journal, 8–13.

30. Hawley, "Autobiography," 12; Miller, Diary, September 13, 1855, 13; Foreman, "Missionaries," 201–2.

On Saturday, November 10, 1855, President Miller, still staying at the Croft residence, received a new group of elders. The St. Louis Stake authorities, on October 7, 1855, had called George B. Higginson, Henry Eyring, William Bricker, William O. Flavel, as well as James Case from Manti, San Pete County, Utah Territory. Higginson wrote that "Bro Kinney our Teamster, was an old Hunter and kept our Larder well filled With Wild Turkeys, Quails, and Prairie Chickens that Abounded in that Wild Region. Once and a While we came to A farm House, and sometimes Passed through Small Villages, and Backwood Hamlets, the People as a General thing Treated us very Kindly, and all went along Smoothly until we came to the City of Springfield Mo."[31] Elder Flavel decided at Springfield that he would not go on the mission.

Higginson called it "his Apostacy" and said that Flavel "was full of Lucifer" and mean words. According to Higginson, Flavel tried to whip up mob action against the elders, "but the Lord, through the firearms we had, persuaded them to let us Pass on our way Quietly." Once they crossed into the Indian Territory, the missionaries located "old Nauvooers" by the name of Hackshaw who were living on one of the farms of a Cherokee chief named Tom Taylor. Hackshaw informed Eyring that the mission headquarters was located at a community of former Wightites on Spavinaw Creek, about eighteen miles from Hackshaw's homestead on Chief Taylor's farm. He described them as "sheep who had lost their Shepherd" until joining the Latter-day Saint church under the direction of President Miller and his missionaries.[32]

Higginson and the new missionaries found at the junction of Prior's Creek and Grand Saline "a large Branch of the Church" of "Mostly Cherokees." He believed that the Holy Spirit's power was being poured out on the Native Americans, particularly the gift of healing. He noted some examples. One "Partly White" elderly Cherokee woman, who had been unable to use her limbs for twelve years, was baptized for healing; she walked home after that. One of the elders, John A. Richards, benefitted from the healings. A three-quarter-white Cherokee lady was "[h]ealed of a disease of 7 years" by the elders in a blessing that involved the laying on of hands. She married Elder Richards, and when "she died a good Saint," he inherited slaves and livestock as well as "Cattle and Sheep farms."[33]

---

31. Miller and Miller, Journal, September 13, 1855, 16; Foreman, "Missionaries," 202; George B. Higginson, letter to Andrew Kimball, Esq., March 1892.

32. George B. Higginson, letter to Andrew Kimball, Esq., March 1892.

33. George B. Higginson, letter to Andrew Kimball, Esq., March 1892.

The missionaries continued having some success into 1856 as they proselytized the Latter-day Saint cause and created a sense of community. Two examples involved one marriage and more baptisms. On Thursday, November 15, William Hawley married Nancy Matheny, a stepdaughter of Jacob Croft, followed by a wedding supper. On December 9, President Miller baptized six more converts: Stephen Maloney and wife, Enoch Hacksaw and wife, Rebecca Hewitt, and Jeannette Goudy. On January 20, 1856, John and Sylvia welcomed a new daughter to the family named Sarah—named for her grandmother.[34] Several days later, death came to the community. William Slade notified President Miller on February 1 that Elder Robert C. Petty, who had been ill since the previous summer and was staying at the Slade home, would not live long. Slade and Miller rode to Petty's aid and comfort. Early the next morning on February 2, at 2:45, the young elder passed. He was buried the next day in the Joseph M. Lynch "burying ground between Grand River and the Spavinah."[35] Petty's death, far from home, saddened the "Saints of the Indian Territory Mission" and the remaining missionaries—President Miller, Henry Eyring, W. N. Cook, Jonathan A. Richards, William Richey, and Geo Higginson.[36]

Troubles befell the Latter-day Saints with federal authorities in the Cherokee Nation. The agent for the Cherokees, George Butler, had ordered Sheriff Jefferson Hicks to apprehend and escort Miller and deliver him to the commander of Fort Gibson. He would then be given to the authorities in Van Buren, Arkansas, confined in jail, and "then they expected to try him for something, no one seemed to know what. However, the Sheriff, after having a talk with Dr. Robert Daniel Ross, one of the counselors of the nation and a nephew of the Chief, refused to serve the writ." Miller and Butler met. Miller believed Butler "a gentleman, but had

---

34. Foreman, "Missionaries," 203; Hawley, "Autobiography," 12.

35. A Petty descendent wrote in 2008, "I went to the Spavinaw Valley and learned that the Mormon Colony was in Spavinaw and that the old Spavinaw cemetery was located on the banks of the Grand River. In 1922 the Spavinaw Dam was constructed, and water was pumped the distance of 65 miles. The old Spavinaw Cemetery was moved to the present day Spavinaw/Strang Cemetery. If Elder Robert Cowan Petty was buried in this cemetery and his body was found in this area, his remains will be at the Spavinaw/Strang Cemetery, and his grave will be unmarked and unknown. If his body was not recovered from the old cemetery, if that is where he was buried, his body will lay under Lake Spavinaw." M. Shane Symes, "Robert Cowan Petty, 1812–1856."

36. Miller and Miller, Journal, February 3, 1856, 20. Foreman, "Missionaries," 198, 204–5; George B. Higginson, letter to Andrew Kimball, Esq., March 1892.

been imposed upon; he had, on investigation" realized matters were different than he had thought. Croft knew Butler for several years, and Butler had a good opinion of Croft.

Apparently, Lewis Rogers, one of Jacob Croft's neighbors, had complained against Miller "for counseling the brethren to leave the nation to gather to Zion." Butler also "promised Elder Miller that the writ would not be served, and if it became necessary for Elder Miller to leave the nation, Mr. Butler would inform him of the same by letter and not issue another writ." Miller and Butler discussed Latter-day Saint theology, "but Mr. Butler advised Elder Miller not to preach in the settlement any more for the present. He was convinced that Mr. Rogers, a Methodist, was meddling with the affairs of the Saints at the instigation of the priest." President Miller put aside preaching and went to work for a short time for Jacob Croft.[37]

Elder Miller's call to Zion (Utah Territory) and, perhaps, the problems with the federal authorities heartened the Spavinaw members "to go to Zion in the West." President Young had written the previous November to President Miller that his "instructions to those whom you baptized, who do not belong to the nation, to gather to these vallies as speedily as their way may open, are correct and you will continue them, but the Cherokees who are baptized may remain there." Young suggested that the Latter-day Saint Cherokees could possibly, if practicable, be placed in a suitable central gathering place in the nation, but that they could live "for the present, in those places" they were then living.[38]

John Hawley wrote that "the gathering [to Utah] was strongly impressed upon our minds. We wished to be with the church . . .[but] hated to leave father behind." Pierce Hawley still would not accept Brigham Young's leadership. He believed that Young had been responsible for the Church taking the Hawley property across the river from Nauvoo in Lee County without compensating the Hawleys after they joined the Black River Pine Mission in Wisconsin. Pierce Hawley believed the Black River Saints in 1844 were also supposed to get the *Maid of Iowa* in return for the last raft of timber from the Wisconsin mills delivered to the Nauvoo

---

37. Foreman, "Missionaries," 206; Miller and Miller, May 3, 1856, 24; George B. Higginson to Andrew Kimball, Esq., March 1892; Butler to Gov. Thomas S. Drew, in Morris L. Wardell, *A Political History of the Cherokee Nation*, 119–20; Grant Foreman, *The Five Civilized Tribes*, 412–13; Carolyn Thomas Foreman, "Dr. William Butler and George Butler, Cherokee Agents," 169–70.

38. Brigham Young, letter to Elder Henry W. Miller, November 28, 1855.

landing. Young had supposedly, according to Father Hawley, "kept us out waiting in Nauvoo for a week till the church could make a trip with our steamboat up some small river" and never returned the boat. John Hawley said that his father felt that the Utah church leadership "never intended to let us have our property and this all struck in father's craw." Pierce Hawley instead wanted his children to endure on "the boarder of Zion till Joseph [Joseph Smith III] would take" the authority, mantle, and place of his father, Joseph Smith Jr.

Jacob Croft next wrote to the old patriarch, who replied that he believed the truth was not with the Brighamites and that its leader was a pretender and an imposter. Hawley advised Croft to go to Nebraska Territory and wait "till the Lord raises up the man to lead us to sion [sic]." Neither Jacob Croft nor the grown children of Father Hawley would follow the old man's advice. Pierce Hawley died two years later, still in Indian Territory. John remembered that those who had not followed their father's advice "are the ones that suffered the most. But we are not going to cry of spilt milk, for in the resurrection we will have to confess to Him."[39]

President Miller, on June 3, 1856, visited the immigrants on a staging ground where William Slade, the Hawleys and their friends, and other travelers were preparing for the journey to Utah. Miller also discovered a Texas complement led by Elder Benjamin L. Clapp. Elder Miller spent several days in the neighborhood, assisting the Saints in preparing for the trip. Miller organized the train with Jacob Croft as Captain; William Slade, the Chaplain; John Hawley, Sergeant of the Guard; and Stephen A. Duggins as company clerk. Miller accompanied the emigrants, keeping a journal of their experiences, until the Croft Company reached its jumping off point, just seven miles from Kansas City. Miller bade them farewell and moved on to St. Louis to meet with Church authorities. He returned by steamboat to Kansas City, journeyed south, and reached Spring Creek in the Indian Territory on August 20, 1856.[40] Two months earlier, Brigham Young wrote to Erastus Snow (probably in St. Louis) to "please inform" Brother Henry W. Miller of the Cherokee Nation "that he is honorably released" from his mission "and permitted to return home" because of poor health.[41] Miller soon returned to Salt Lake City.

---

39. Pierce Hawley, letter to Jacob Croft, June 6, 1856; Platt and Hawley, *House of Hawley*, 49; Hawley, "Autobiography," 13.

40. Miller and Miller, Journal, June 3, 1856, 26; June 22, 1856, 27; August 22, 1856, 30.

41. Brigham Young, letter to Elder Erastus Snow, June 30, 1855.

The followers of Joseph Smith Jr. were to be found on the plains and prairies and in the mountains of the West all the way to California. The decision of many like the Hawleys was to go to the Latter-day Saints in the far West. Strands of Mormonism, originating in Nauvoo, ran variously to dissenting communities in Wisconsin, Michigan, Texas, Iowa, the Indian Nations, California, and elsewhere. The Hawleys left the Nauvoo church, then later the Wightites. Now the family split again, leaving the father and mother in the Indian Nations. The death of Joseph Smith Jr. led to dissension and spreading clusters of opposing communities. Smith's legacy was widespread and diverse, moving from the Mississippi and Missouri River valleys across the American territories covering plains and mountains all the way to California.

John Hawley stood in June of 1856 as a symbol of this important facet of the Latter-day Saint emigration to the West Coast before the rails linked the continent. The Latter-day Saints were instrumental in turning the story of the West into an even broader and more diverse movement, of the extraordinary web of religious beliefs and extended family connections. He reflects Smith's legacy, and his story becomes an essential narrative for telling much more about the Latter Day Saint Restoration movement in the West.

CHAPTER 4

Wagons West to Utah Territory

1856

"Only the All-seeing Eye saw and only the All-seeing Ear heard all the occurrences in that long and wearisome journey."

The Jacob Croft Company, with sixty-five souls, included almost thirty members of the Hawley clan and close friends in the summer and fall of 1856. Their company was one of nearly twenty Church and independent companies organized and sent to Salt Lake that year. Hawley's autobiography devotes two sentences about the Jacob Croft Company's journey to Salt Lake City. Perhaps to John, the journey was part of his everyday life on the frontier and borderlands. He had been born in the backcountry, lived as a child in Missouri, and made the journey from the Wisconsin wilderness to the Texas Hill Country frontier as a teenager. He was twenty-eight, married, and influential among his neighbors, and remained so as they moved into the Indian Nations. Perhaps the journey to him was no more dangerous and exciting than a road trip today would be from Los Angeles to Kansas City. Nonetheless, Hawley and hundreds of thousands of immigrants like him from 1841 to 1869 were engaged in an epic migration.

Estimating Mormon deaths on the immigrant trail has become problematic. For instance, Kip Sperry in 2006 estimated that about 250 Latter-day Saint wagon companies helped transport a good portion of the "some eighty thousand Mormons . . . west to Utah" from 1846 to 1869, with a mortality rate of about 7.5 percent. Accident, gunfire, disease, exposure, and other incidents took almost six thousand lives on the immigrant trail to Utah Territory. Another study in 2014 inspired by Melvin Bashore speculates that the percentage of Mormon deaths on the trail was much lower than Sperry's findings. Bashore and his colleagues suggest that the total Mormon immigrant death percentages are inflated by Sperry due to the uncertainty of the total number of deaths in the Martin and Willie handcart companies of 1856. Bashore offers a more conservative estimate, stating that the "Willie and Martin handcart companies suffered a mortality rate of 16.5 percent," but that number may significantly underrepresent the actual number of deaths in those companies.[1] If so, then the average percentages of Mormon deaths in the wagon companies are skewed.

Death in the West from disease, accident, or mayhem was constant whether in the backcountry or on the immigration trail. For example, six years earlier in Texas, the Hawleys had been living at Zodiac along with Sylvia's parents, Heber and Sally Johnson. A colony member, Spencer Smith, had been traveling away from Zodiac with Heber Johnson and replied in a round-robin letter sent by his wife. Johnson was not feeling well, probably because his wife (Sylvia's mother) had recently died. Smith wrote that cholera had been devastating the "coast [near] in San Antonio small village 60 miles from this place," and perhaps "200 died of the cholera this season." In acknowledging all that tragedy of death, he was also acknowledging his wife's news that their youngest daughter, one-year-old Clarissa Carmelia, had just passed from the fever and chills.[2]

Some estimates of deaths for the whole of the Oregon Trail alone range from twenty to thirty thousand, averaging ten to fifteen graves per mile. Merrill Mates wrote that "between 1849 and 1853, Asiatic Cholera was the greatest killer on the trail. The disease continued to appear during the 1850s, but its appearance considerably diminished after 1853." Peter D. Olch, in conflict with the Brigham Young University Mortality Project, repeats the estimation "that the overall mortality rate on the Oregon-California Trail was 4 to 6 percent of those starting west."[3] Tom Cropper, a thirteen-year-old cowhand and teamster, witnessed the effect daily after crossing the Platte: "The Company now was traveling 'the old Mormon Trail,'" along which he saw Mormon graves almost daily.[4]

Bashore's study cites Peter Olch's estimation that "the overall mortality rate on the Oregon-California Trail was 6 percent of those starting west." The study points out that the Mormon Trail was significantly shorter than

---

1. Kip Sperry, "Migration, Emigration and Immigration Records," 61–68; Tad Walch, "New Study: Mormon Pioneers Were Safer on Trek than Previously Thought, Especially Infants."

2. Anna C. Smith, letter to Spencer Smith, 1850.

3. Peter D. Olch, "Treading the Elephant's Tail: Medical Problems on the Overland Trails."

4. Merrill Mattes, *The Great Platte River Road, The Covered Wagon Mainline via Fort Kearny to Fort Laramie*, 85; Thomas Waters Cropper, "History of Thomas Waters Cropper."

the Oregon Trail. The Croft Company had to cross portions of Kansas and Iowa to reach the Mormon Trail near old Winter Quarters. Recent data also indicate that the mortality rate along the Oregon Trail may have been lower than estimated by Olch in "Treading the Elephant's Tail: Medical Problems on the Overland Trails."[5] The researchers conclude that Mormon immigrants totaled 56,042 immigrants "from 1847 through 1868." Their data states that the Mormon Wagon Companies suffered "1,910 deaths, giving a mortality rate of approximately 3.41%. Of these, there were 930 female deaths (3.48%) and 944 male deaths (3.27%)." The figures are somewhat higher than the national mortality rate for the "same time period [which] was approximately 2.5% to 2.9%," indicating that immigrant rates were about fifteen to thirty percent higher.[6] Death rarely came from Native Americans, and more often from bad sanitation, inadequate meal preparation and food storage, untreated water, and living outdoors from late spring to late fall while sheltering from the elements under wagon tops and tents when available. The journeyer's old companion of disease accompanied the pioneers as they trekked toward the westering sun. Tuberculosis (consumption), measles, cholera, dysentery, pneumonia, pertussis (whooping cough), and smallpox so dreaded by the Native Americans laid the weak low forever.[7] John Jacques' handcart company that summer of 1856 suffered from a "diarrhoea [that] prevailed in the camp." So many immigrants were ill that some had to walk and not ride."[8] Death by livestock or wild animals, drowning, maiming, shooting, and other physical injuries stalked the unwary, the weary, and the fatigued on the trail.

According to Peter D. Olch, wagons wheels were the cause of most physical injury and death. With some frequency, children and adults apparently slipped while getting out of a wagon and fell beneath the wheels. William Thompson Newby recorded in his diary the first known instance of a vehicular death in 1841: "July 18—A very bad road. Joel J. Hembree son Joel fel off the waggeon tung & both wheels run over him. July 19—Lay buy

---

5. Melvin L. Bashore, H. Dennis Tolley, and the BYU Pioneer Mortality Team, "Mortality on the Mormon Trail, 1847–1868," 113.

6. Bashore et al., "Mortality on the Mormon Trail," 114–15.

7. Olch, "Treading the Elephant's Tail," 25–31.

8. J[ohn] J[aques], "Some Reminiscences," 1; also in Journal History of the Church, November 30, 1856, 33–38 (hereafter cited as Journal History). John Jaques, 1827–1900, a devoted LDS member, an English convert immigrant, lost his oldest daughter (age two) during the tragedy. An intellectual, he wrote very well, serving in editorial newspaper positions and as an LDS assistant historian.

Joel Hembree departed this life about 2 oclock." The second major cause of bodily injury and death on the trail came from firearms. Stampeding livestock ranked third.[9] An example of a shooting death was recorded by John Bidwell in 1841 after a James Shotwell pulled a firearm from a wagon "with the muzzle towards him in such a manner that it went off and shot him near the heart—he lived about an hour and died in full possession of his senses."[10]

Injuries and accidents and unforeseen circumstances were commonplace in every pioneer company. In one of the handcart companies that summer of 1856, John Jacques recorded that "Ellen Cantwell was bitten by a ten-rattle rattlesnake, which was subsequently killed, but the girl was not fatally affected. On the 18th a woman named Stewart was missed. Several men went to search for her, but she got into camp before they did, though much exhausted after staying out all night and having been vigorously serenaded by wolves."[11]

Captain Croft's company, fortunately, lost no one.

As events progressed during the traveling season of 1856, pioneer history and lore of the wagon train and handcart companies detail how complex, tiresome, long, and boring the trail was for many, yet tragic for others. The travelers' experiences were a mixed bag: some experienced seemingly banal incidents, such as those of the Croft wagon train, while for others that season, particularly the members of the Willie and Martin handcart companies, incidents boggle comprehension. The narrative cannot grasp the event's horrifying miseries leading up to the desperate camp at Martin's Cove in present-day Wyoming. The two companies started late in the season, and the weather trapped them in Wyoming. The best estimates suggest several hundred Latter-day Saints died from starvation, lack of warm clothing, poor shelter, and failure to find warmth.[12]

Twenty-two years after the Martin and Willie handcart tragedies, John Jacques, a member of the companies, was asked to give one man's context to the inexplicable horror of it all:

> Some people have supposed that, in the course of these papers narrating the journey of the fifth company of handcart emigrants across the plains in 1856, I should "tell it all." They need have been under no apprehension

---

9. Olch, "Treading the Elephant's Tail," 25–31.
10. John Bidwell, *A Journey to California*.
11. J[aques], "Some Reminiscences," 1; Journal History, November 30, 1856, 33–38.
12. For more on these disasters, see my reviews and the works of David Roberts, *Devil's Gate: Brigham Young and the Great Mormon Handcart Tragedy*; and Tom Rea, *Devil's Gate: Owning The Land, Owning The Story*.

on that point. I could not tell it all. I do not know it all. No human being could tell it all. No human being knows it all. One pair of human eyes could see and one pair or human ears could hear only a small portion of all that transpired in the course of that eventful expedition. Scores of incidents occurred outside the ken and the cognizance of any one observer in or with the company. Only the All-seeing Eye saw and only the All-seeing Ear heard all the occurrences in that long and wearisome journey.[13]

Bad weather and blizzards trapped the two handcart companies (Willie and Martin) "near Devils Gate. Hundreds of men, women, and children died of the exposure, exhaustion, and starvation . . . even with the massive rescue effort." In historian Will Bagley's estimation, the Willie and Martin companies were "the worst disaster in the history of America's overland trails."[14]

However, President Young's letterbook for January 1857 displays his continued enthusiasm for the handcart experiment. Writing in a letter to Apostle John Taylor in New York City, Young still believed the handcart experience revealed "a happy and important reality" because the handcarts demonstrated the "principles of equality and less cost." He also noted the surviving young women of marrying age had found suitable husbands.[15]

While the routine activities of the Hawleys and their traveling companions seem inconsequential in comparison, the horrific experiences of the two handcart companies still remind the reader today that they exemplified the rule that proper preparations and planning were essential to western travel in North America. The Jacob Croft Company with its large Hawley group, along with the other wagon trains and the handcart companies, was only one of many companies of Mormons that traveling season. Several included immigrant companies from Texas. Reports noted that Latter-day Saint missionary leaders in Texas, including Benjamin Lynn Clapp, William M. Allen, and Andrew Bigler, had been released from their mission calls so that "a good number of the Texian Saints [could prepare] for the spring emigration" to gather to Zion.[16] Some of

---

13. J[aques], "Some Reminiscences," 1.
14. Will Bagley, *Blood of the Prophets: Brigham Young and the Massacre at Mountain Meadows*, 52; Will Bagley, "'One Long Funeral March': A Revisionist's View of the Mormon Handcart Disaster."
15. Brigham Young, letter to John Taylor, January 1857.
16. "News From Elders," 5.

the Spavinaw-area members such as the Crofts, Mathenys, and Croppers would resume their journeys that began in 1853.[17]

The magnitude of the migration in which the Mormons of Spavinaw joined in 1856 cannot be overstated. Economic historian Gregory Grossman has written in concrete terms that this was a "remarkable feat of organization, discipline, and endurance." More than the entire population of Nauvoo and its surrounding areas (16,000) trekked "in 3,000 wagons with their flocks and herds and families in great hardship for some 1,400 miles" to settle "in the Great Basin of the American West, a vast, forbidding, almost empty region of arid and rugged terrain with extremes of temperature."[18] The Hawleys and comrades attest to the truth of that suggestion.

Harvey Harris Cluff noted quite rightly that faith drove the first sets of Mormon pioneers into the West and on into the vastness of the Utah Territory. In his own unique dialect, the reader can hear Cluff's tone and voice as he writes,

> The "chambers of the Lord" was a very appropriate name for the Vallies of the Mountains. Our enemies had forced us into the grandest place of protection to be found on the American Continant. But during this tedious and difficult Journey, we did not know the advantages or disadvantages that we would meet. We were going by faith in the promices of God and in the prophetic utterences of the Prophet Joseph Smith. Day after day, month after month we travelled on our journey Westward realising that sufficient was our Strength for the requirements of the day, deeply imbued with the idea of finding a safe abiding place beyond the power and menace of wicked men; all of which gave Strength to our navel and marrow to our bones. There was even more than that to stimulate and make one realise, under the circumstances, that we were loosing nothing in being driven from the face of our Countrymen by our Countrymen. Even in the desert there was more satisfaction in facing the painted savage warrior on his own hunting grounds

---

17. Cropper, "The Life and Experience of Thomas Water Cropper." Several memoirs by Cropper narrate decades of his experiences in the west from Texas to Utah. Consult Cropper, "History of Thomas Waters Cropper"; Cropper, "The Life and Experience of Thomas Waters Cropper," 22–26.

18. Gregory Grossman, "Central Planning and Transition in the American Desert: Latter-day Saints in Present-Day Sight," in his words "a compressed version of a paper presented at the Annual Conference of the European Association for Comparative Economic Study, Barcelona, Spain, September 2000." Clark expands Grossman's number to "70,000 of the estimated 300,000 people who crossed the plains from the 1840s to 1860" were Latter-day Saints. See David L. Clark, "Violence and Disruptive Behavior on the Difficult Trail to Utah, 1847–1868," 83.

and the wild buffalo on his range, than to get a little consistant friendship or Sympathy from Gentiles.[19]

Jacob and Sebrina Croft financed their journey to Utah in part by selling some of their African American slaves to Cherokee Chief Stand. Titles—to thirty-seven-year-old Patricia, four-year-old Andrew, and two-year-old Landy—warranted "to be sound in mind and body" were sold for $1,300. John and George Hawley witnessed the sale.[20] The Crofts did not sell all of their slaves. Thomas Waters Cropper, the young cowhand on the journey, reminisced in 1932 that "[t]heir slaves came with them—at least some of them did—particularly one named Dan, a trusted slave and an expert with cattle drove the biggest team."[21]

By 1856, more than a decade of travel experiences had created expectations of caravan life on the Mormon Trail.[22] The Mormons depended on William Clayton's odometer and guidebook to get them to Salt Lake Valley. Wagons were much more likely to be those associated with farm work and regular life rather than the Conestoga of lore, often holding a ton and more of freight and passengers. The sides canted upward as lofty as five feet above the wagon bed, onto which a structure could be temporarily (or permanently) attached to bows with a covering of canvas-material types treated to increase rain resistance. Water barrels, chains, and at least one hundred feet of rope were customary gear, along with grease containers for sockets and wheel bearings. Travelers rendered buffalo and wolf parts when necessary to replace the absence of commercial grease. Many wagons carried replacement axles, tongues, spokes, and other items that could be packed under the bed.

Food supplies were the heaviest and bulkiest portion of the wagon load as well as the most important. A successful journey depended on a dogged, gritty expenditure of animal and human muscle and sweat, "so foods high in calories were favored." Hunting large game animals, trapping of fowl, and gathering prairie and mountain greens, roots, and berries could supplement a diet but could not guarantee adequate foodstuffs to

---

19. Harvey Harris Cluff, Autobiography, Journals, and Scrapbook, 1868–1916.
20. Cherokee Nation Collection in Western History Collections of the University of Oklahoma, published in R. Halliburton, Jr., *Red over Black: Black Slavery among the Cherokee Indians*, 114.
21. Thomas Waters Cropper, quoted in *Millard County Chronicle*, January 14, 1932.
22. For an excellent detailed description of the material culture of the overland trail, consult Will Bagley, *So Rugged and Mountainous: Blazing the Trails to Oregon and California, 1812–1848*, 134.

survive the trail. Dorinda Moody Slade, a Hawley neighbor in the Indian Nations and Pine Valley, was reported to have remembered that "on the road to Utah: Their main sustenance was cornbread, pigweed green, fish and buffalo meat. The latter would be jerked and taken along to help them on the way."[23] By 1856, the supply points at Scotts Bluff and Fort Kearny and Fort Laramie and Fort Bridger were limited and costly.

The Croft Company typically would have roughly 6.5 tons of flour, 5 tons of bacon, 650 pounds each of coffee and salt, and 1,300 pounds of sugar. Thus, coffee with bread and bacon were the staples of the menu. Dried and packaged rice, fruit, beans, pickles, baking soda, and other items may have expanded the basic diet. Portable chicken coops were attached to some wagons, and milk cows often accompanied families with small children. Smaller and lighter iron cooking kettles were preferred, along with the coffee pot, frying pans, tin cups, plates, and eating utensils. Pioneers were aware of the dangers that came with inadequate and untreated supplies, as well as the diseases that accompanied such conditions: dysentery, scurvy, and other sicknesses. Thomas Waters Cropper wrote that Croft Company supplies were obtained in part by selling twenty-five head of cattle.[24]

Will Bagley has written concisely that "the men and women who went west during the 1840s realized they might as well have stepped off the edge of the earth" because "it was unlikely they would ever see again those they left behind."[25] Lillian Schlissel has powerfully noted that immigration to the West not only moved women from their daily gender-oriented tasks to also performing work linked to men, but also forced them to endure the separation and perhaps termination of "long-lived, intimate loving friendship[s]" they had created and nurtured "with other women in the settled communities of the East."[26] Schlissel noted that the eastern world of American men and women "had been ordered by a separation of sexes. The delineation of the culture's 'sexual spheres' place women in life-long contiguities with other women." The western immigration ruptured "the high levels of emotional fulfillment within their own group" and forced women to cope with new and increasingly stressful situations on the trail.[27] Although the women of the Jacob Croft Company were veterans of frontier life and movement along America's borderlands, this

---

23. Ella Lloyd Beckstrom, "Dorinda Melissa Moody's History."
24. Cropper, "Life and Experience."
25. Bagley, *So Rugged and Mountainous*, 176.
26. Quoted in Lillian Schlissel, *Women's Diaries of the Westward Journey*, 87.
27. Schlissel, *Women's Diaries*, 88.

eight-hundred-mile trek to Utah Territory must have appeared intimidating to men and women both. And it must have been even more for men and women from the settled communities east of the Mississippi and the countries across the ocean.

Women suffering the "dissolution of bonds with other women" and other emotional ties aggravated the physical hardships endured on the journey. When these women wrote longingly of the home, they also meant their close bonds with mothers, sisters, and friends, and they grieved over the loss of those relationships which had provided the structure and the emotional support of their lives. This sundering of their emotional life with women and with the familiar world of womanly affairs, one may surmise, lay at the root of the antagonism to men that marks the pages of so many diaries of the journeying women. In almost all the early stages of frontier life—the trail itself and the first settlements—women strove to reestablish the traditional norms of sex roles and work patterns. Thus, there are numerous diary accounts of mothers insisting that their young daughters wear sunbonnets and gloves on the wagon trains. Once the settlements were established, wives, mothers, and young girls found themselves caught between "old" and "new" lifestyles. The diaries provide remarkable records of ambivalence, of anxiety, and sometimes of exultation as women moved toward new expressions of freedom and self-assertion.[28]

The Jacob Croft Company moved out on June 23, 1856, from their first encampment near Spavinaw. Thomas Waters Cropper narrated in his daily journal the company's trip across the plains and mountains to valleys in the far-away mountains. He remembered that the trip began with 150 to 200 head of cattle, some horses, 3 Croft wagons, and a buggy. Cropper's half-sisters, Nancy and Amelia, were married to William Hawley and Isaac Hawley. Isaac Hawley and Sam Bertice drove two of the wagons. Jacob Croft had the buggy, while Stephen Duggins piloted the Croft family wagon. George and John, the other Hawley brothers, had their own wagons. The large Slade family needed three more wagons of their own. Others driving wagons included Enoch Hackshaw and Robert Lloyd [Loyd]. The younger boys, including George and Tom and Leigh Cropper, were tasked with managing the cattle. A "meeting [was held] and

---

28. Schlissel, *Women's Diaries*, 87–88. Also see Adrietta Applegate Hixon, *On to Oregon! A True Story of a Young Girl's Journey into the West*, 12.

organized the [the sixty-five-member company] electing Br. Jacob Croft, Captain; Br. Wm. [Rufus] Slade, Chaplain; Br. John Duggins], Clerk."[29]

John Hawley, as Sergeant of the Guard, would have been responsible for the camp's safety. His duty included ensuring that each member of the company acted in accordance with the company rules. He would have been accountable for rousing the camp each morning and having it in bed each night. The camp would be secured at night by drawing the wagons into a circle, tongue to stern. He would have supervised the construction and maintenance of the corral when in use. Weaponry had to be clean, functional, and at hand.[30]

The initial journey on bad roads from Spavinaw took almost a month to a camping area several miles west of Kansas City. The first week from Monday to Sunday, June 23rd to 29th, the Company covered less than forty miles to a point a few miles north of the Neosho River. The party held church services on Sunday the 29th. The second week from June 30th to July 6th, the wagons and animals made better distance—about fifty miles to a Sunday camping site at Drywood Creek, just across the Kansas border. Much of that week had been spent looking for straying horses, oxen, and cattle. The company covered eighty-four miles the third week, despite a broken axel on the Croft carriage. The travelers bivouacked near a spring some miles from Kansas City on July 15, 1856.[31]

The next ten days the company consolidated, bringing sick members forward who had been left behind at camp, searching for lost animals, and preparing for the westward trek. The Jacob Croft Company would have performed similar tasks as the Swiss immigrants did later that year in the Kansas City area: "The fixing of tents under the trees in the wood, the building of a campfire, the baking of our bread in baking kettles, the washing of our clothes and the tending" of young ones. "But, some of the work was hard many were the privations that we were beginning to feel, we still felt happy."[32] Cropper noted that twenty-five cattle were sold to

---

29. Grant Foreman, "Missionaries of the Latter Day Saints Church in Indian Territory," 207.
30. Clark, "Violence and Disruptive Behavior," 86–87.
31. Cropper, "History."
32. Quoted in Polly Aird, *Mormon Convert, Mormon Defector: A Scottish Immigrant in the American West, 1848–1861*, 127.

outfit the needs of the journeyers.³³ Once ready the company began to move along the Kansas River to Uniontown.³⁴

Croft, Hawley, and the other adults who had experienced many years on the American borderlands now encountered new challenges as they crossed the western prairies and far mountains. Breakfast would be served about six in the morning, and the travel would finish about five in the afternoon. Then an hour of rest, or 'nooning,' for man and animal. The oxen grazed while still yoked. A wagon team would hold a place in the column a day at a time. The advantages and disadvantages were equalized by rotating one day at a time from front to rear to the middle. Open terrain allowed several parallel columns to move, decreasing the amount of dust one had to endure. In close terrain, the column moved in single file. Tom Cropper and the other cowhands in the Croft Company began a learning curve in handling the trail herd. At first, cows that birthed caused "considerable trouble" by backtracking their offspring who had been given to local ranchers. The young riders soon learned to kill the calves instead, peeling and taking the skins ahead so that the cows would follow.³⁵

The Croft Company never camped twice on the same ground. They averaged between fifteen and twenty miles daily, moving only half the day on Saturday then stopping to camp and wash up. Sunday was celebrated with morning services then followed by a half day of travel. Tom Cropper recalled, "We always traveled a little every day, no matter what the conditions." At day's end, the company would create a roughly circular encampment, enhancing security against animals and strangers by chaining the tongue of each wagon to the tail of the wagon ahead. An opening at either end allowed movement of animals in and out of camp. Fires were made of young willows during season, or drift wood, burnable debris left by earlier travelers, or from "prairie coal" (dried buffalo dung). Access to water from the Platte made it of little concern until travelers reached the South Pass. Few boiled the water, which when done was "to kill the wiggle-tails." Untreated drinking water factored heavily into the mortality rate on the trail.³⁶

The pioneers still found means and time to enjoy themselves when possible. Polly Aird wrote about the experiences of a group of Latter-day Saint immigrants traveling two years earlier who "began to appreciate the

---

33. Cropper, "History."
34. Foreman, "Missionaries," 206–7.
35. Cropper, "History."
36. Cropper, "History."

scenery and enjoy themselves despite the heat, dust, work, and daily trials. In the evenings, they sat on oxen yokes around campfires and sang hymns, and when the bugle called, they assembled for prayer." One immigrant recorded: "my soul rejoices as we march Zionward and views the land which the Lord has blest for the gathering of his Saints."[37]

As the Croft Company entered "Indian country,"[38] the wild cattle and horses would have been entrusted to Sergeant of the Guard John Hawley. On one occasion, the animals were enclosed in a log stockade about eight feet high. Cropper's narrative gives no further details. The company may have been at Fort Laramie or a federal Indian Agency, or a holding pen somewhere on the North Platte used by other companies. The cattle took some time to quiet down while four or five of the boys "on horseback rode around and around the stockade trying to quiet them before we left them for the night. Finally, they all laid down and we were at the point of leaving them when like a clap of thunder they were on their feet running and trampling each other until they went over the top of the fence and broke the pickets off, making a hole big enough for them to get out." The riders rode as fast as possible to head off the herd, "swinging our hats and hollering at them to try to stop them." The cattle ran for nearly a mile and then eventually allowed the cowhands to lead them back to the stockade. The boys repaired the fence, only to have to repeat three more times that night the sequence of uncontrolled animal frenzy, broken fence, stampede, and round up. By morning, nine cattle had disappeared, for which the local Indian Agent compensated Captain Croft at twenty dollars apiece.

The Croft Company followed the Platte River "for two hundred miles and came to a bridge where we crossed to the other side. Near was Fort Kearny where a garrison of soldiers were stationed." Sam Bertice, the company teamster, volunteered "to join the soldiers" at Fort Laramie; and Tom Cropper was moved from herder to Bertice's job. He crossed the Sweet Water River "twenty-six times in twelve miles" along the trail. The company now was traveling "the old Mormon Trail," and saw as many as twenty graves a day where people had been buried along the route. The thirteen-year-old would pilot the wagon from Fort Kearney to Salt Lake City then "down to Fillmore."[39]

---

37. Aird, *Mormon Defector*, 130.
38. Cropper's term, offensive in our time, may be merely the writing of an old man denoting the difference of living in the 'civilized' Indian Territory compared to the life of the Plains tribes.
39. Cropper, "History"; Cropper, "Life and Experience."

Tom Cropper recalled the numerous buffalo on the Platte, surrounding "our train on all sides. One day they bolted right through our train and tipped over three wagons. The wagon bows were broken, and the contents of the wagons spilled around on the ground, but no one was injured, and no serious damage was done." His horse "Tobe" had earlier belonged to Indians and apparently had been trained to run buffalo. One day, the horse "was champing at the bits and acting like he wanted to give chase, so I decided to run up to one of them. After about a quarter of a mile run I got up to one." Cropper had some difficulty in making his horse return to the train. The Saints made bison a regular part of the diet. They cut up and hung the "choicest parts" to dry on lines strung on the wagon sides. Cropper "never lost my appetite for 'Jerked' meat."[40]

The trekkers often encountered other immigrants on the road. Tom Cropper remembered that "there was one Hand Cart Company ahead of us and one behind us. A four-mule team from the one in front waited for us and asked for donations for their company. We gave them a ton of flour, a beef and some other provisions. We expected to catch up with them any day, but we lost a number of our work oxen and had to break more, so they beat us to Salt Lake City by two days."[41] Thomas Bullock noted on the 22nd of September that he had "camped with a company of brethren from the Southern States, many of whom had left Lyman Wight, and [inaccurately wrote that they] had been re-baptized by Elder Preston Thomas, also a large company of Saints with Captain [Jacob] Croft, near the Warm Spring." Thomas's company earlier in 1853 consisted "of poor Englishmen, a couple of Scotsmen, and some wealthy Texas families with their slaves," but no runaway Wightites. The confusion resulted from Thomas's earlier mission to Texas that brought converts to the Indian Nations in 1853, and that the Croft Company (with former Wightites converted by Miller) was camped nearby to Bullock's camp in 1856. Bullock confused the two companies.[42]

A week later, a party led by Apostle F. D. Richards and Elder Daniel Spencer, noted in the *Deseret News*, had "camped with [Jacob] Croft's company consisting of 58 persons, 14 wagons, 80 yoke of oxen, 30 horses, and 130 loose cattle; they are principally from Texas and the Cherokee

---

40. Cropper, "Life and Experience."
41. Cropper, "History."
42. Thomas Bullock, "Interesting from our Missionaries on the Plains," 2. Thomas Waters Cropper, quoted in the *Millard County Chronicle,* July 31, 1930; Daniel H. Thomas, *Preston Thomas, 1814–1877, A Biography*, 34.

land. They were healthy and in good spirits, and gave us a most hospitable reception. This was the last company passed by us on the road."[43] The Croft Company had apparently passed the other companies on the trail.

Native Americans would impede the progress of the Croft Company every so often. The warriors would ride into the camp, or form up across the trail, and require toll in the form of salt and other foodstuffs. On reaching the Platte River, the Croft Company encountered "a very large camp of savages—mostly women and children. The men were hunting buffalo. The women came into our camp with all sorts of indian [sic] finery—moccasins, shawls embroidered with beads and porcupine quills. They wanted to trade for salt, bright colored cloth, or flour. They would give about fifty cents in moccasins for a pint of salt or ten cents worth of glass beads."[44] The company encountered no violence with the Native Americans.

Robert L. Munkres's estimation of Native American threat to wagon train immigrants before 1860 had increased through the years because of the growing encounters between the races: on the trail, at "traders' tents, cabins and posts"[45] as well as the military installations. A typical series of encounters included the one below:

> May 30   passed Scottsbluff) Passed two French Traders' cabins and three Indian Lodges with them.
> June 1   Came onto the Platte River again and passed a Traders tent of French and Indians. . . . Passed three more Trading Posts.
> June 3   passed Fort Laramie).
> June 4   Passed a Traders' Post and about twenty Indian Wigwams with them.
> June 8   Passed 2 trading posts; saw no Indians.
> June 9   Passed a Trading Post and an Indian Wigwam.
> June 10 Passed a Traders Station today and an Indian Lodge with it.
> June 11 There was a Traders Station and six Indian Lodges with them.
> June 13 Passed two Trader's tents and an Indian Lodge with them.
> June 14 Independence Rock) Here is a white Trader as usual, with an Indian Wigwam.
> June 16 We passed two traders tents today.

---

43. Franklin Richards and Daniel Spencer, "Journey from Florence to G. S. L. City," 2.

44. Cropper, "History."

45. Robert L. Munkres, "The Plains Indian Threat on the Oregon Trail Before 1860," 218.

June 21 We have passed a Trader and a blacksmith shop today and are in sight of an Indian Town.
June 22 Passed a Traders and a Blacksmith shop today.
June 26 Green River Ferry) Here is quite a town. Five or six cabins and four or five stores and one Indian wigwam.

Munkres used the entries of sixty-six diaries and determined that an "overwhelming majority of the diarists and their companions encountered no overt threat of attack while passing through present-day Nebraska and Wyoming." Most negative contacts seemed to be theft "motivated by the hope of plunder" with "more than one out of every three parties . . . very likely to receive the attention of a raiding party." Munkres appears to be equating presence with a threat, which may be an uncertain assumption. When comparing Unruh's comments, some of the encounters may have been driven by issues with certain tribal groups other than raiding. The opportunity for commerce, whether trading or raiding or collecting tribute and passage fees, surely can be suggested as reasons why some tribe members were attracted to the white immigrant routes.[46]

Comments over a period of years by Latter-day Saint pioneers may have exaggerated the lack of danger from the horse-mounted tribesman. Harvey Harris Cluff wrote: "To look a Savage in the face all painted for war, was indeed horrowfying, but a little flour, sugar and coffee made the face of the Savage more humanterian. And he proved a closer friend than our white brother." Almost forty percent of the emigrant wagon trains had almost no contact with the Native Americans.[47]

The Jacob Croft Company, nevertheless, during the last five weeks on the road had reason to be careful. On September 7 and 9, 1856, the company members learned from Californians returning to the east "of the increased hostility of the Cheyennes" and the killing of several of the members in Almon W. Babbitt's ox train. Tom Cropper recorded, "Of the four teamsters in that train two were killed and one wounded; and a woman named Wilson (as was presumed from the tracks) was severely wounded and taken prisoner, and her child, about two months old, was

---

46. Munkres, "Plains Indian Threat," 218.
47. Munkres, 198–99, 204; Pierson Barton, "Journal of Pierson Barton Reading, In His Journey of One Hundred Twenty-Three Days Across The Rocky Mountains From Westport On the Missouri River, 450 Miles Above St. Louis, To Monterey, California, On The Pacific Ocean, In 1843," July 3, 1843, 162; Cornelia A. Sharp, "Diary of Mrs. Cornelia A. Sharp: Crossing the Plains from Missouri to Oregon in 1852," May 29, 1852; Cluff, Autobiography.

murdered. The wagons were plundered, but, as we subsequently learned, most of the property was retaken by Captain Wharton of Fort Kearney." Another Californian told them of "his wife killed, and his boy, some 3 or 4 years old, taken prisoner."[48]

According to Franklin D. Richards and Daniel Spencer, the commanding officer at Fort Kearny had

> doubts of his ability to maintain the post, for want of troops. Mr. Babbitt had left Fort Kearney for Utah a week previous, accompanied by Thomas Sutherland and a driver. . . . As we were leaving the fort for our camp on the north side of the Platte, a discharged soldier came to Capt. Wharton with the news of another massacre by the Cheyennes. This soldier had accompanied Thomas Margetts and James Cowdy, and their families, from Laramie and on returning from a buffalo hunt, when about 125 miles from Fort Kearney, found the wagon plundered and the murdered remains of his traveling companions.[49]

Almon Babbitt was killed by Cheyenne later that same month. His and his companions' grave sites were visited by a widow of Babbitt and her brother, Joel Hills Johnson.

Johnson recorded:

Friday, June 5th. This morning we started early to cross the river to Fort Kearney. . . . We saw Captain Wharton . . . [who] said that they had no doubt but what Colonel Babbitt was murdered by the Indians [and on]Sunday, June 7th. This morning started early and nooned on the Prairie Creek near where A. W. Babbitt's train was broken up last fall by the Indians. We saw the graves where those that were killed were buried, but the wolves had dug them up and devoured them, for we saw their bones, hair and grave clothes scattered about the ground. We camped for the night at the crossing of the creek.

> Yes, dead by the thousands have we passed,
> Entombed along the road,
> When Michael's trump must call at last
> To stand before their God,
> Where all receive, for thought and word
> And every deed, their just reward.[50]

The difficulty of the trip did not recede the closer the company came to its destination. Not only were the pioneers concerned with the Native Americans, but the women also discovered during the final weeks to Salt

---

48. Cropper, "History."
49. Richards and Spencer, "Journey from Florence to G. S. L. City," 258.
50. Joel H. Johnson, 1802–1882 Autobiography (1802–1868).

Lake City, once above the Great Plains, that their work would become even more difficult. Males outnumbered females in many of the wagon companies as high as ten to one, although counting the male-to-female percentage in the Latter-day Saint trains would have been reduced because of the number of families and those with plural spouses. In Hawley's experience as a young man, plural families had included a polygamous company from Wisconsin to Texas in 1845 and 1846, and his own brother George had at least two wives in the Croft Company (the sisters Ann and Sarah Hadfield and possibly a third, the teenage Hawley ward, Jenet Condie).

Men and women would have to cope with walking through the dust thrown up by the wagon wheels while keeping children and animals in sight and safe from the rigors of the road. Once in the higher elevations, Lillian Schlissel wrote, as

> the men were needed for more pressing chores, the women drove the teams of horses or mules. When the wagons were being inched up the mountain passes of the Rockies, the women worked behind, carrying large rocks to set beneath the wagon wheels to keep them from backsliding. Many diarists fairly exploded with bitterness as the hard journey erased the more graceful tributes by which eastern society had flattered women and hidden the inequalities of their station.[51]

Tom Cropper closed his trail account with, "We finally crossed the Great Divide where the streams ran west instead of east. Then we reached Bear River and went down Echo Canyon, crossing the stream 46 times. There were no bridges at that time. We came up over Little Mountain, also Big Mountain and down Immigration Canyon to Salt Lake City and camped on Immigration Square, where the City and County Building now stand. This was on the eleventh of October, 1856." The *Deseret* News simply reported on the 15th that the Jacob Croft Company had arrived.[52]

John Hawley's entry concerning the westward passage is the shortest of all his entries in the autobiography. He only wrote, "So it is we went to Utah and we had a very pleasant time crossing the plains rejoicing and dancing as we went. We left Kansas City on the 24th of July, 1856, and landed in Salt Lake October the 11th."[53] Whether whimsy or the result of being extremely busy with security duties as Sergeant of the Guard for some sixty individuals and more than two hundred animals had kept him from daily record-keeping remains unknown.

---

51. Schlissel, *Women's Diaries*, 88.
52. Cropper, "Life and Experiences"; "Arrived," 253.
53. John Hawley, "Autobiography of John Hawley," 13.

CHAPTER 5

Welcome to Zion

October 1856 to September 1857

"THE SISTERS TO TEACH THEIR SONS & DAUGHTERS THE PRINCIPLES OF RIGHTEOUSNESS AND TO IMPLANT *A DESIRE IN THEIR HEARTS TO AVENGE THE BLOOD OF THE PROPHETS.*"

The Hawleys first resided in Ogden City at or near Bingham Fort, located in what is now downtown Ogden, Utah. John and George rented a sawmill from a "G. Farr." This may have been the site of the first saw and grist mill established in Ogden Canyon in 1850 by Loren Farr.[1] The Hawley brothers also contracted with their former Texas neighbor, John H. Taylor, living in Weber County, for eighty acres each for farming.[2]

John Hawley wrote that "The Consecration Law was then taught to us" by the Ogden leadership, who directed the members to consecrate their properties to build up the Church as the fiscal agent for the literal Kingdom of God on earth. One in every three Mormons did consecrate, including President Brigham Young, deeding nearly $200,000 himself to the Church.[3] John and Sylvia, desiring to be in conformity with "the ordinances of the gospel," deeded all their property to Brigham Young as the "Trustee and Trust" of the Church. Before deeding their property, John had tithed one-tenth of all his property with "Father Bingham," probably Erastus Bingham of Ogden, who served as bishop during the 1850s.[4]

Receiving a "stewardship" in return for consecrating their property, the Hawleys then controlled their assets and chattels. John believed that "if we should prove faithful to the kingdom in rendering an account of

---

1. In March of 1850, by special request of President Brigham Young, Loren Farr moved to Ogden to take charge of the northern settlements. He built the first sawmill and grist mill north of Salt Lake. See Rhea Farr Wiggins, "Lorin Farr."
2. John Hawley, "Autobiography of John Hawley," 13.
3. Gustave O. Larson, "The Mormon Reformation," 47–48.
4. "Settlers in the area built *Bingham's Fort* under the direction of Bishop Erastus Bingham and lived there from 1853 to 1856," as stated in Webcrhistory, "Home Page & 1849–1869 Chronology."

our Stewardship yearly, we would then be entitled to all the blessings of the kingdom."[5] Every year the Hawleys accounted for how they handled their stewardship. Hawley was perturbed for years after the Church introduced the Order of Enoch. He noted that "there was quite an excitement in the south about the Order of Enoch." Many of the Dixie members joined, but Hawley thought it "all useless for those that had come to the Law of Consecration as I had to take, as I thought Enoch lower. So I never connected myself with this inclination."[6] The United Order, however, was not organized until after the Hawleys left Utah Territory. He may have confused it with the Zion's Cooperative Mercantile Institution, which was organized in 1869 as a closed Church-directed economic and mercantile system to develop local cooperative businesses throughout the territory.

After settling in Ogden, John and Sylvia were baptized yet again to conform to the Latter-day Saint revival movement that became known as the Mormon Reformation; it was the LDS leadership's institutional response to the religious, social, and political pressures of outsiders arriving in the Valley and the Territory, particularly after 1849.[7] The motivation for rebaptism involved the membership's supposed wickedness, and God's punishments rolled out on them. The intent was to correct evil works while sanctifying the Church and anointing the people for the Second Coming. The leadership wanted to separate the Church and its members from the concerns and desires and influences of a profane world.

In September of 1856, a few weeks before the Croft Company arrived in Salt Lake Valley, several general authorities spoke on issues outlined by President Young. The purpose was to align members' lives with the covenants they had made when joining the church. At Kaysville, President Jedidiah M. Grant, second counselor in the first presidency, included directions to be clean "in their persons and dwellings," to organize "families in order, carefully cultivating their farms and gardens," and "to gather into and build up the fort and settlement." He then "concluded by praying that all those who did not feel to do right might have their way opened to leave the people and Territory." The Latter-day Saints who would "not come forward" and renew their covenants by repentance, confession, and

---

5. Hawley, "Autobiography," 13.
6. Hawley, 21.
7. Hawley, 13. Hawley commented in retrospect on one of his vexations—the repetitive baptism in the LDS and RLDS churches for the remission of sins: "We will end this being baptized for the remission of sins by and by."

baptism should be counted "as heathen men and publicans, not numbered among the Saints," and shunned.[8]

Jedediah M. Grant foreshadowed the movement when he spoke to the membership at Provo, Utah, on July 13, 1855. He compared the church wards to trees with "branches" that needed to be cut off. "The Kingdom would progress much faster" with the diseased branches gone, Grant threatened. He continued, stating that he "would like to see the works of reformation commence," with every man walking "to the line, then we would have something like union." The audience was urged to refine themselves, to fuse the sacred and the profane in their lives, and to cleanse their "houses, lots, farms and everything around yon on the right and the left, then the Spirit of the Lord can dwell with you."[9]

The Hawleys were caught up in the Reformation and its catechism that commenced at the October conference. The basic recommitment of a member to his or her covenants was based on the principles of the imminent Second Coming—that members had to be convicted and confessing of their sins. They had to earnestly seek forgiveness through rebaptism and walk a godly walk. Leadership framed declamations with such ferocity that members were pushed into a fanaticism that is difficult for modern readers to grasp.[10] George Armstrong Hicks, a member from childhood to adulthood and who went from active member to apostate, wrote that at his community of Spanish Fork the "wildest bombast was preached as the Gospel of Christ," and that the Church could only be renewed if evil people were removed.[11]

The Reformation took hold in southern Utah Territory. Devout Latter-day Saint and frontier scout, John Chatterley, thought it was "insane . . . reli-

---

8. William Willes and Gilbert Clements, "Great Reformation," 4.

9. Address delivered by Jedediah M. Grant in Brigham Young, July 13, 1855, *Journal of Discourses*, 3:58–61.

10. Hawley, "Autobiography," 13. William P. MacKinnon, "'Lonely Bones': Leadership and Utah War Violence," 121–78, discusses the role of implicit and real violence in the Reformation. Further reading should include William P. McKinnon, *At Sword's Point, Part 1: A Documentary History of the Utah War to 1858*, vol. 10; David Bigler and Will Bagley, *The Mormon Rebellion: America's First Civil War, 1857–1858*. Also see Eugene E. Campbell, *Establishing Zion: The Mormon Church in the American West, 1847–1869*; Larson, "The Mormon Reformation," 47–51; Paul H. Peterson, "The Mormon Reformation of 1856–1857: The Rhetoric and the Reality," 59–87; and Will Bagley, *Blood of the Prophets: Brigham Young and the Massacre at Mountain Meadows*.

11. George Armstrong Hicks, *Family Record and History of George Armstrong Hicks*.

gious fanaticism" that required the Saints to separate from the Gentile world while awaiting the Second Coming. He alleged that a secret conspiracy of fellow Mormons in Cedar City cautioned Chatterley "to look out for myself, as I was doomed, as it was concluded by a majority in one of their meetings, that I must be put out of the way; and knew too much, and was much opposed to their hellish murderous conduct." He feared discussing some who allegedly left for California but then disappeared. After the warning, Chatterley made it his custom to tread carefully.[12]

Hawley recorded no incidents of violence in his personal experience of the Reformation. He found it an "exciting time," as the "catechizers came to my house on their mission" to explore their sins, such as adultery. "[T]hey wished to know if we wanted to be catechized separately. We told them no, for thank God we had not broken the covenant we made the time we was joined in marriage" at Zodiac, Texas. John and Sylvia were then rebaptized for the remission of sins.[13] In 1857, John "was being walked

---

12. Robert H. Briggs, "The Mountain Meadows Massacre: An Analytical Narrative Based on Participant Confessions," 313–33. Chatterley's account is on page 320.

13. Hawley, "Autobiography," 13. For more on the Reformation, see Polly Aird, Jeff Nichols, and Will Bagley, eds., *Playing With Shadows: Voices of Dissent in the Mormon West*, 51; Ronald W. Walker, Richard E. Turley, and Glen M. Leonard, *Massacre at Mountain Meadows*, 282–84; Briggs, "The Mountain Meadows Massacre," 330n26. On November 3, Brigham Young introduced a list of thirteen questions for the brethren. This list evolved into a list of twenty-six questions that were posed in personal interviews within the privacy of one's own home rather than through public exhortation. Ward teachers visited each family in the ward and catechized the people with some of the following selected questions. See Larson, "The Mormon Reformation," 53–55.

1. Have you shed innocent blood or assented thereto?
2. Have you committed adultery?
3. Have you betrayed your brother?
4. Have you borne false witness against your neighbor?
5. Do you get drunk?
6. Have you stolen? [This question was expanded into seven additional questions specifically asking about the use of fields, animals, lost property, strays, irrigation water, and borrowing and branding.]
7. Have you lied?
8. Have you contracted debts without prospect of paying?
9. Have you labored faithfully for your wages?
10. Have you coveted that which belongs to another?
11. Have you taken the name of the Lord in vain?
12. Do you preside in your family as a servant of God?

by Brother Wilford Woodruff" in the Endowment House, and "the conversation came up about the excitable times we had had." John confessed that he was not satisfied with some of the "revengeful speeches that had been indulged in by some of my brethren." Woodruff told Hawley that he believed "some of our brethren had gone farther with this reformation and vengeance than they ought." This conversation occurred several weeks before the massacre at Mountain Meadows.[14] Woodruff wanted to know how Hawley had responded to the catechism, and Hawley replied that he "had nothing to confess." Woodruff told Hawley: "You are an exception worthy of imitation. I wish we as a Quorum of the Twelve could of did truthfully as you did in this, but to our shame there was but three that had to confess to adultery." Hawley did not ask who these three were, but he suspected Woodruff of being one of them.[15]

Public plural marriage was another change to which John Hawley had to adapt. They were facts of everyday life in territorial Utah. He had become painfully aware of the doctrine in 1845 in the Lyman Wight Company when he unwittingly paid courtship to a young second wife of another man.[16] Lyman Wight tried to force Sylvia Johnson, the woman whom John loved and to whom he was espoused, to marry Spencer Smith as a concurrent wife.[17] George Hawley himself had three wives.[18] Although John Hawley remained monogamous, he seriously contemplated the mat-

---

13. Have you paid your tithing in all things?
14. Do you teach your family the gospel of Salvation?
15. Do you speak against your brethren or against any principle taught us in the Bible, Book of Mormon, Book of Doctrine & Covenants, revelations given through Joseph Smith the prophet and the Presidency of the Church as now organized?
16. Do you wash your body and have your family do so as often as health and cleanliness require and circumstances permit?
17. Do you labor six days and rest or go to the house of the Worship on the seventh?
18. Do you and your family attend ward meetings?
19. Do you oppress the hireling in his wages?

14. For a more descriptive role of Elder Woodruff's participation in the Reformation, see Thomas G. Alexander, "Wilford Woodruff and the Mormon Reformation of 1855–57," 25–39.

15. Hawley, "Autobiography," 14.

16. Melvin C. Johnson, *Polygamy on the Pedernales: Lyman Wight's Mormon Villages in Antebellum Texas, 1845–1858*, 57.

17. Hawley, "Autobiography," 9–10.

18. Brigham Young, letter to Zadok K. Judd, February 24, 1860.

ter during his thirteen years in Pine Valley, and he nearly took a second wife. Eventually, the doctrine of plurality caused him, in significant part, to break with the Latter-day Saint church in Utah.[19]

Apostle Erastus Snow of St. George supported the principle of plural marriage in his part of the Mormon Kingdom. In one example, Snow advised Brigham Young that William F. Butler should have a second wife, stating that the man had not had "very much satisfaction in his marriage" because Snow thought the woman was "partially deranged."[20] According to Lowell C. Bennion, the St. George Censuses in 1862, 1870, and 1880, recorded that about thirty "percent of St. George's husbands had more than one wife."[21] Ten years after the Hawleys came to Dixie, a local census by church leaders recorded that about forty percent (or 67 of the 170 families) were polygamous.[22]

Men dominated the Hawleys' Utah. Talks by W. W. Phelps and Brigham Young in the October General Conference of 1861 are representative of these relationships. Phelps told the listeners in the Tabernacle that Eve had fifty-six children, twenty-eight of each sex, and "that Adam had many wives." President Young reinforced what Phelps said. Young also counseled, "[I]f a man is faithfull & should his wife leave him & be married to another without his consent there is no power in heaven or on earth that can prevent him from claiming her in the resurrection." Two paths, apparently, existed for a woman to lawfully leave her husband. If she became "alienated from" her spouse, then the husband's duty would be "to give her a Bill [of divorce] and set her free." Even if they co-habited afterward in fornication and were punished by death, she would "come up in the morning of the resurrection & claim all of her rights & privileges in the marriage covenant." The second way reinforced the submission of a wife to husband.

---

19. John Hawley, "Experiences of John Hawley," 234–35. Robert Hawley, a descendant of John Pierce Hawley, in conversation with the author, on September 28, 2002, said family traditions remember that John was not at all serious about marrying a second wife.

20. Erastus Snow, letter to Brigham Young, November 7, 1869.

21. Lowell C. Bennion, "Mapping the Extent of Plural Marriage in St. George, 1861–1880," 27–28.

22. James Godson Bleak, *The Annals of the Southern Utah Mission: A Record of the History of the Settlement of Southern Utah*, 151. The annals include typescripts and manuscripts that form the narrative of the St. George Stake. Bleak used documents from ecclesiastical accounts, official records, texts, files, papers, letters, and narratives to create a cornucopia of documentary material not only for the southwestern portions of the territory but also for Arizona, Nevada, and eastern Arizona.

Young counseled that should a wife desire another man higher in authority who "is willing to take her & her husband gives her up there is no Bill of divorce required in the case it is right in the sight of God."²³

Apostle Orson Pratt's series of lectures reinforced the authority of the patriarchal leadership dominating the Mormon culture. He gave advice to women to not "unite herself in marriage with any man, unless she has fully resolved to submit herself wholly to his counsel . . . and to let him govern as the head." Pratt counseled that a woman should be single rather than married and "rebel against the divine order of family government, instituted for a higher salvation." Rebellion against the male head of the marriage union would lead to greater condemnation. He also informed the prospective plural wife of rising in her spouse's affection by her own merits, not by subterfuge against the other wives.²⁴ Orson Pratt wrote in *The Seer* that "it is far better for her not to be united with him in the sacred bonds of eternal union, then to rebel against the divine order of family government, instituted for a higher salvation; for if she altogether turn therefrom, she will receive a greater condemnation."²⁵

Nonetheless, Eugene E. Campbell and Bruce L. Campbell "have revealed that 1,645 divorces were granted by Brigham Young during the period of his presidency and . . . they do indicate that many Mormon marriages during this period (pre-1890) were unstable and that official attitudes toward divorce were lenient." Since Brigham Young could not "grant civil divorces terminating monogamous marriages," and was the only Church leader who could grant divorces for polygamous marriages, the logical conclusion is that the great majority if not all the 1,645 divorces were of a polygamous nature.²⁶

Zerah Pulsipher, a member of the First Seven Presidents of the Seventy and a Church quorum subordinate only to the First Presidency and the Twelve, moved in 1862 to the Southern Mission in Dixie. His counsel about

---

23. James Beck Notebooks, October 8, 1861. Note that Beck has an annotation on the opening page of this entry. It is written perpendicular to the main text, in different ink color and right over the diary entry itself: "I do not vouch for the correctness of this by any means as my experience is that the memory of man is treacherous. – JA Beck."

24. Orson Pratt, "Celestial Marriage," 183–87. Pratt's first wife divorced him in part for marrying many much younger women.

25. Pratt, 173–76, 183–87.

26. Eugene E. Campbell and Bruce L. Campbell, "Divorce among Mormon Polygamists: Extent and Explanations," 4–23.

how a man should behave towards his wives and children offers an idealized insight into the family world of southern Utah at that time. He counseled that the wives' "acts of kindness to" their husband would define the extent of his love for them. A father can love "good children" (equating a wife to a station of childishness), and "if the destroyer comes to take one of them, which will he give most likely the one he cannot keep, of course." Pulsipher counseled that children should not be whipped in anger. Daughters should never be with men that are unknown to the father. He begged "you mothers to take care of your children while they are with you."[27]

This is the plural wife patriarchal world that the Hawleys understood from Wisconsin to Texas, and from the Cherokee Nation to Utah Territory. And within that world, the Hawley family life continued. Some of the Zodiac children intermarried with those of other families, and some of those marriages were polygamous. Notable was Harriet Wight, a daughter of Orange Wight and Sarah Hadfield, who had come with her mother and stepfather, George Hawley, to Utah Territory. Orange himself had set precedence for spousal exchange, marrying Marion Sutherland, the first wife of William Curtis. Orange, Lyman Wight's son, had long known George Hawley and was a senior member of the Texas colony. George's courting of Sarah and betrayal of Orange moved him into the ranks of the plurally married and beyond Lyman Wight's good graces.[28]

Harriet Wight married Wilbur Bradley Earl in 1867 of Pine Valley; he was one of three brothers who spent their lives on the Utah-Nevada border. All three brothers practiced polygamy. Harriet was the second wife of Wilbur Earl, joining Mary Langley as a sister wife. She was one of several young former Wightites, including several children of John H. Taylor in Weber County, who are known to have entered polygamy in Utah Territory. It was to Harriet Wight Earl's home that her father, Orange Lysander Wight, would come in the late nineteenth century after a lifetime on the American frontier as a Texas Ranger, rancher, and farmer. He would rejoin the Latter-day Saint Church in Utah.[29]

---

27. Terry Lund and Nora Lund, *Pulsipher Family History Book*, 32; Zerah Pulsipher, "History of Zerah Pulsipher, As Written by Himself."

28. Johnson, *Polygamy on the Pedernales*, 82, 170–71.

29. Johnson, 184; Turk, "Mormons in Texas," 43, 77–78; Joseph Ira Earl, "Journals from the Life and Times of Joseph Ira Earl," 19–20, 37–38, 235; Orange Lysander Wight, "Recollections of Orange L. Wight, Son of Lyman Wight." As early as 1858, Wight had written to Wilford Woodruff inquiring

In 1877, more than fifty percent of St. George's inhabitants were connected as spouses or children or families. This was not unusual in the Latter-Day world in the West and certainly not for the Hawleys. In Lyman Wight's Texas colony, from 1845 to 1857, plural marriages connected at least seventy percent of the members, including nearly forty percent of the adults and more than sixty percent of the families.[30] The Hawleys and their neighbors' Mormon world in Utah abounded with plural husbands, wives, families, and communities.

During the April Conference of 1857, the Hawley brothers were called to the "Rio Virgin River about 350 miles south near the Arizona Territory line."[31] The call ended the brothers' hopes for running the Farr sawmill and farming the Ogden land they had bought from Taylor. The thirty-eight families, including the Hawleys and others, many of them southerners, departed almost immediately. Led by Samuel Adair and Robert Covington, the Covington Company[32] settled at what was first known as "Adair Springs" and then renamed Washington City.

A Church branch was established with southerners Robert D. Covington chosen as a presiding elder, and Harrison Pearce and James B. Reagan serving as counselors. Texans William R. Slade, William Hawley, Joseph Hatfield, Preston Thomas, and Sims B. Matheny joined them.[33] The area was known to the Saints, but it was undeveloped. The Mormons had explored the Iron and Dixie regions as early as December 1847. The Spanish and Mexican padres and traders had been traveling through the area since the 1770s. C. Gregory Crampton wrote that "by the time the Mormons arrived in the Great Basin, the region they occupied was pretty well known," but they "had the region to themselves and quickly utilized any advantage that fell to them resulting from the work of those who had preceded them." The Southern Utes were not queried as to their opinion of these changes. The Latter-day Saints sped up establishing routes and connections to California, where they intended to expand permanently,

---

after Sarah and the children and requesting that she reply to his letters. Orange L. Wight, letter to Stephen Wight and Wilford Woodruff, September 17, 1858.

30. Johnson, *Polygamy on the Pedernales*, 152–60. Further research should identify such populations in other Utah LDS communities, such as Manti and Bountiful, during this period.

31. Johnson, 14.

32. Freddijo Passey Burk, *Joseph Hadfield Story: An Incredible Odyssey*, 164, 168.

33. C. Gregory Crampton, *Mormon Colonization In Southern Utah And In Adjacent Parts of Arizona and Nevada (1965)*, 65. Bleak, *Annals*, 22.

although by 1857 their growing conflict with the federal government was undercutting those aims.[34]

Jefferson Hunt and Howard Egan had led wagon trains through southern Utah to California and back even before Apostle Parley Pratt's exploring trip of fifty men came to find possible settlement locations in the territory's southwest at the end of 1849. Hunt opened the passage from Parowan to present-day Enterprise and southward to Mountain Meadows, then beyond into the desert and on to California. Reaching the junction of the Rio Virgin and Santa Clara rivers, Parley P. Pratt then turned his party north through Mountain Meadows and east toward what would later become the villages of Cedar City, Parowan, and Beaver. Pratt made the determination that Center Creek (Parowan) and Beavers Creek (Beaver) would make for good first settlements.[35] Parowan was named and settled in 1851. In January 1852, John D. Lee led a small exploring party to the Rio Virgin, returned north, and settled at Harmony that year.[36]

By the following year, Parowan and Beaver's populations had reached 392 and 455, respectively. Jacob Hamblin and other Latter-day Saint missionaries began a settlement on the Santa Clara River just above its junction with the Rio Virgin.[37] The meeting of the Washington County court at Harmony in 1856 gave "control of water, timber, and grass of Pine Valley" to "C. W. Dalton, L. W. Roundy, John Blackburn, and Robert Richey for the purposes above specified" and "also the control of the water, or springs in Grass Valley." A proviso that the men "must subserve the interest of the settlements" was a prominent part of the declaration. That proviso would cause problems in the next decade as the population began to grow along the lower Virgen and Santa Clara rivers.[38]

As the settlers labored that summer at Washington and Santa Clara, the Pine Valley Mountain loomed as a beacon of green timber and cooler

---

34. Crampton, *Mormon Colonization*, 16.
35. Crampton, 26–27.
36. Bleak, *Annals*, 3, 12. See William B. and Donna T. Smart, *Over the Rim: The Parley P. Pratt Exploring Expedition to Southern Utah*; Thomas D. Brown, *The Southern Indian Mission: Diary of Thomas D. Brown*.
37. Jacob Hamblin is one of the most intriguing characters in the story of southern Utah, its settlements, and Indian missions, because of his understanding and compassion for indigenous peoples and their cultures. Consult Todd M. Compton, "Becoming a 'Messenger of Peace': Jacob Hamblin in Tooele," 1–29; and Todd M. Compton, *A Frontier Life: Jacob Hamblin, Explorer and Indian Missionary*.
38. Bleak, *Annals*, 20.

weather to the north of Santa Clara and Washington and to the west of Harmony. When the crop nearly failed that first year at Washington, a few settlers went up to the Piedes mission at Tonaquint on the Santa Clara and others moved elsewhere.[39] The Santa Clara and Ash Creek emerged west and east in the valley at "the very heart of the mountain," then flowed south and east to the various villages settling on its base.[40] Hamblin was located to the west of the valley on the north end of the Mountain Meadows.[41]

That summer of 1857 under the sun and in the incredible heat, the settlers at Washington dug ditches, cleared brush, and planted a crop that nearly failed. They built a "pole" bowery and arbor by placing them "vertically in the ground with brush as a roof. The sides were open and it had a dirt floor and was built in the meeting house block. It was used for church and civic programs until an adobe building was built in 1861 near the same location." The County Court of Washington County made William R. Slade Sr. a Justice of the Peace, a School Trustee, and a Selectman of the County Court, and John Hawley served as an appointed Constable.[42]

Brigham Young had also called Jacob Croft and his sons-in-law, Stephen Duggans, Isaac and William Hawley, and Sims Matheny, to settle Dixie. Croft and his sons-in-law, Sims Matheny and William Hawley, had earlier moved to Fillmore. Their neighbors in Fillmore petitioned to have Croft remain and build a flour mill. Young granted a request for Croft with Hawley and Matheny to work on his Fillmore mill.[43]

John Hawley had placed his wife earlier with her sister, Lucy Johnson Kelting, in Provo, then went down to Washington and put in his "crop such as cotton and potatoes." Once the southern branch was established, John "returned to Provo with a recommend from my Bishop to get my endowment before I returned with my family to the south." The Hawleys would have traveled the forty miles to Salt Lake City to receive their endowments. John described the ritual:

> Here we passed through the ordeal of washing and anointing with oil and we was brought under oath to avenge the blood of the Prophets and Patriarch Joseph and Hyrum Smith. We also received the signs and tokens of the Melchizedek and Aaronic Priesthood and also the grips of the Sign of the

---

39. Crampton, *Mormon Colonization*, 65.
40. Elwood Mead, *Bulletin 124: Report of Irrigation Investigations in Utah*, 207, 223.
41. Crampton, *Mormon Colonization*, 66.
42. Bleak, *Annals*, 27–28.
43. Brigham Young, letter to Jacob Croft, December 2, 1857.

Vale and the sure sign of the Vale as also disturbs and also a new name by which we should be called from the grave.

John moved into the Sealing Room, passing to the right of Brigham Young at the head of the alter. Sylvia passed to the left. Standing, the couple took "the grips of the sure Sign of the Vale and . . . Brigham sealed us together." They were "pronounced worthy to come forth in the first resurrection and pass the Gods on to our Celestial Glory and exaltation."[44]

The Hawleys participation in these ceremonies bound them in a unique fellowship with their fellow co-religionists, which joined their lives in a fusion of the hallowed and mortal worlds that defined Latter-day Saint culture. The Hawleys departed immediately for the southern country "with a heart full of love to God, to think we was worthy of the highest glory that has been received." Only by sinning against the Holy Ghost could deprive them of this blessing. Quite soon, the Hawleys, particularly John, had other concerns with which to deal.

As the Hawleys journeyed the trail to Washington, so did the Fancher-Baker emigrant wagon train. Hawley said they traveled with the company for three days, overtaking it near Beaver. Hawley discovered that "they was pretty much all men of families and had a quite large drove of cattle all going to locate in California." The captain told Hawley that they had problems in Salt Creek and Provo. "He said, 'We have a Dutchmen with us, a single man, and he has given us all the trouble we have had. He would not obey orders but was sassy with officers in these places and it all originated by our cattle being grazed on there herd grounds, but we intend observe the laws and the rules of the territory.'" Hawley concluded in one of the great understatements of Utah history—he was "satisfied the Saints gave them more trouble than they ought."[45]

Just north of the Meadows, Jacob Hamblin had established a small village and ranch. For years, travelers had rested there "for a time on the cool (near 6000 feet high) meadows, in preparation for the long" four-hundred-mile trek to San Bernardino across the deserts ahead. Tragedy shredded the tranquility of Mountain Meadows in 1857. Hawley wrote:

> Well we left this camp as we traveled faster than they did. By the time we got home which by the way was called Washington, John D. Lee and other officials was having their interpreters stirring up the Indians to commit hostilities on this camp of emigrants. However they landed safe in their destiny

---

44. Hawley, "Autobiography," 14.
45. Hawley, 14.

stopping place, Mountain Meadows. Here they were to wait till the other company came up and then they were both to travel together from here. But alas they met with death by the Indians and whites worse than all. Their fate comes unto them after they surrendered and gave up their arms according to report. To say the least of this tragedy, it must of been heart rending to those that witnessed and helped to do the deed.[46]

The company may have included as many as 140 immigrants with about two dozen wagons, scores of draft animals, and as many as several hundred cattle. The party had rested the night before at the springs some thirty miles southwest from Cedar City, about seven to eight miles northwest from the upper portion of Pine Valley, and two miles south of Jacob Hamblin's ranch. On September 7, 1857, Mormon militia from southern Utah, accompanied by a few Native American freebooters, surprised the immigrants with an early morning assault on the wagon train at Mountain Meadows.[47] The initial long-range rifle and arrow attack at dawn took down fifteen to twenty immigrants, many of them males of fighting age. Nonetheless, immediate counterfire from the survivors broke up the first frontal assault and threw the attackers back. The defenders formed a defensive lager, chaining the tongues of the wagons to the beds of those in front of them. Fighting pits and deep furrows were dug inside the lager, and for five days the siege continued. On the 11th, cut off from water, running low on ammunition, and with dead bodies and the dying and wounded within the enclosure, the survivors made a fatal error. They permitted Iron Brigade Militia Major John D. Lee to offer surrender terms. It may be surmised that he may have offered guarantees as a Mason to the other Masons in the lager.

Lee told the emigrant party that the militia would protect them from the warriors if they surrendered, turned over the weapons, and left the area under guard. Separating the immigrants into three groups—the wounded and very young children in wagons at the front, then the women and older children, followed by the men each under escort of a militia member—the Arkansans left their position and trudged down the road for a mile. The generally agreed upon version is that at the cry of "Do your duty!" each militiaman shot his prisoner while painted white men

---

46. Hawley, 14.
47. Men assigned to the militia units are found in the Iron Military District, 1856–1857, Muster Rolls, October 10, 1857. Officers and other ranks were ordered to Mountain Meadows individually or in small groups, not as units. John Hawley, George Hawley, and William Hawley were members of the Brigade.

and Native Americans assaulted the women and older children from the brush. Major Lee and others cut the throats of the wounded in the wagons. Seventeen young children were left, whom the killers thought would not be good witnesses if they survived, and who, according to the doctrine of blood atonement, were not condemned to die. Two years later, the federal government located the surviving children and returned them to their families in Arkansas.[48]

John Hawley boldly answered the question of his supposed involvement in the massacre. He wrote that he had "been asked a number of times, 'Were you in that massacre?'" John D. Lee accused him by name of being there; thus, Hawley wrote, "[A]s I lived in southern Utah at the time of this massacre, they have thought that I must be the man." John Hawley's brothers George and William were on the killing ground. William may have had to be chained to a wagon wheel because he opposed the massacre. John Hawley, at a Washington meeting, angrily denounced the planning and the killing of men, women, and children at the direction of local priesthood and militia leadership. He believed that those who accused him of not siding with the brethren had been among the killers at the Mountain Meadows. "The men spoke . . . and declared to us that the dividing line was then drawn between Jew and Gentile, and all must die that passed through the Territory who were not of our faith." Having just returned from Salt Lake City, Hawley was called on to speak "and proclaimed with as much zeal against the work of death (done by them as I then supposed) as they did for it." Hawley believed his opponents met in secret to see if he should be killed, "but as I had a balance of power in their meeting, the vote stood in favor of my living." William Alma Young, who participated in the Massacre and testified at John D. Lee's trials, was sent to him to warn him off, telling him: "Bro. John, you came very near losing your life for what you said yesterday; and I have been sent to tell you to be more on your guard." John told Young that he would back his words in "proclaiming against that deed of murder, you will kill an innocent man; but you may tell your brethren that I will stand on what I said."

President Young's message arrived that day, ordering that the wagon train should pass, to "treat them as you would like to be treated were you passing through their own land." Young's letter restored to John some standing in the community.[49]

---

48. Crampton, *Mormon Colonization*, 70–71.

49. John Hawley, letter to Bro. Joseph, June 12, 1884. William Alma Young was related to John H. Young, either a nephew or a half-brother. John H.

William Alma Young, at fifty-two, known as "Uncle Billy," was the oldest member of militia at Mountain Meadows. He claimed he was ill on September 11, 1857, and watched the mass murder from the vantage of the militia camp. Not indicted for the murders, Young never identified John Hawley as a participant or present at Mountain Meadows, although he identified others involved in the bloodbath: his battalion commander, John D. Lee; his platoon leader, Harrison Pearce; and William R. Slade, James Mangum, John M. Higbee, Philip Klingensmith, Oscar Hamblin, and William Bateman. All these men were well-known to both Hawley and Young. They were all known members of the community of southern Utah.

The community knew their local ward, stake, and militia leaders and members were, at the time, attacking the Fancher-Baker immigrant party. The records of the Cedar City Female Benevolent Society on the 10th (the day before the killings) state that the sisters were counseled

> not to be fearful in these troublesome times . . . that these were squally times, and we ought to attend to secret prayer in behalf of our husbands, sons, fathers, and brothers. Instructed the sisters to teach their sons & daughters the principles of righteousness and to implant a desire in their hearts to avenge the blood of the Prophets. Sister Hopkins said that she with sister White had visited the sisters in the middle lines, that they felt well and manifested a good spirit, and was desirous to do well, and to improve,[?] advised them to attend strictly to secret prayer in behalf of the brethren that are out acting in our defence.[50]

Two days after the massacre, Stake President and Iron Brigade Colonel William H. Dame counseled "at some length . . . the brethren . . . upon the necessity of our being wide awake all the time, and of preparing for the future."[51] Whether the sisters were aware earlier that a mass execution was going to occur is not clear, but the desire "to avenge the blood of the Prophets" indicates they had a solid idea of what was happening. The priesthood meeting reveals Dame's intent to form community solidarity to cover up the tragedy.

California newspapers issued the first reports within two weeks; too many people knew of the heinousness crime. With the United States

---

had married Priscilla, John Hawley's sister, in 1846 at Austin, Texas. Laurel Hawley Stubblefield, *Pierce Hawley 1788–1858: A History of His Family and Their Conversion to The Church of Jesus Christ of Latter-Day Saints*, 31; Hawley, "Autobiography," 7.

50. Cedar City Ward Relief Society Minute Book, September 10, 1857.

51. Parowan Utah Stake Melchizedek Priesthood Minutes and Records, September 13, 1857.

Army marching on Utah Territory because of the Latter-day Saints' resistance to constitutional and republican government, the perpetrators knew the federal government would become involved.[52] Major James Henry Carleton, in the aftermath of the Utah War, investigated the crime officially and issued a report in 1859. When one of the mass murderers, Philip Klingensmith, a former Cedar City bishop, confessed, a five-year investigation with the entire nation avidly paying attention ended in 1877 with only one man being executed by firing squad: John D. Lee. The Church restored John D. Lee's plural sealings and priesthood in 1961.[53]

Subsequent archaeological evidence has emerged. Before Governor Michael Leavitt's order for a hasty reburial of human remains mistakenly exhumed at Mountain Meadows, Dr. Shannon Novak, a well-qualified forensic anthropologist working for and reporting to the Office of Public Archaeology, worked within the short time frame to examine and evaluate the remains before reinterment. Some of the stories of the massacre were verified. Historian Gene Sessions argued that "the bones reveal nothing that historians have not known since 1859 when Major Carleton reported that 'nearly every skull I saw had been shot through with pistol or rifle bullets.' . . . I do not believe that they would reveal anything I do not already know from the historical record about how the emigrants were killed and who did it." However, research reveals that only two men who were reported to be at Mountain Meadows possessed revolvers. According to the militia muster rolls of October 10, 1857, Ira Hatch and John Hawley had revolvers. Hawley may have been lying about his role at Mountain Meadows, or he may have given his weapon to one of his brothers or even someone else. The muster rolls must be considered in the light that pistols were used during the massacre, and the records reveal that only Hawley and Hatch had such weapons.[54]

The event continued to affect John Hawley as well as the others in southern Utah, including those who had made Pine Valley their home.

---

52. For a good understanding of the Utah War, consult Bigler and Bagley, *The Mormon Rebellion*, and McKinnon, *At Sword's Point*.

53. Juanita Brooks, *The Mountain Meadows Massacre*, 376.

54. Shannon A. Novak, "The Mountain Meadows Massacre"; Shannon A. Novak, *House of Mourning: A Biocultural History of the Mountain Meadows Massacre*; Shannon A. Novak and Derinna Kopp, "To Feed a Tree in Zion: Osteological Analysis of the 1857 Mountain Meadows Massacre," 85–108; Shannon A. Novak and Lars Rodseth, "Remembering Mountain Meadows: Collective Violence and the Manipulation of Social Boundaries," 1–25.

Hawley recalled in 1858 that Colonel Albert Sydney Johnston (spelled "Johnson" by Hawley) and Judge Cradlebaugh entered the territory to end the Utah War. Hawley reported that several of the perpetrators, who Latter-day Saint general authority Anthony W. Ivins later described as "rough wild men of the frontier," hid from the officials. Although, according to Hawley, they were in no real danger—only their guilt pursued them. He compared their awareness of their guilt to the comfort of the Holy Spirit, except where the latter comes only on condition of repentance; the guilty consciences were always present with the slayers.[55]

Various accounts of memorializing the victims uncovered the continuing tension between the Saints and the "Gentiles." One example is an incident when Brevet Major James H. Carleton and elements of the First Dragoons constructed a rough cairn, twelve feet high and fifty feet round. From red cedar was fashioned a cross with the "inscription 'carved deeply in the wood': 'Vengeance is mine: I will repay, saith the Lord.'" Four years later, Brigham Young and a traveling party halted at the crumbling monument; "the wooden cross and its inscription . . . still stood above the rock cairn." Amending the inscription, Young spoke aloud, supposedly uttering, "Vengeance is mine; and I have taken a little," or words to that effect. Then he raised "his arm to the square," later wrote massacre participant Dudley Leavitt, and in five minutes there was not one stone left upon another.[56]

Three years later, Lorenzo Brown rode from Pine Valley to visit Jacob Hamblin at his ranch. He passed a new monument of cobblestone and earth topped by an unfinished wood cross. It had been re-erected on May 27 and 28, 1864, by the officers and other ranks of M Company, California Volunteers to memorialize the victims of the massacre. Brown described the scene: "On one side of the cross is inscribed Mountain Meadow Massacre and over that in smaller letters is vengeance is mine & I will repay saith the Lord." Brown noted in his journal, "Someone has written blow [below] this in pencil. Remember Hauns mill and Carthage Jail."[57]

---

55. Anthony W. Ivins, letter to Mrs. G. T. Welch, October 18, 1922, 3; Hawley, "Autobiography," 17.

56. Quoted in Bagley, *Blood of the Prophets*, 142, 229, 247.

57. The Journal of Lorenzo Brown, 1823–1890, July 1, 1864.

CHAPTER 6

The Hawleys of Pine Valley

Part I

"He was burned to a crisp ... but still, we felt sure that we planted him for a glorious resurrection in the morning of the first."

The coming of whites to Pine Valley likely began with Riddle and the first of two racially motivated killings between 1856 and 1858. Isaac Riddle claimed to have discovered the valley in the early part of 1856 while chasing a cow from the west. He thought the valley "the most beautiful sight I had ever beheld." Sometime after the settlers came to the valley, Jacob Hamblin wrote that Paiutes had retaliated against the Mormons for killing one of their own. The Paiutes, following tribal custom in choosing a victim to balance the reciprocal nature of revenge killing, "observed local Mormons closely and selected," according to Hamblin, an old English immigrant named Freestone, who was "without wife or children, and was 'not worth anything.'" They fell upon him and crushed his skull with rocks. In fact, Isaac Riddle had killed earlier a native, for whom Freestone was ritually sacrificed.

Riddle's motive for the killing was rooted in grim deeds a decade earlier from 1844 to 1846 when he was a teenage hunter for the James Emmett Company in the Iowa and Nebraska wilderness. The local natives had deliberately been killing game in an attempt to drive the settlers away. They succeeded to the extent that the emigrants' families suffered from malnutrition, so much so "that one squirrel or duck was divided between the four families that constituted [one] party. Our rations ran short, and for some time we lived on one-half pint of corn per day to each individual." In 1858, Riddle wrote to Brigham Young that he shot the "impudent" Indian at Pine Valley because he had killed a "lot of critters." In the letter, he told Young that he had confessed and been rebaptized.[1]

---

1. Todd M. Compton, *A Frontier Life: Jacob Hamblin, Explorer and Indian Missionary*, 129; Isaac Riddle, letter to Brigham Young, December 9, 1858; William G. Hartley, *My Best for the Kingdom: History and Autobiography of John Lowe Butler, a Mormon Frontiersman*, 149.

Jehu Blackburn and Robert Richey with Riddle set up a small sash saw that year and furnished milled products to the regional Latter-day Saint settlements as well as other communities nearby in Nevada and Arizona, including Pioche, Bunkerville, Mesquite, and Littlefield.[2]

Thirty miles to the south, John Hawley moved to Washington and then on to Pine Valley. At thirty-one, he was in the prime of his life. Born into pioneer heritage, he had lived on the ever-moving frontiers of western America. He lived in and accepted a religious culture in a climate of weather extremes, as well as the religious community in which the temporal and spiritual united daily, imbued with an eternal meaning. From his baptism twenty years earlier by William O. Clark, John was a life-long follower of Joseph Smith's restoration.[3] The Hawleys and their friends and neighbors from Texas and the Indian Nations hewed a communal living in the far southern mountain valleys of the Great Basin.

The Hawleys, along with several other families, moved to Pine Valley before the planting of 1858. As the excitement in Dixie waned from the events of the Reformation and the massacre at Mountain Meadows, the pioneers' lives focused on making a living from the arid land. John and George Hawley had worked hard that first year at Washington, building homes, farming, and constructing a cane mill. James G. Bleak recorded in the Annals of the Southern Mission that "the first communal work engaged in [at Washington], was to construct irrigation ditches. This, with the plowing, planting, and shelter making kept all very busy. Night watching added an additional duty, to protect growing crops from incursions of horses and other stock." Bleak noted that each family had about a pound of cottonseed, which they planted.[4] The Hawleys' cotton crop failed, however, and they did not do much better with corn and wheat. They sold the cane mill to John D. Lee for $82 and rebuilt it on his land. They also sold him a "Hawley lot" and sixteen acres for $150 and moved on to Pine Valley, "it being situated in a high altitude with good pine timber."[5]

---

2. "Improvements in the South," 413; Hazel Bradshaw, *Under the Dixie Sun: A History of Washington County by Those Who Loved Their Forebears*, 350–51; Wanda Snow Petersen, *William Snow, First Bishop of Pine Valley, A Man Without Guile*, 119–20.

3. John Hawley, "Autobiography of John Hawley," 2.

4. James Godson Bleak, *The Annals of the Southern Utah Mission: A Record of the History of the Settlement of Southern Utah*, 22.

5. Burk, *Joseph Hadfield Story: An Incredible Odyssey*, 179; Hawley, "Autobiography," 16, 17. Lee noted that he had arranged "with Jno. & Geo. Halley to deliver & put

The Hawleys and friends, woodworkers all, knew they were moving to lumbering country. A federal government bulletin many years later noted in 1903 that the original settlement at Pine Valley was "a milling center," not an agricultural community, obtaining lumber, timber, and other wood products for the surrounding communities. Although timber and milling operations dominated Pine Valley's first decades, water needs and subsistence farming were realities from the beginning. Authorities believed that the Santa Clara River would supply sufficient water for the communities to the south, but timber and water grants in Pine Valley stipulated they must "subserve the interests of the settlement."[6] The valley basin rested due north then east from St. George, about thirty-five miles on rough roads for many years. The basin stretches about five miles from east to west and two miles from south to north with an exit north into Grass Valley then to Pinto, where travelers may journey east and west. The location is one of "the beauty spots of the earth" with good soil for crops but "too high in altitude for maturing most fruit crops," wrote Wanda Snow.[7]

John Hawley became the presiding elder and "acted the part of a Bishop as well" for the Pine Valley Branch, a position he would hold until 1867. The authorities then organized a ward with William Snow as bishop and Hawley as his first counselor.[8] William Snow Petersen was a brother of Apostle Erastus Snow and a polygamist. Apostle Snow thought of Hawley as a friend and worthy member in the cause but had doubts about his full commitment to the principle of plural marriage. The apostle also did not choose Samuel Knight, the worthy first counselor in the bishopric of Santa Clara Ward, as the new bishop in that ward specifically because Knight also would not participate in plural marriage. Knight would become a member of the high council of Saint George Stake only a few months after Erastus Snow's death in 1888.[9] That issue, and undoubtedly kinship, led the apostle instead to appoint his own brother, who did have multiple wives.[10] The branch was attached administratively to the Santa Clara Ward

---

up my caine mill a[t] Washington (a 3 Roler) for 82$." John D. Lee, *A Mormon Chronicle: The Diaries of John D. Lee 1848 – 1875*, 220.

6. Frank Adams, "Agriculture Under Irrigation in the Basin of the Virgin River," 235.
7. Petersen, *William Snow*, 119, 120.
8. Bleak, *Annals*, 34, 66, 94, 151; Hawley, "Autobiography," 18.
9. Bleak, *Annals*, 691.
10. William Snow (1806–79) an older brother of Erastus Snow, replaced John Pierce Hawley as the theocratic and secular leader at Pine Valley. William Snow, Excerpts From the Diary of William Snow. Samuel Knight (1832–1910), an

until transferred to the St. George Ward in 1862.[11] John Hawley also became the road supervisor responsible for the building and improvement of the road to the Washington area, while William Slade served as Justice of the Peace in Pine Valley as he had in Washington.[12]

The Hawley clan and kin and other settlers resided in what one writer called freedom's abode in the "Mountains High." Some of the families included those of George Hawley with his three wives, sisters Sarah and Ann Hadfield, and the teenager Jeannette Goudie (sometimes known as Janet or Jenet Condie); John and Sylvia Hawley; and Joseph Hadfield. William R. Slade's family joined them in the move, living there part-time for some years. John Hawley, although not the oldest son and brother, had been the clan and former Wightite community leader for some years, and now became the leader of the Pine Valley community for almost a decade. His leadership characteristics were based on his physique, personality, and dedication to the faith. Hawley was a "large boney, very powerful man, was quiet slow speaker, very unassuming . . . not excitable blustering kind at all." Photographs of Hawley and his brothers reveal a common face and countenance of family physiognomy. They were big, strong men—assets in frontier survival. John was sturdy, dependable, and willing to follow counsel, exactly the type of leader the Church wanted for one of its smaller yet vital outposts.[13] John's willingness to serve emphasized the point of unity for church and state on the frontier. He served as a constable, a road supervisor, a presiding elder, and later first counselor to Bishop Snow. He also served as the school superintendent for almost a decade. He directed both the regular and church schools held first in a primitive log building, and later in a newer building.[14]

The year of 1859 ended in tragedy for the Hawleys. On November 10, 1859, their toddler, John, was sleeping on a bed. The house took fire and the bed on which young John was sleeping caught the flame. Before the fire could be put out, John wrote heartbreakingly, "he was burned to a crisp . . .

---

interpreter of American Indian languages, served in Utah's Dixie from 1854 in the Southern Indian Mission and later at Santa Clara. Arthur Knight Hafen, "A Sketch of the Life of Samuel Knight, 1832–1910."

11. Bleak, *Annals*, 34, 72.
12. Bleak, 32.
13. "Sketch of James H. Jennings."
14. Bleak, *Annals*, 27–28, 34, 66, 94, 105, 111, 148, 151, 153, 158.

but still we felt sure that we planted him for a glorious resurrection in the morning of the first" resurrection.[15]

Eight months later, Snow wrote to Young from Pine Valley, then a "settlement [that] has some fifteen or sixteen families." He informed Young that from Pine Valley, he would travel "the Santa Clara crossing it several times for fourteen miles, thence across [illegible] of Damaron Valley & the volcanic Crators [sic] to St George 32 miles from this place." A new route from Damaron Valley, six miles shorter, would travel through Santa Clara to St. George. This route made the distances almost the same from Cedar City to Santa Clara or the "route by Toquerville and Washington." He did point out the route was not as "smothe" as the older road, "but we have just been working improving it nearly all the way and I deem it now equal if not superior to the old road especially for the downward trip."[16]

The millers and loggers built Upper Town, as it was known, nearer the east end of the valley. The initial millers "[set] up on Spring Branch" and "[t]he men lived across the road north in dugouts in what is now Claude Bracken's field." Dugout residences were not unusual in early pioneer Utah, and some claimed they could be comfortable. For instance, one memoir recorded that in Palmyra, Utah County, the settlers fashioned livable dugouts:

> The dug-outs were places dug in the ground, usually four or five feet deep, with steps leading down into the room from one end, and a roof usually made of willows and mud. The dugouts were quite warm and comfortable during the winter, there being a fire-place the opposite end of the entrance. They were generally without windows, so in order to get light, the door must be left open, or the open fire depended upon for illumination.[17]

The men directed the water flow into a horseshoe shape down "a steep embankment where it then flowed through a millrace to a waterwheel to furnish the necessary power." The settlers organized their community politically and religiously. Prominent members of Lyman Wight's "Texas Epidemic,"[18] as members of Wight's colony had been described more than fifteen years earlier by George A. Smith and Ezra T. Benson, had settled and remained on the east end of the valley for several years until a flash

---

15. Hawley, "Autobiography," 18.
16. Erastus Snow, letter to Brigham Young, September 9, 1862.
17. Fred Woods, "Immigration to Utah and Early Settlement of Spanish Fork," 31–46.
18. George A. Smith, letter to Brigham Young, October 7, 1848; Bennett, *Mormons at the Missouri*, 226.

flood devastated the community. Moving some houses and property a half mile or more to the west, the survivors raised Lower Town.[19]

The settlers constructed a small log school with a dirt-covered roof close to the first mill east of the creek with the first cemetery, where John Hawley presided over religious and other gatherings. Daniel Tyler, a Mormon Battalion member, was the first school teacher, and William Snow taught later for a short time. School teachers at that time were paid from tithing in-kind goods. Almost all comments from local historians agreed that the schooling was substandard. John Hawley and the other former Wightites and Texans at Pine Valley probably would have supplied a "Rules for Teachers" like the one used at Burnet County, Texas, about the same time. The rules were:

1. Teachers each day will fill lamps, clean chimneys.
2. Each teacher will bring a bucket of water and a scuttle for coal for the day's session.[20]
3. Make your pens carefully. You may whittle nibs to the individual taste of the pupils.
4. Men teachers may take one evening each week for courting purposes, or two evenings a week if they go to church regularly.
5. After ten hours in school, the teachers may spend the remaining time reading the Bible or other good books.
6. Women teachers who marry or engage in unseemly conduct will be dismissed.
7. Every teacher should lay aside from each pay a goodly sum of his earnings for his benefit during his declining years so that he will not become a burden of society.
8. Any teacher who smokes, uses liquor in any form, frequents pool or public halls, or gets shaved in a barber shop will give good reason to suspect his worth, intention, integrity, and honesty.
9. The teacher who performs his labor faithfully and without fault for five years will be given an increase of twenty-five cents per week in his pay, providing the Board of Education approves.[21]

Samuel Hamilton served as postmaster. Within a short time, perhaps as many as thirty families were living in or near the valley. Many of the children had no shoes that first year because the only pair they owned had

---

19. Petersen, *William Snow*, 120; Hazel Bradshaw, ed., *Under Dixie Sun: A History of Washington County by Those who Loved Their Forebears*, 181.
20. The Pine Valley school stove was plant burning, so a requirement would have dictated who would donate the cord of wood.
21. "Rules for Teachers."

fallen apart. Shoes were not essential for summer play, but with the cold and the snow, the children needed them as necessary gear for school. The one shoemaker in the community took care of the boys before the girls because the boys worked in the fields, and he probably took care of the men before the boys. Some of the girls did not attend school that first term.[22]

Brigham Young visited the new branch in Pine Valley in 1859, as he explored the area to locate a permanent center place for a stake near the junction of the Rio Virgen and Santa Clara Rivers. According to Hawley, Brigham told the settlers that many more would come to the area and advised them to save their money, "for we want to buy all the Senators and all the editors and all the delegates and judges sent there. That is all the men of influence, for said he, money will buy all, but they are not of the same price." Young told his listeners that by bribing the officials, "we shall have peace in our territory."[23]

On this visit, Hawley asked Young why the followers of Wight's colony in Texas were excommunicated with Wight in 1848. Young said he had received a letter from Wight "signed in his own handwriting" that denied Young's authority over him. Wight's letter to Young was a response to his excommunication by Apostle Orson Hyde at Winter Quarters for Wight's pamphlet titled "An Address." It denied the authority of the Twelve to control his movements and to order him to Utah with his followers. Wight believed only the deceased Joseph Smith Jr. and John Smith, President of the Council of Fifty, presided over him. Reaffirming the action, in December 1848, President Young and Apostle Amasa Lyman were present when John Smith as "senior member of the Fifty" once again pronounced the excommunication of Wight and his followers. Wight, who had argued that his age in the Twelve and in the Fifty made him senior to Young, was younger than John Smith. Young told Hawley that he [Young] had, somewhat accurately, "predicted that when Lyman was cut off many that was with him would return to the church."[24]

Hawley asked President Young about the incident in 1844 involving the Maid of Iowa. The members of the Wisconsin pine company had expected to exchange a raft of lumber in return for the steamboat but

---

22. "History of Washington County," 351; Petersen, *William Snow*, 136, 149; Bleak, *Annals*, 65–66.

23. Hawley, "Autobiography," 17.

24. Hawley, 17. See Johnson, *Polygamy on the Pedernales*, 112–123, for his discussion on the crisis of authority in the LDS Church from 1844 to 1848 as Young prevailed over the challenges within the Twelve to lead the LDS Church.

ended up with neither lumber nor steamboat. Lyman Wight told them that Young had deceived them. This embittered many of the company who would form the core of Wight's colony in Texas. Young told Hawley that Bishop George Miller was guilty and that he and the Twelve could do nothing about it. In fact, Miller had no choice in the matter, for he had to honor a contract with a Mr. Morrison and Mr. Cahoon who, in return for $100 monthly, had leased the boat. Hawley accepted Young's version, thinking it was plausible and straight.[25] In fact, Joseph Smith had been the authority who signed the papers along with four others.[26]

Hawley as the road supervisor for construction between the valley and Washington had crews removing stones from the road to ease President Young's journey south in 1859. According to Hawley, Young had a vision that "burst upon him and he saw a great city with steeples and spirals and also a temple." Hawley noted the prophecy as well as the context that it was a day's work to "break thru the crust li[k]e frozen snow. But this city had to be built for Brother Brigham had seen it spiritually and said it must be done."[27] The present-day city St. George grew from the vision.

John wrote that he and George purchased a share in a sawmill. For some years, they worked at the mill. George also worked at the Riddle lathe and shingle mill. Like their working days in Wisconsin, Texas, and in the Indian nations, the brothers carpentered and set wheels and made looms. John remembered that "for years loom making was a good business, as our women had to spin and weave their wearing apparel initially." Paying about $50 a year in-kind tithing because "it was all labor and no cash" indicated the Hawleys made ends meet at Pine Valley and not much more.[28]

By 1861 the first sawmill was being updated, while two more were being erected. The population increased accordingly. Water power drove the up-and-down sash saws, known as muleys, of those older mills. By 1862, the Eli Whipple mill could produce 4,000 to 5,000 board feet in a single day; and plans were being made to add a lathe

---

25. Joseph Smith, contract with Arthur Morrison and Pulaski S. Cahoon, June 15, 1844; Hawley, "Autobiography," 6, 12–13, 18.

26. Joseph Smith, contract with Arthur Morrison and Pulaski S. Cahoon, June 15, 1844. See also Levi Moffet vs. Charles Ross, 1844–1845.

27. Bleak, *Annals*, 32; Hawley, "Autobiography," 18.

28. Hawley, "Autobiography," 16, 17; Beckstrom, *O' Ye Mountains High*, 25.

and shingle mill.²⁹ Erastus Snow wrote to Brigham Young in September 1863 that he had "just returned from Pine Valley, where three saw mills are in successful operation. Lumber and shingles are becoming sufficiently plentiful to enable our citizens to prosecute their buildings with spirit and vigor."³⁰ The small Whipple mill had burned down in the latter part of 1862 but was rebuilt immediately. The fourth and fifth mills, the Burgess plant and Gardner's Mill, owned by father Robert and son William, were rapidly constructed. Gardner's mill established a new standard of technology. People would gather at Gardner's to watch a circular saw nicknamed "the elephant," driven by steam power.³¹

Apostle Erastus Snow, leader of the Southern mission at the newly established community at St. George, understood that timber, water, and roads were keys to the community's success. Within a month of the pioneers' arrival at the new community above the junction of the Santa Clara and Rio Virgen, Snow wrote to Brigham Young, "We have, as yet, found no good saw timber nearer than Pine Valley, I have examined in company with Bro's Robert Gardner and Thomas Forsythe, and find it to be abundant, of a fair quality, and easy of access." He noted that "a good wagon road can be made from here to Pine Valley in a distance of thirty miles, not, however, without considerable labor." He expected Eli Whipple and Thomas Forsythe, with a few men, to depart for the valley. Forsythe would repair and operate the older mill, while Whipple would build a new one.³²

As the mills grew in number and technology improved, the economic power struggle for control of the lumber industry intensified. By 1863, the Hawleys were apparently no longer mill owners and had returned to making their living with their woodworking and carpentry skills as well as subsistence farming. Lorenzo Brown, a long-time Latter-day Saint and new settler at Pine Valley, said John and George Hawley by then were in arbitration for John Alger's shingle mill.³³

The continuing needs for building materials in St. George led Apostle George A. Smith that summer to inquire of Apostle Erastus Snow if the production of milled lumber could be increased. The Washington County Court appointed a committee composed of Jacob Hamblin and mill owners Robert Gardner and Robert L. Lloyd to distribute their allotments of the

---

29. Bleak, *Annals*, 65–66.
30. Erastus Snow, letter to Brigham Young, September 28, 1863.
31. Bleak, *Annals*, 58, 65–66, 74; *Pioneer Pathways*, 351.
32. Erastus Snow, letter to Brigham Young, January 5, 1862.
33. *Journal of Lorenzo Brown*, 146.

pineries to the Snow, Whipple & Gardner Mill; the Messr Burgess Mill; and the Thomas Forsyth Mill, indicating the continuing and close interaction of church, government, and business. The mill owners were centralizing and increasing their power.

Two years later (1865), the owners colluded in pricing milled products as follow:

1. $40 per each 1000 board feet of building lumber, fencing and flooring, and finishing lumbering,
2. $50 per each 1000 board feet, and
3. finishing lumbering at $70 per 1000 board feet.

Four years later in 1869, the County Court of Washington County notified the mill and landowners that the government would continue its oversight of the timber and its use.[34]

The daily lives of the Pine Valley settlers were like all the other pioneers who had to scrape and scrabble a living from Utah Territory. The clay or rock fireplace substituted for metal cookstoves, which came later. Bringing the light of civilization to the wilderness challenged the people literally and figuratively. In an era before oil lamps and electricity, each household depended on its own homemade "common candle or brush light." Many in the beginning used "a cup or saucer filled with grease, with a rag for a wick—this crude lamp was much used by the early pioneers." Candle-molds would eventually be found in almost every home.[35]

The transmission of the written word was highly desired but took time to flourish. The first newspaper in St. George, if short-lived with only fifty-one issues, was *Our Dixie Times*, later renamed *The Rio Virgin Times*.[36] It was published from January 22, 1868, to November 1868. *The Veprecula* or *Little Bramble* began a semi-weekly, four-page handwritten publication in May 1864 and closed in June 1865. Local historian Loren Webb notes that "it wasn't your ordinary newspaper since little news was carried in the semi-monthly." The four contributors (Orson Pratt Jr., George A. Burgon, Charles L. Walker, and Joseph Orton) wrote under pen names. Orson Jr. made it clear that he thought knowledge should be based on empirical evidence. His principles led to trouble that fell upon him. After Pratt Jr.

---

34. Bleak, *Annals*, 77–78, 81, 118, 189–90.
35. "Sketch of the Life of Bishop William Davis"; Zaidee Walker Miles, "Pioneer Women of Dixie"; Eleanor Cannon Woodbury Jarvis, "The Home as a Manufactory."
36. Bleak, *Annals*,159.

was excommunicated in September, "Ego," Guglielmo Gustavo Rosetti Sangiovanni, replaced him. The telegraph line, bringing its swift tongue of lightning, became operational from Salt Lake City to St. George in 1867 and reached San Francisco in October of that same year.[37]

Flint and steel often supplanted the use of scarce matches to start a fire in the hearth. The shovel, hoe, handsaw, and cut cradle were the tools for nurturing crops, growing grain, and controlling grass. A person traveled no faster by foot, horseback, or wagon. The settlers' lives revolved about the geographical and sociological centers of their lives, school, and church. The school with its young hearts pumped the lifeblood of the community while the meeting house fed the soul. At Pine Valley, presiding elder John Hawley supervised all those needs.[38]

Local historian Wanda Snow Petersen in her history of Pine Valley quoted Elizabeth Snow's description of just how difficult it was to create a physical community in Utah's Dixie:

> Of all the territories colonized by the Mormon church, this Dixie Mission was by far the most difficult.[39] Of all the God-for-saken lands that any human beings were even asked to carve a town out of, that Dixie country was it . . . a hole bounded on the north by red sandstone cliffs, on the east and west of black lava rock, and on the south by the muddiest dirtiest river imaginable [that could change] from a muddy lazy course . . . [into] a raging ferocious torrent, sweeping everything before it the rest of the time.[40]

Temperatures ranged near 80 degrees in April and up to highs of 116 degrees into October. Hot "dusky winds blew" alkali and red sand over the valley floor covered only by "cactus, mesquite, and sage brush," through which sneaked "rattlesnakes, lizards, gila monsters, and the coyote." The desert, the heat, the aridity, and the animals tried the pioneers' physical and moral strength.[41]

The settlers used wagons and tent shanties to construct a substantial material infrastructure with their own wits and hands, with human and

---

37. See Seth Millington Blair Diary and Autobiography; Bleak, *Annals*, 150–51, 159. See also, Loren Webb, "Southern Utah Memories: Newspapers of Washington County, Utah, 1864 to 1994 — Part 1 of a two-part series."

38. "Sketch of the life of Bishop William Davis"; Bleak, *Annals*, 65–66, 148, 158; Petersen, *William Snow*, 136, 149; Bradshaw, *Under Dixie Sun*, 351.

39. Several descendants of the pioneers of the missions at the Muddy and the Hole in the Rock Mission and Elk Mountain may disagree with Elizabeth Snow's comments.

40. Petersen, *William Snow*, 93.

41. Petersen, 93.

animal sweat. They used and recycled resources locally and imported minimal supplies from Salt Lake City and California. Called to St. George in 1861 with her family, Ellen B. Ray Matheny wrote that they "encountered all the discomforts and privations which were such prominent features of the southern mission in its earlier years." The Mathenys were not the only families to spend the first two years in St. George living in tents.[42] Phoebe Jane Boggs Prince later recalled that first winter they sheltered in a shed and the wagon box, the latter being the supply room. After the crops were planted, Phoebe and her family were excited as her father built the one-room hut.[43]

Being an apostle apparently did not get Erastus Snow a house more quickly than anyone else. On February 12, 1863, he wrote to President Young, who was then on the road north of St. George:

> I wish to inform you that finding the log cabin down at Heberville in danger of being used for fuel, I hauled the logs to this city, and am now using them for a temporary habitation for Artimisia and her children. Please indemnify the proprietors and charge in A/c. The remainder of my family are still in their tents. I have commenced a house but have not been able to finish for want of lumber. . . . The frosts have been unusually severe for "Dixie" during the past winter. We have had but little rain compared with last winter. One of the most copious rains of the season is now falling: and not a little interfering with our paper as it drops through the tent.
>
> Rheumatism has prevailed to some extent in this place owing to our exposed condition in our tents during these frost nights. From the same cause my own health has been somewhat impaired during the last two months.[44]

Clothing was as rudimentary as their shelters. The pioneers cut up "wagon covers and tent cloth" and replaced clothing as it wore out. Despite being stiff and scratchy from the rough seams, the clothing was sturdy and lasted years before store-bought fabrics of various sorts became available. Straw hats were created carefully, a little bucket molding the crown; Sunday meeting hats were whitened to brilliance with sulfur and heat in a tightly enclosed space. Soap came from the yucca root, which, when soaked in water, produced "fluffy suds" from which clothes and hair came out smelling sweet. The whites, however, would yellow, so sub-

---

42. Minerva White Snow, "Biographical Sketch of the Life and Labors of Minerva White Snow," 302.

43. Bradshaw, *Under Dixie Sun*, 241.

44. Erastus Snow, letter to Brigham Young, February 12, 1863.

stitutes for yucca soap had to be found.[45] The stores in St. George were thirty-five miles at the end of a bad road, so home manufactures were even more essential in Pine Valley. After the men sheared the few sheep, the women and girls washed, dried, and corded the wool. The spinning wheels spun yarn, and then "stockings and other pieces of wearing apparel" were knitted.[46] Mary Dart Judd, one of Bishop Zadok Knapp Judd's wives, was proud that she "spun the first peas of cloth that was made of cotton raised in the mountains of Utah and mission raised the seed that stocked all southern Utah."[47]

Pioneer life in Dixie was harsh. Danger from the arid desert and mountain environment of southern Utah, northern Arizona, and the deserts to California challenged the wagon trains in 1849 led by Church leaders Jefferson Hunt and Howard Egan. They lost fourteen men to the environment, hunger, thirst, and injury.[48] Bishop James Leithead on the Big Muddy had to report to Erastus Snow, in the summer of 1869, that the Davidson family, a husband, wife, and teenage son, became separated from a company making the sixty-five-mile trip northeast from the community of St. Thomas to St. George. The family did not have appropriate shelter, and the water ran out. They sent their son ahead on a horse for help. He did not make it. Their sunbaked, blistered bodies lay for at least a day before being found and buried.[49]

---

45. "History of Washington County," 350.
46. Petersen, *William Snow*, 136.
47. Quoted in Compton, *Jacob Hamblin*, 150.
48. C. Gregory Crampton, *Mormon Colonization in Southern Utah and in Adjacent Parts of Arizona and Nevada*, 26–27.
49. Aaron McArthur, *St. Thomas: A History Uncovered*, 31–32; Bleak, *Annals*, 184–185.

CHAPTER 7

The Racial Divide and Theocracy in Greater Dixie

"I KNOW NOT TO THIS DAY, WHY AND WHEREFORE THEY WERE SLAIN, NOR HAVE I EVER LEARNED OF ANY ACCUSATION AGAINST THEM BEYOND SUSPICION OF COMPLICITY, OR OF HARBORING SPIES FROM HOSTILE BANDS."

John Hawley's flexible interaction with his social and physical environment combined with his devotion to religion and community open an important window into the narrative of the Mormon West. However, for whatever reasons, Hawley did not choose to elaborate on some important aspects of the religious landscape. We must look over his shoulder through this window to discuss what he did not write. Historian W. Paul Reeve in *Making Space on the Western Frontier*[1] examines the roots and struggles of Mormons, miners, and Southern Paiute for contested space in southwestern Utah and eastern Nevada. His study is evidence of Dr. Archie P. McDonald's saying that "land fashions the man." John Hawley's life is proof positive of that comment. However, if one were to evaluate the history of those southwestern lands solely by Hawley's writings and the public records of his time, the researcher would conclude neither Native Americans, black Americans, nor miners crossed his way during those years at Washington and Pine Valley.

This chapter cannot include a detailed and careful inspection of the complicated relationships between the Utah settlers and Native Americans, for that would require a book in and of itself. However, the confusion of interaction between Anglo-Americans and American Indians in Dixie is much more complicated than the mantra of "Brigham Young said be kind" and that feeding them was better than fighting them. Death and near extermination of Indians became the whites' first inclination when-

---

1. See W. Paul Reeve, *Making Space on the Western Frontier: Mormons, Miners, and Southern Paiutes*. The groups struggled to dominate the terrain and consecrate it according to the images of each groups' myths. Reeve explores the dynamic nature of that clash according to the needs of three very different worldviews.

ever they felt threatened.² Adding confusion to the ethnic interactions in St. George, the settlers there in 1878 offered to help the Indians become self-supporting. Indian interpreter and missionary Augustus P. Hardy, recorded by Bleak in the *Annals of the Southern Mission*, reported that the "St. George United Order proffered to the Indians of Chief Moqueak . . . some eight acres of good land situated near Price," close to the junction of the Santa Clara and Virgen rivers, south of St. George. Hardy told Moqueak that "we will plow the land, and we'll furnish the seed, and sow it for you." The Indians were to water it, to take good care of it, and "raise all you can for your own use and to be a blessing to all who raised it." Church leadership told Moqueak that the land was "not to be used by those who are lazy and will not work," with the final admonition that the settlers do "not wish you to suffer and die for want of food, but we cannot give you food to waste."³

While Moqueak and his small family clan accepted the offer in Washington County, the Circleville Massacre twelve years earlier had revealed what happens when the white community felt threatened by Indians who did not immediately submit. Lieutenant General Daniel H. Wells of the Utah territorial militia wrote in May 1866 to Brigadier General Erastus Snow: "You will doubtless have heard of the troubles at, and near Circleville [ten miles from Panguitch], before this reaches you. I do not well see how the brethren there and in other places could have done less."⁴ Both men knew that the resolution to "the troubles" at Circleville could have and should have been far less severe. Snow wrote to General Wells that he thought the settlers killed fifteen to eighteen Piedes. He added, "I know not to this day, why and wherefore they were slain, nor have I ever learned of any accusation against them beyond suspicion of complicity, or of harboring spies from hostile bands, but whether those suspicions were well founded, I know not." Major James T. S. Allred had "arrested and disarmed" the prisoners. Snow explained to Wells that "he left instructions with Colonel William Dame to see that the prisoners were treated kindly."⁵ No record of such directions from Snow to Dame exists.

---

2. For a bibliography of the continuing violence between Mormons and American Indians in the West, see Todd M. Compton, *A Frontier Life: Jacob Hamblin, Explorer and Indian Missionary,* footnotes to pages 27–29.

3. James Godson Bleak, *The Annals of the Southern Mission: A Record of the History of the Settlement of Southern Utah,* 498.

4. Bleak, 134.

5. Erastus Snow, letter to Daniel H. Wells, May 28, 1866.

The Mormon militia established Fort Sandford in March 1866 at the mouth of Bear Creek. The fort protected routes "to Parowan and Beaver from Panguitch and Circleville." Silas S. Smith was the fort commander. Subject to Smith's command, the Circleville inhabitants captured and then "annihilated a band of captive Paiute Indians, including helpless women and children." Joseph Fish, a long-time pioneer in the area, wrote in his memoirs that the Paiutes "were disarmed and kept as prisoners. One night they attempted to make their escape and they were nearly all shot down. Some thought that the attempted escape was imaginary and only used as a pretext to kill them." Community opinions were contradictory. Some thought the murders were "a butchery, that it was not justifiable . . . while some said that they were in league with the hostiles and should be treated as the hostiles were, shot wherever found." The Mormon militia members slit the throats of nearly thirty bound men, women, and children, and then buried the bodies in the basement of a mill.[6]

The Mormons did not distinguish the American Indian tribes and clans as different nations and peoples and instead identified them by one color and race. Historian and anthropologist Robert F. Borkhofer Jr. wrote "that at the time of European arrival there were some 2,000 native cultures and many mutually unintelligible languages in the Americas. Whites flattened these into a single racial category 'for the purposes of description and analysis' and 'for the convenience of simplified understanding,'" and "have tended to generalize from the characteristics of a single tribe (or small group of tribes) to all Indians. They have spoken and written as if all Indians are interchangeable." Thomas F. Murphy argued that the "Book of Mormon's image of the Lamanite perpetuated this reductionistic error." The Mormon scripture offered a way that the American Indians could escape their racial debasement. The path was that of "the glorification of Lamanites, as envisioned in the Book of Mormon . . . [involving] the Christianization, assimilation, and whitening of the Lamanites." The theology of Joseph Smith Jr. insisted that "the status of a Lamanite was something to be saved from, not aspired towards."[7]

---

6. Joseph Fish, *Life and Times of Joseph Fish: Mormon Pioneer*, 105–6. See also Albert Winkler, "The Circleville Massacre: A Brutal Incident in Utah's Black Hawk War," 4, 13; Sue Jensen Weeks, *How Desolate Our Home Bereft of Thee: James Tillman Sanford Allred and the Circleville Massacre*.

7. See Richard Drinnon, *Facing West: The Metaphysics of Indian-Hating and Empire-Building*, xvi; Robert F. Berkhofer Jr., *The White Man's Indian: Images of the American Indian from Columbus to the Present*, Preface–Chapter 1; Lori

Although John Hawley did not write about them during his Utah years, his views on the American Indians probably did not much differ from other Mormons. Christopher C. Smith believes that for the English, and likely the Anglo-Americans later, race "was mostly a vague notion meaning something like peoplehood. Anglo-Americans essentialized the races, but also saw racial 'character' as changeable and determined by environment, culture, and the supernatural more than biological heredity," more so for Native Americans than Africans and their descendants. Intolerance was mutable against them and "never quite so straightforward as racism against Africans." Anglo-Americans believed Africans always were black and never assimilable. Smith, following historian and sociologist Alden T. Vaughan's reasoning, notes that "Englishmen of the early colonies articulated their prejudices regarding 'culture, not color,'" and that the colonists would convert the natives into a new breed of "neo-Englishmen."[8] The Latter-day Saints took it a step further to mean that the American Indians, through Mormon proselytizing, could be turned into a "white and delightsome" people as prophesied in the Book of Mormon.

Various theories on race developed from about 1680 to 1760, one being "whites first in the South and then in the North came to see Indians as racial 'tawnies,' distinct from racial whites." The Anglo-American image of Native Americans began to weaken and became "more susceptible to racial—as distinct from cultural—bias than it had been in the previous century." Smith noted that competing race theories developed in the century before and during Hawley's lifetime. Quasi-scientific "polygenic" models argued that different types of humanity developed from separate and varied species. The "monogenists," on the other hand, steeped in the scriptural absolutism of the Word, asserted the unity and common descent of one human species following a literal comprehension of the Bible. By the 1850s, according to Thomas F. Gossett,[9] polygenism was largely the domain of scientists, while evangelicals and their clergy championed monogenism. Both sides viewed colored races as fundamentally inferior; polygenic racism was much more extreme and "frequently denied that the

---

Elaine Taylor, "Telling Stories about Mormons and Indians," 72–75, 82–85; Thomas W. Murphy, "Imagining Lamanites: Native Americans and the Book of Mormon," 86–88; Christopher C. Smith, "'The Whites Want Everything': Mormon Conquest of the Wasatch Front and Range, 1847–1851," 27–29.

8. Alden T. Vaughan, *The Roots of American Racism: Essays on the Colonial Experience*, 5–12.

9. See Thomas F. Gossett, *Race: The History of an Idea in America*.

nonwhite races were people at all and maintained that missionary efforts among them were wholly wasted."[10] Monogenists much more than polygenists believed that religious evangelism (think Latter-day Restoration missionary efforts to the Lamanites) to be not only a duty and commandment but also commendable and productive.

Latter-day Saints and the American Indians, however, are joined at the hip theologically in Mormonism, being the risen and fallen portions of the House of Israel in the Americas, with defined roles of redeeming the Lamanites and humanity in general. The Book of Mormon, observes Christopher C. Smith, arrived on the literary scene at this confused, transitional moment in the history of American race theory. The book reflected the slightly older language of color that racialized American Indians as "dark" or "black" rather than red (1 Ne. 12:23; 2 Ne. 5:21; Alma 3:6; Morm. 5:15), and it used a blend of environmentalist and essentialist language, presenting dark skin color as hereditary and inferior but not unchangeable. Within just a few verses, it could assert that Lamanites' "hatred was fixed" by their "evil nature," but also that divine grace might redeem them (Enos 1:13–20).[11]

Thus, in a confusing welter of race theory and divine promises being acted out in the primitive and dangerous environment of southwestern Dixie, the results were a puzzling pattern of Latter-day Saints not only killing American Indians but also baptizing them in high numbers. For example, Bleak reported in March 1875 that almost all the "Shebits" were baptized and "became members of the LDS Church." On March 17, 19, and 23, ninety men and eighty women were confirmed members, and twenty-seven children were blessed.[12]

The Mormons considered Native Americans to be a threat. The truth, however, is that the Indians were in greater peril from the Saints who overemphasized the danger to themselves and retaliated in violence when they felt endangered. There were cases where the white settlers, particularly the women, thought themselves in danger. For instance, according to Latter-day Saint women, Indian men would appear when the men and boys were gone and try to extort food and other items. Julie Jeffrey wrote about "the unnerving habit" of Indians "appearing silently wanting food or just a look at a white woman and her children. Many white women believed that native men were particularly aggressive when white husbands were away from

---

10. Quoted in Smith, "Whites Want Everything," 30.
11. Smith, 31.
12. Bleak, *Annals*, 392–99.

the homestead. They found the Indians scavenging for food frightening, especially when the men had weapons." Whites took to punishing Indians, sometimes in strange ways. For instance, Jacob Hamblin had one Indian, named Enos, sent on a mission for horse stealing, an unusual punishment without further explanation by Hamblin, while six others who had been stealing were whipped by other Paiutes at Hamblin's insistence.[13]

No racially inspired killings occurred around Washington and St. George. However, the farther one was from St. George, the higher the apparent risk for conflict between the Saints and Native Americans. Two examples involved the Elk Mountain Mission in 1855 and a Hamblin-led mission to the Navajos in 1860. At the new Elk Mountain Mission near waht is now Moab in 1855, despite the initial good relationships between the missionaries and local Utes, matters quickly unraveled in suspicion as the settlers erected stone buildings and sowed crops, which the tribe members raided. In September, several young Ute warriors and other freebooters killed three Saints and stole some cattle. The settlers killed several Utes and wounded as many as a dozen in turning back the initial assaults. The two sides then negotiated a settler withdrawal from the valley. Permanent settlement did not resume until 1877.[14] Another incident was the murder by Navajos of teenage George A. Smith Jr., son of the apostle, on the eastern side of the Colorado River in the fall of 1860. He was a member of one of Jacob Hamblin's annual trips south of the Colorado River. Curiously, this was the only fatality in the decades of Hamblin's trips to Hopi and Navajo territory in northern Arizona.[15]

The world of racial conflict surrounded the world of John Hawley at Pine Valley. In 1864, some forty miles to the west of the valley, Latter-day Saints emigrated to Meadow Valley in eastern Nevada because of drought in Santa Clara and reports of mineral wealth in the west. Bleak was incorrect in suggesting that "the influx of prospectors and miners . . . attracted a number of Pi-ute indians." They had been there long before whites came to

---

13. Julie Roy Jeffrey, *Frontier Women: The Trans-Mississippi-West, 1840–1880*, 72–73.

14. Compton, *A Frontier Life*, 163. See also Tom McCourt and Wade Allinson, *The Elk Mountain Mission: A History of Moab, Mormons, The Old Spanish Trail and the Sheberetch Utes, 1854–1855*; John W. Van Cott, *Utah Place Names: A Comprehensive Guide to the Origins of Geographic Names: A Compilation*; Daughters of Utah Pioneers, *Grand Memories*; Eugene E. Campbell, "Brigham Young's Outer Cordon: A Reappraisal," 220–253; Elk Mountain Mission Journal, May–October 1855; William B. Pace, autobiography.

15. Compton, *A Frontier Life*, 179–83.

Dixie or miners seeking metal came in what the whites called the western valleys of eastern Nevada. Friendly relations deteriorated, and Bleak insisting that "kindness was taken advantage of and [the Native Americans] became exacting in their demands." Incidents on the 23rd and 24th of July resulted in near violence and theft of livestock. About this time an Indian chief died, according to Bleak, and the tribal leaders demanded the settlers provide a white man to be killed to accompany their chief on his spirit journey across the veil of death. When the Paiutes decided to push the issue, the whites resisted and took five Indians as prisoners, whom they killed while the prisoners were supposedly attempting to escape.

Historian W. Paul Reeve tells another version of confrontation that year between the miners and the Indians. According to the surviving witness tales, all of whom were informed by whites, several Indians were abusive to a white woman who drove them out of her shanty brandishing a piece of firewood. That night, Indians stole some livestock. The next day, the settlers caught five Indians in the act of threatening a white miner. After the settlers took the Indians as prisoners, a fight broke out. An Indian stabbed the miner, and all five were killed during the brawl or hunted down and dispatched. No whites died. President Snow, when informed of the actions, wrote in reply to J. D. L. Pearce: "At 2 p. m. of yesterday I received Bp Bunker's letter from Panaca bearing date of the 24th. I deeply regret the necessity for killing your Indian prisoners. I fear it will render conciliation more difficult." Apostle Snow endorsed Bishop Bunker's "policy of taking no prisoners, but killing thieves when taken in the act. I hope, however, that God will over–rule it for the best."[16]

The killing continued in 1865 in the valleys to the west of St. George and Pine Valley. This time Indians, miners, and Mormons were involved. An Indian named Okus murdered a miner for his belongings. When captured by Gentiles, "he was chained," Bleak writes, "and putting one end of a chain around his neck and attaching the other end to the horn of a saddle, set off at full speed for Meadow Valley, 10 miles, which they made in one hour and ten minutes." Okus named two more Indians who "were indirectly concerned in the murder." A party led by a Mr. Woodman tracked the group of "three men, two women, and some children; they killed the men, letting the women and children go. Two of these men proved to be the ones indicated by Okus. The other had borne a good character; but Mr Woodman and party said they all shot their arrows very

---

16. Bleak, *Annals*, 100–101; Reeve, *Making Space On The Western Frontier*, 26.

wickedly at the company." An Indian's character did not matter when he was defending his life from armed whites.[17]

In January 1866, Navajos who had been raiding settler territory for years killed Dr. James Whitmore and William McIntyre near Pipe Springs, Arizona. Militia, led by some of St. George's most distinguished citizens, recovered the bodies after intense interrogation of Paiute prisoners, probably including torture. Perhaps as many as ten Paiutes were executed by the militia at or near Pipe Springs. The Saints acted with a summary vengeance, neither taking prisoners nor seriously investigating the incident, even after the local Paiutes insisted the Navajos had done the killings. Jacob Hamblin concluded: "They killed the wrong Indians." This "vengeance killing" of innocent Indians had dire consequences. On April 2, 1866, brothers Joseph and Robert Berry and the latter's wife, Isabella, were murdered in retaliation for the execution of Indian relatives. First reports held the wife was raped and then dispatched by gunshot and arrows. Bleak's report of April 15 indicates the bodies were not mutilated, suggesting perhaps the woman was not violated.[18]

By 1867, capital punishment was not rare for offenses committed by Indians. Erastus Snow wrote Brigham Young that February:

> A few thievish Piedes in this region evidently served as guides to the navajoes in their January raid and subsequently stole a few horses and cattle upon Navajoe Credit. Indian "Bill" an old offender and ring-leader of these rogues was arrested, acknowledge the truth and "went up the Spout" a few days ago. A few of his abettors are a little sour over it, but I think they will make no fuss about it for fear taking the same journey. I have appointed a meeting to have a general talk with all the Piedes on the River at this place on next Tuesday week.[19]

The darkly jocular comments of "going up the Spout" and "no fuss about it for fear taking the same journey" defined a clear line that justice for Indians was different from white men.[20]

Historian James Bleak conveyed a telegraphic message to President Brigham Young in February 1870 reporting the killing of a Native American by members of the local Mormon militia. Navajos had been raiding north and east from Hebron and Iron Springs. For almost two

---

17. Bleak, *Annals*, 130. White descriptions of American Indians as "wicked" and "impudent" and "saucy" often preceded killing them.
18. James A. Bleak, letter to George Albert Smith, April 13, 1866.
19. Erastus Snow, letter to Brigham Young, February 24, 1867.
20. Erastus Snow, letter to Brigham Young, February 24, 1867.

weeks the militia had been tracking "fresh signs" but had not been able to catch their prey. Finally, Thomas Walker telegraphed Bleak to tell him "of a Navajo raid. Men were started out in pursuit. – Arrived at Iron Springs at dusk; found two Pi-edes at the houses, who acted in a very suspicious manner and the boys felt justified in firing at them, which they did, and killed one, the other succeeded in getting away. The boys supposed that they were Navajos, and did not ascertain the facts until after the indian was shot." The militia was shooting first and asking questions later.[21]

John Hawley's writings ignore the devastating ravages wrought by the whites on the Native American culture of Dixie during his time in southern Utah. Whites had entered southern Utah before 1850 and had solidly settled in by 1859. Gary Tom and Ronald Holt noted that the original Paiutes of the St. George area were gone when Anthony Ivins, mayor of St. George and a livestock operator in northern Arizona, was instrumental in establishing "the first Paiute reservation . . . in 1891 on the Santa Clara River west of St. George. . . . The Paiutes who had originally [been] residents of the reservation area were either dead or had moved—most to the Moapa reservation in Nevada or to Cedar City. This fact illustrates the devastating effect of white colonization since the riverine core of the Paiute homeland and its center of densest population" lay on the axis straddling the Santa Clara and Rio Virgen river lands.[22]

Edward Leo Lyman has noted that epidemics destroyed the tribal clans in Dixie. Most disturbing is that historian James Bleak failed in the *Annals* to record, as he should have, the overwhelming rupture of Indian life and patterns of survival because of white settlement. There had been reports of epidemics among the Nevada Paiutes: a cholera plague, and, a little before 1860, an epidemic of diarrhea and "passage of blood" (which may have been cholera again) in Muddy Valley (sixty miles south and west from St. George), in which deaths were so numerous that bodies were "dumped into a near-by gully." Todd Compton concluded that "the settling of St. George and Santa Clara in 1861 by Mormon colonists had already caused," no matter how unintentional, "a precipitous decline in the Paiute way of life." The expiry of the native culture continued.

John Stucki, quoted in Compton, recorded that after the Swiss immigrants came to Santa Clara in late 1861, "a horrific epidemic" destroyed the Santa Clara Paiute community there:

---

21. Erastus Snow, letter to Brigham Young, February 24, 1867, 6–7.
22. Gary Tom and Ronald Holt, "The Paiute Tribe of Utah," 141.

Wigwams [were burning] along the sides of the South hill and the edge of the Santa Clara Bench close to our town. They had the habit of burning their wigwams whenever anyone died. I remember that we could see wickiups burning every day for a while. . . . They died off so fast that there were hardly any left in a short time and the white brethren went in mass one day to bury dead Indians. Although Santa Clara Valley seemed to be almost alive with Indians, afterward there were hardly any to be seen.

Stucki reports no whites were sickened by the illness.

Historians Todd Compton and Leo Lyman place the blame squarely on the Latter-day Saints. Compton has written, "White disease, white appropriation of water resources, and overgrazing from the whites' cattle" reduced "this Paiute homeland to a few scattered bands." Jacob Hamlin's initial encounters in 1854 with the "extensive Tonaquint villages" had quickly reduced their numbers by 1870 and after to "only a memory."[23] In 1878, Augustus P. Hardy, a linguist and evangelist for the local Native Americans, addressed a St. George priesthood meeting and made what Leo Lyman described as "one of the most shocking reports ever uttered in southern Utah." Hardy told the congregation, with Apostle Wilford Woodruff presiding, the native population of roughly "three or four hundred persons when the Southern Indian Mission was founded [only twenty-four years earlier] in 1854" had been reduced to "only two Tonaquint Paiute men [who were still residing] near the Santa Clara River." The once "extensive cultivated land" no longer existed, now reduced to perhaps a dozen acres. Indian Missionary Hardy concluded his report to "the Priesthood Meeting [about] the condition of the natives. Some twenty-five families made their homes in St George and vicinity, they made their living chiefly by begging some, however, worked. These were most of the Shebits tribe. Only two – Quan-tun and Tutegabits Charley – remained of the number body of To-o-no-quints, or Santa Clara indians, which numbered some three or four hundred in 1854, when Jacob Hamblin, Thales H. Haskell, Samuel Knight, and Augusts P. Hardy first visited them. The report set forth that five and a half acres of the eight acres given to the indians at Price last month, had been sown to wheat for them, and the remainder would be planted by themselves with corn, melons, squashes &c."[24]

The story of the inhabitants on the lower Santa Clara and Rio Virgen is not one of racial or cultural equity or fairness. The narrative of the

---

23. Compton, *A Frontier Life*, 354–56.

24. Edward Leo Lyman, "Southern Paiute Relations With Their Early Dixie Mormon Neighbors"; Bleak, *Annals*, 498–99.

ethnic divide in southern Utah reveals the settlers' responsibility for the disappearance of the original inhabitants. Todd Compton stated that "in the 'New Western History,' a major theme is whites moving into an area, destroying the Indian's environment and ecosystems (especially through overgrazing, overhunting, taking over water supplies), then the Indians are at a loss when their means for survival is gone, and thus the whites have forced them into dependence on the whites. (Of course, then the whites looked down on them for begging.)"[25]

The Latter-day Saints, including the Hawleys and their neighbors, along with the other white settlers in Santa Clara, St. George, Washington, Pine Valley, and elsewhere, were responsible for the destruction of the Indian habitat. The local whites excused their role in the devastation of the first peoples in religious terms that hid the racist and ethnocentric content of their condemnation and argued that the "fallen" natives were suffering the natural and inevitable circumstances of being a dirty, diseased, and uncivilized people.

Black Americans, on the other hand, were a nonentity to John Hawley. He mentions nothing about free people of color or African American slaves in his autobiography or any other of his writings. He did not include Dan, for instance, a black slave teamster for Jacob Croft in the 1856 emigration company from the Indian nations. John does not mention that he and his brother witnessed the sale of Croft slaves, who were both Dan's fellow workers and property, to finance their master's trip to Utah Territory.[26] A few black Americans did live in Utah Territory. Robert M. Smith owned twenty-six slaves in Utah County, for example, in 1850.[27] A photograph of Parowan Stake President William H. Dame and his wives taken in the 1860s shows unnamed black servants standing on the porch behind them.[28] The Southern Mission historian James G. Bleak listed John Burton, one of the first pioneers that settled Parowan

---

25. Todd Compton, e-mail message to Melvin C. Johnson, September 30, 2016.

26. R. Halliburton, *Red over Black: Black Slavery among the Cherokee Indians*, 114; Thomas Waters Cropper, quoted in "Millard County Chronicle," January 14, 1932. However, there is no listing for Dan in the Jacob Croft Company registry of members in the wagon train. See "Jacob Croft Company Reports, 1856."

27. United States Census (Slave Schedule), 1850.

28. Census records in Parowan or Iron County identify only John Burton by color and name. 1856 Utah Statehood Census. The record lists John as living with Sidney R. and Betsy Burton in 1856. Perhaps as many as five (certainly less than ten) blacks lived in the Red Creek Post Office region of Parowan, meaning

in 1851, as "colored."²⁹ Burton, the chattel property of Susan McCord Burton Robinson, was probably not freed until the Congressional act in 1862 terminated slavery in the territories.³⁰ He died in 1865, and his remains are in the Parowan Cemetery. The Hawleys had arrived in Dixie in 1857. John Hawley would have known about John Burton even if he had not met him.

Slaves were present in Dixie. The Washington County records document the masters of male "servants" sixteen years of age and older as responsible for paying the same poll tax as those levied "of six day's labor on all white male per-sons over the age of 16 years. Ten hours a day, or $2⁰⁰ per day cash."³¹ John Burton was an active member of the Church in Parowan. He contributed fifteen dollars towards the construction of the rock meeting house. James Henry Martineau recorded the slave's participation in a Thursday evening of fasting in his journal for January 5, 1860: "Br. J. A. Hall spoke in tongues, and John Burton (a slave) interpreted. The burden of Br. Hall's word was to the effect great and important events were now being consummated in the work which we would soon hear of, and the importance of living our religion."³² John Anderson West, a member of the slave owner's extended family, condescendingly told a story recorded by his grandson William Thomas Morris, that the "old Negro who they called 'Black John' . . . would often preach in their testimony meetings and the burden of his sermon was, 'Brudders and Sisters, wen the good Lawd calls old Black John, I'se a gwine, I'se a gwine, over Jordan to meet my Lawd.'"³³ Hawley and his opinion on African Americans, even those members of the church, probably would have coincided and reinforced the racial aloofness of Martineau and the casual dismissiveness of Morris.

Of fervent religious path-keepers, the Dixie settlers had plenty.

Paragoonah in 1860. About a dozen individuals born in Australia are on the roles. Some numbers in the colored/black column are erased.

29. Bleak, *Annals*, 5. John Burton (1797–1865) was a slave who, according to family lore, later became a freedman. Burton was originally gifted as property to Susan McCord. Also known as "Black John," "Faithful John," or "Burton Robinson," he lived near the home of McCord and Joseph Lee Robinson in Parowan and was a member of the Church of Jesus Christ of Latter-day Saints.

30. Alfred H. Kelley, Winfred A. Harbison, and Herman Belz, *The American Constitution: Its Origins and Development*, 433.

31. Bleak, *Annals*, 31.

32. James H. Martineau, Parowan Utah Stake History, 1851–1980, 61.

33. Don E. Burton, *The History of Faithful John Burton*; Parowan Ward general minutes, 1851–1926.

Theocracy dominated life in Utah Territory before and after the Hawleys left Pine Valley in 1870. A theocratic desire by the Utah church leadership drove a compulsive attempt to integrate Latter-day Saint economic and political independence from the United States. Economist Gregory Grossman has reasoned that the "religion's basic tenets are central to understanding" the Latter-day Saint integrated economic system in Utah. Because the Saints believed that Christ's Second Coming would happen soon, a sanctified people must become

> materially suited as well as spiritually and morally perfect. Accordingly, their whole socio-politico-economic system and its institutions and policies were crafted to serve the *ultimate goal under pressure of time.* This overarching purpose comprised two partly mutually competing tasks: *development*, the technical and economic task of constructing—from naught and against severe odds—a country with a functioning economy worthy of the Advent, for themselves and an expected rapidly growing population; and the quest of *utopia*, the educational and socio-psychological task of raising a community of the highest moral and ethical standards in line with the tenets of the faith, also worthy of the Advent. Under the direction of strong leadership and with great determination and speed, the Saints proceeded to construct their Zion, build villages and towns and an extensive irrigation system.[34]

The Latter-day Saint leadership struggled in Utah Territory with the laws of the Republic and Territory as well as the hostility of outsiders, immigrants, indigenous peoples, and outlaws. The Church priesthood leaders strove for unity in matters temporal and religious to govern themselves and thwart outsiders.

Group solidarity helped the Saints ensure their secular and religious goals. Unity of purpose, will, and action led to security for the entire community as early as 1846 and 1847, during Brigham Young's leadership. An example can be found at Ponca Camp in what is now northeastern Nebraska. Instead of launching its thrust in 1846 toward the Salt Lake Valley, Young ordered the forward company into a winter encampment. The pioneers' lack of unity severally and jointly caused disruption in the camp of six hundred. Newell Knight, a member of the camp high council, lamented that division in the camp resulted in the failure of a planned short-distance cattle drive because the men would not work in harmony. Knight wrote that he felt an "earnest desire . . . that a union may be effective with this people for I fear lest perils will follow, like they formerly

---

34. Gregory Grossman, "Central Planning and Transition in the American Desert: Latter-day Saints in Present-Day Sight."

did unto the Nephites and the children of Israel when they fell into transgression." Knight wrote that his troubled heart caused him to exhort his "brethren to humble themselves before the Lord and be united, for union is the key to power and strength," and that the Saints surely had need of such a combination to help them overcome all the troubles that challenged them.[35]

The priesthood members in the Intermountain Basin, including John Hawley, ruled the community and people both secularly and religiously. Seth Blair, a southerner and convert to the Church, revealed the desire of some for theocratic control in an 1851 letter to Senator Sam Houston. Blair thanked the senator for his assistance in Blair's selection as United States District Attorney for the territory. He also mentioned the general belief among the Latter-day Saints that they anticipated "a millennial reign upon the Earth . . . [that will] grant constitution wrights [sic] to all men religiously or politically." In other words, the Saints expected Christ to arrive in their lifetimes and rule all humankind.[36] Blair repeats the refrain to Brigham Young four years later from Port Sullivan, Texas: "My Beloved Friend & Bro: [Blair thanks his Heavenly Father] for the blessed spirit of God that dwells with me and further for that kind & most Heaven Spirit of union that draws me towards as the Head of the Church of our Holy Father on the Earth . . . for you with your Sacred Councillors that hold authority in connection you over the people & Kingdom of God . . . you was called of God to become a Savior of men."[37] Blair believes Young is superior to all humankind in his relation to God.

Political and temporal behavior in Dixie in the following years reflected Blair's belief in the singularity of the Latter-day Saint kingdom in the West. Church leaders, including John Hawley, presided over civil and religious matters in southern Utah. Bleak's entries in the *Annals* during the 1860s demonstrate priesthood authority being involved in the affairs of all people, both members and Gentiles, in striving for unity. In March 1862, the Washington and Santa Clara "elections revealed that 'the Lord permitted us again to have the men of our own choice to rule over us.'" The minutes of the St. George stake conference at the end of May 1863 recorded that "'temporal matters as well as spiritual duties' were the concerns of the Conference." In a postscript to a letter from President Brigham Young to William Crosby that fall, to which Apostles Erastus Snow and Orson

---

35. Newel Knight Autobiography, circa 1871, 2177–78.
36. S. M. Blair, letter to General Samuel Houston, December 1, 1857.
37. Seth M. Blair, letter to President Brigham Young, January 7, 1855.

Pratt were both privy, the settlers were to be prevented from "selling their cotton to go out of the territory." During that year of 1863, according to John Hawley, George A. Smith advised those in Dixie to arm themselves "with the weapons of death. . . . I think this was universally observed. In fact, we was as a general rule more willing to fight for the kingdom than live its doctrine."[38]

The Church into the 1860s, well after the massacre at Mountain Meadows, possessed a willingness to use military force to compel the inhabitants of the southwest to obey counsel. General Daniel H. Wells, the militia commander and second counselor to Brigham Young in the first presidency, sent orders to Colonel William H. Dame, the military leader in the Iron Military District during the militia's murderous activities at Mountain Meadows several years earlier. Wells advised the Iron Brigade commander that it would be "wisdom for each settlement to keep a guard night and day . . . [so that people are not] carried off in the night time." In other words, the equivalent of a militia quick reaction force should be prepared for immediate action "without bluster or hurry to attract undue attraction" and to "fill all the vacancies in the companies." In effect, the order implied that no one was permitted to leave without the church leadership's notice and permission.

Church leaders resolved temporal and secular matters in Dixie. In 1863, Orson Pratt Sr., Erastus Snow, Jacob Gates, and James G. Bleak addressed wards meeting "up the Rio Virgen" at Harrisburg, Grafton, Toquerville, and Virgin City. The leaders advised "the people there . . . to build a neat, commodious, well finished, meeting house, to also be used as a school house . . . temporal matters as well as spiritual duties were treated upon by the speakers; the planting of corn on an extended scale, to provide against scarcity of bread-stuffs was enjoined upon the farmers." Later in the summer, church authorities had to settle water rights on the Santa Clara as drought dried up orchards and vineyards.[39]

The *Annals* reflected that the Dixie priesthood leaders took their duties seriously. The St. George Stake Conference during the first week of September 1865 exemplifies a dedication to priesthood harmony. Instructions from Apostle Erastus Snow, Henry Harriman, and Jacob Gates of the first quorum of seventy, the area patriarch, and members of the high council and bishoprics "were timely, the exhortations to faithful discharge of duty were fervent and words of encouragement to continue in

---

38. John Hawley, "Autobiography of John Hawley," 20.
39. Bleak, *Annals*, 62, 80, 84, 95.

the path of duty . . . [and] unity of action." During the same conference, Apostle Erastus Snow urged that the road at Pine Valley be improved.[40]

Consequences followed for those who did not follow counsel in striving for a unity of action. On May 1, 1868, the members in conference at St. George were counseled on the necessity "of becoming <u>One</u> in temporal things as well as in doctrinal and government affair." At the end of conference, some of those who had been found guilty "for unfaithful conduct" were cut off (excommunicated) from the Church. A year later President Brigham Young noted that "when the Saints live as they should . . . [all] will be spiritual to them."[41] The leadership stepped up its efforts in the years of 1868 and 1869. Probably prepared and counseled by President Young, Erastus Snow and John W. Young opened a new ministry at St. George and the surrounding areas to urge the members in the performances "of daily duty as . . . [an] union in temporal and spiritual affairs in elections and all other civil or domestic duties."[42]

A letter from Erastus Snow to Brigham Young in 1869 summarizes the extent of the co-mingling of his temporal and spiritual duties: "I have, hitherto, for many years, performed the duties of a Presiding Bishop over all this southern country, and everything temporal, as well as spiritual, civil and military; emigration and tithing . . . but as business and settlements increasing I find it difficult to do justice to all these various departments without more efficient aid." In reinforcing spiritual unity, Snow believed that other rival Latter Day Saint organizations were *persona non grata*. For instance, the apostle, while on tour with his entourage that same year, excommunicated Elder Richard C. Gibbons in 1869 at Fort Hamblin. Gibbons had been handing out "tracts and publications" for the RLDS Church, led by Joseph Smith III, the son of Joseph Smith Jr.[43] Gibbons' chastisement may have been of some interest to John Hawley a few miles away, who was investigating RLDS doctrines himself at the time.

Brigham Young, Erastus Snow, and other Church leaders were impressed with the dedicated hard work of Church officers and members in the region's communities. John Hawley is just one example of a few then hundreds and later thousands of Dixie men and women who combined both church and community in their lives. John had grown to adulthood in Lyman Wight and George Miller's common-stock communities in Wisconsin and Texas.

---

40. Bleak, 129, 146.
41. Bleak, 162–63, 181.
42. Bleak, 160.
43. Bleak, 146, 160, 163–64, 181, 187.

He had been trained to accept the economic covenant of common-stock property. With other colonists, he "entered into [a covenant] and that was we would have to take as Lyman said 'the orders of God' and those days was days of order to do as we was told and in this we was well schooled." John and George's eleven years in Wight's colony prepared them well to serve in the Latter-day Saint communities of Utah Territory.[44] The Hawleys, born and bred on the borderlands and frontiers, lived the daily reality of the Latter-day Restoration, unifying church and state as they created their family life in the mountain valleys of the Great Basin.

---

44. Melvin C. Johnson, *Polygamy on the Pedernales: Lyman Wight's Mormon Villages in Antebellum Texas, 1847–1851*, 54; Hawley, "Autobiography," 6.

CHAPTER 8

The Hawleys of Pine Valley

Part II

"Sometimes during a dance, a pair of shoes would pass from one pair of feet to another so many times that at the end of the dance the owner of the shoes could not find them."[1]

While on business in Beaver in 1862, John and George Hawley met and became "acquainted with a man by the name of Stephen Farnsworth, the man that had the great vision at Nauvoo before Joseph's death." This was a prophetic vision tale that was apparently known at the time locally but has not had much of an impact in histories and family records. More than foretelling of the Mormon saga coming west, the Farnsworth Vision superbly illustrates the need to create a sanctified, millennial people.

Farnsworth used terms that millwrights, woodworkers, and coopers, such as the Hawleys, instinctively understood. The vision heralds the Twelve's rigorous preparation of both church and members for the coming hardships and persecutions and depicts the Church triumphant and apocalyptic in the final days. Farnsworth, on his way to the temple at Nauvoo, remembered

> that a drizzling rain set in and as far as his eyes could extend, he saw the Saints moving west, but he did not see Joseph or Hyrum in the move. He saw the twelve with Brigham at their head and they went west a long ways in the wilderness and he saw the twelve with a mallet apiece and the church in a long tub. And the twelve whooped the church with iron hoops and commenced driving these whoops with their mallets. So tight did they drive these hoops that it seemed to him that they would soon be squeezed to death. He saw some break the ranks and they fled to our enemies, but the majority stuck to the tub and those that would stand squeezing was the ones that was prepared to redeem Zion. He saw them go up to the Center Stake of Zion and the people

---

1. Quoted from William A. Wilson, "Folklore in Dixie: Past and Present," 524.

of that land sunk in the earth so terrible was there [sic] presence. The earth opened and swallowed them up and in this way Zion was redeemed.²

John noted that Farnsworth had told the narrative in various ways.

The vision reinforced the Twelve's authority as legitimate heirs to Church leadership following the deaths of Joseph and Hyrum Smith. The prophetic vision required them to fashion the Church members in the west (the tub) with mallets (the priesthood authority). The "iron hoops" are the guidance and direction given by the priesthood, and the "hoops" were so tightened that Farnsworth thought that church members "would soon be squeezed to death." Some members did fall away and join the Saints' opponents. Bishop Joseph Lee Robinson recorded that in the vision that Brigham Young and the Twelve had been hammering on the hoops holding the barrel, which represented the Latter Day Saint church and membership. The barrel burst. Nearly one-half of the members of the church ran away.³ However, "the majority" that stayed with the Church and endured the contraction and compression "was prepared to redeem Zion," wrote Hawley. The "Center Stake of Zion" was so powerful that "the people of that land sunk in the earth so terrible" as if swallowed by it, so that "in this way Zion was redeemed." The power of the vision narrative so impressed Hawley that he could record it clearly twenty-three years later.⁴

John Hawley as presiding elder exemplified the religious and secular power of Farnsworth's vision as an instrument of redeeming the citizens of Pine Valley for Zion. He preached on a short mission that year with "others of like authority" to exhort and teach in the northern settlements. The presiding leadership in Salt Lake City apparently thought "a change in preaching" in the various communities was beneficial from time to time. Hawley, conforming to his understanding of his role in the church, instructed his audiences "to live to the law of God and to keep the commandments and to honor the authority."⁵

Hawley had no difficulty in tightening the hoops of religious authority. One example involved Lorenzo Brown, a friend of his brother George. On January 12, 1864, John Hawley, as presiding elder, interviewed Brown, who complained later in his diary that he thought Hawley was

---

2. Quoted in John Hawley, "Autobiography of John Hawley," 19. See also Stephen Farnsworth Vision, 1844.
3. Joseph L. Robinson, Autobiography and Journals, 20–21.
4. Quoted in Hawley, "Autobiography," 19; Farnsworth Vision.
5. Hawley, "Autobiography," 19.

prejudiced against him. John did not hesitate to give counsel when he felt it was needed. On another occasion, concerned that the morning services were sparsely attended, John requested "all hands" come to service that evening. John spoke at length and "requested the abolishing of card playing." Toward the end of April 1866, Brown got into a brawl with George Bryce over mill business. They paid fines of $2.50 and $1.00, respectively. The next Sunday Presiding Elder John Hawley used Lorenzo's name and the incident as examples to avoid. John never mentions Lorenzo Brown in his writings, while the Brown's index to his diary mentions the various Hawleys no less than seventy-two times in five years.[6]

Hawley also preached in St. George when called to do so. In November 1866, Charles Lowell Walker noted in his diary that Hawley, D. H. Cannon, William P. McIntire, J. W. Crosby, and Jacob Gates spoke from the bowery. Cannon and McIntire "spoke on the rise and progress of the Church." Hawley preached that keeping the covenants would lead to the Saints having "the spirit of them" to "live them." That evening Crosby talked about Conference and matters in Great Salt Lake City, while Jacob Gates spoke on a variety of topics, including Joseph Smith, "the Book of Mormon, [and] setting up the Kingdom of God on Earth." He said seeking happiness in the world "without the aid of the Holy Ghost" was folly.[7]

The life of the Utah Territory pioneers, however, was not all work and no play. The people of Dixie were not shy when it came to entertaining themselves. Several days after the pioneers' arrival, the men put a large tent belonging to Asa Calkins up on the Adobe Yard in St. George. William Wilson reported the bowery "was also their first dancing place," and "the pioneers danced at Christmas" in 1861. Not only were Church meetings held there but also the first Christmas social "with wrestling matches, hop-step and jump contests, foot races, and a program of singing. Later that evening a dance was held, with Oswald Barlow's orchestra that provided the music for this first dance." William Cowley played snare drum in Barlow's band. Barlow, a fine dancer as well, could play fife and drums. While the "older people danced inside the tent . . . the space outside the tent was cleared for the young people to dance."[8]

The pioneers of Dixie loved to dance. They danced "in church buildings, schools, the social hall, and private homes," and they danced "the polka, the scottische, the quadrille, the Virginia Reel, six nations, the two-

---

6. *The Journal of Lorenzo Brown, 1823–1890*, 153, 165–66, 167–68.
7. Diary of Charles Lowel Walker, 271.
8. Oswald Barlow, "History of Oswald Barlow, St. George Pioneer."

step, the snap waltz, the spat waltz." A "polygamy waltz" was for the "men with more than one wife." For both young and old, dancing was a favorite recreation, and the 4th and 24th of July celebrations always ended in a dance. Lorenzo Brown noted that July 4, 1863, in Pine Valley was celebrated by "all hands [having] a game at ball," an early version of baseball, followed by a "dance in evening."[9]

George Hawley and Lorenzo Brown were close, despite the latter's dislike of John Hawley. For example, on Sunday, May 31, 1863, the Hawleys took supper with the Browns. Two days after that, George rode north with Brown to Little Pinto, and "there struck up the kanyon 5 miles [east] then down [southeast] through a very rough kanyon to J D Lees 5 miles [at Harmony] then 4 miles farther to Hills & stopped for Night." On Christmas evening that year, after sawing at his mill, Brown attended a "very good" dance at the George Hawleys, and another one on New Year's Day 1864.[10]

Remembering these times, Jennie B. Miles recalled: "At the dances some were barefoot, some had cow-hide boots, or heavy shoes. A piece of tallow on the shelf was used to minister to stubbed toes or bruised feet so they could go on with the dance."[11] Folklorist William A. Wilson wrote that "those who had shoes would lend them temporarily to those who were barefoot. Sometimes during a dance, a pair of shoes would pass from one pair of feet to another so many times that at the end of the dance the owner of the shoes could not find them. He would have to wait until the next day when he would find them in the window of the tithing office." [12]

A more substantial material culture replaced the dugouts and the shanties at Pine Valley during the 1860s. Some historians disagreed on who built the "first real house in the valley." Both John and George Hawley had their champions. John "sawed logs and finished the inside with plaster." Wanda Snow Petersen claimed it was George Hawley who built the first house on Spring Branch near the mill, so well-built "that it could be moved later to the lower part of town without falling apart." Time and memory conflated the narrative to one in which the Hawleys built "theirs of sawed logs which were plastered on the inside and boarded up on the outside with vertical boards and batts." After the flood in 1865, John Hawley, William R. Slade, and Joseph Hadfield moved their houses farther west from the

---

9. Wilson, "Folklore of Dixie," 524; Brown, *Journal*, 149.

10. Brown, *Journal*, 152.

11. A. K. Hafen, *Dixie Folklore and Pioneer Memories*, 32, quoted in Wilson, "Folklore of Dixie," 524.

12. Quoted from Wilson, "Folklore in Dixie," 524.

mill on Spring Branch, across from the Old Cemetery. Everyone seemed to remember the quality of the Hawleys' woodworking and house building.[13]

The world of Mormon plural marriage appears strange, even wondrous to the modern reader, and trying to comprehend George Hawley's married life perhaps even more so. A Latter-day husband and father's patriarchal relationships to his wife and children in Utah during the second half of the nineteenth-century was a world apart from American social norms. Every worthy Mormon man held the priesthood and stood at the head of his family; his wife or wives remained subordinate to his religious leadership. Presiding Elder John Hawley dealt with difficult issues concerning his brother's wives in Pine Valley. Brigham Young twice instructed Bishop Zadok Judd of Fort Clara, John's religious leader, to resolve George's quarrels with Sarah and Jeannette, his second and third wives. One of Young's admonitions directed, "If br. George Hawley's second and third wives' statements are correct, as set forth in your letter of Jan. 17, I wish you to request br. Hawley to give each of them a bill of divorce, and if he refuses so to do, disfellowship him." Another instructed the bishop to have George fill out "a blank bill of divorce" from "Jenet" [Jeannette Goudie], pay for it, and file it. George did so. Jeanette married Joseph Hadfield, a long time Hawley clan member, that year on December 25, 1860. The ceremony was performed by Presiding Elder John Hawley, brother of Jeanette's former husband.[14]

The settlers in Pine Valley observed the fulfillment of Young's vision of a city near the confluence of the Santa Clara and Virgin rivers in late 1861. A large company from Salt Lake City came south to found St. George. John Hawley happily noted that the "gathering made lumber business good for us and then we could get a little money occasionally." Two apostles, Orson Pratt Sr. and Erastus Snow, supervised the operation, creating a stake and organizing a high council. Robert Gardner was appointed the presiding bishop for the region. John concluded to pay a good

---

13. Hazel Bradshaw, ed., *Under Dixie Sun: A History of Washington County by Those Who Loved Their Forebears*, 351; Wanda Snow Petersen, *William Snow, first bishop of Pine Valley, A Man without Guile*, 121; Elizabeth Beckstrom and Bess Beckstrom, *O' Ye Mountains High: The Story of Pine Valley Utah*, 24, 183.

14. Brigham Young, letter to Bishop Zadok K. Judd, February 24, 1860; Freddijo Passey Burk, *Joseph Hadfield Story: An Incredible Odyssey*, 188, 362. For a fuller treatment of divorce in plural marriage, see Eugene E. Campbell and Bruce L. Campbell, "Divorce among Mormon Polygamists: Extent and Explanations," 181–200.

sound sum as tithing, for the people of St. George needed it to help them out of the alkali.[15]

The milling and lumber industry in Pine Valley hustled to fill not only the need of St. George's citizens, but the general area as well in 1862 and 1863 as the population grew in Dixie as well as in Pine Valley. More mills came to the valley and added jobs. The county court at Washington that summer appointed Jacob Hamblin, Robert Gardner, and Robert L. Lloyd to apportion the timber rights to three lumber businesses running in Pine Valley: Snow, Whipple & Gardner; Burgess's Mill; and Thomas Forsyth Mill. The county court's decision made it difficult for lumber workers like the Hawley brothers and Lorenzo Brown to prosper in their professions.[16]

Brigham Young visited the Southern Mission at least annually and more in some years during the decade. President Young spoke at Pine Valley in the summer of 1863. He gave "a rattling sermon about stealing and he told us to not be troubled about the loss of property. For said he, there is a day of reckoning coming in which fourfold with interest will be required." The sermon pricked the conscience of Henry W. Miller. After the Croft Company had left Indian Territory for Utah in 1856, conveyance of $30 to Hawley arrived, and Miller who had Hawley's authority to draw the money did so. But he did not forward it to Hawley. John wrote that Miller "never intended to say anything about it. But after this sermon of Brigham's, he came to me and confessed to me and after a month or so he paid me the cash, thirty dollars." John referred to it "as a lucky scare for me."[17]

Sickness and accidents plagued Pine Valley that second half of the year. In July, Lorenzo Brown witnessed what he thought was the "hardest rain I ever saw," raising the creek that ran his mill over nine feet. Eight miles downstream, the raging stream "destroyed everything and drowned 4 children." The beaver colonies on the creek were driven before the flood, injuring "many of them & destroying their dam and houses." The homeless, including Benjamin Gray and families, and that of Jesse Craigham, came to Pine Valley for succor and employment.[18]

Heartbreak struck twice in September within six days. John and Sylvia's toddler, Sylvia Amelia, drowned on the 21st. John wrote of the

---

15. Hawley, "Autobiography," 19.
16. James Godson Bleak, *The Annals of the Southern Mission: A Record of the History of the Settlement of Southern Utah*, 81; *Pioneer Pathways*, 351.
17. Hawley, "Autobiography," 20.
18. Brown, *Journal*, 148–49.

"sorrow and mourning . . . to loose [sic] our children by accident. Here we planted one more which we are satisfied was for a glorious resurrection of the just."[19] Sarah Hadfield, six days earlier, formerly wife of Orange Wight and George Hawley, buried a baby girl she bore on July 25, 1863. The female infant was named Sarah Elizabeth Hadfield, having been given as a surname her mother's family name. Based on an index for the Old Pine Valley Cemetery, Sarah Hadfield (George's plural wife until at least 1860) had moved into the Earl household as a plural wife to Sylvester H. Earl sometime before her oldest daughter's marriage to her husband's son, Wilbur Earl. A year later Sarah joined her daughter, on March 15, 1864, in the Old Pine Valley Cemetery.[20]

Poor housing in mountain winter conditions adversely affected pioneer health, and good housing almost immediately improved it. An example is that of the Brown family. In December 1863, while living "in our open cold shanty," the family of Lorenzo Brown suffered injury and illness. Lorenzo fell and severely injured his hip and had to use a "powerful liniment" to be able to get around. Two of his children, Edward and Benjamin, were stricken with "influenza & canker." Benjamin had "several ague shakes." Daughter Sarah suffered slightly from the ague. Then "John had a severe cold & for 10 or 12 days could not speak loud but kept running about all the time & all this in our open shanty." Once the family had moved into a well-built "warm house where we could nurse & doctor them," the family began to mend. Brown constructed the house with three-inch plank and divided it in the middle with a shingle roof with a matched shingle floor below, and an open space above a good fireplace. A stove stood in another corner.[21]

The Brown, Hawley, Pratt, and Snow families, among others, witnessed a mixture of events affecting the Southern Mission in 1864, including trouble with outsiders, heresy and excommunication, quarrels about water and timber rights, and the expansion to the northwest of new Mormon communities. Joy came to John and Sylvia as another son, William Nephi, was born on January 7th.[22]

On May 5, 1864, Erastus Snow grew concerned about the little Mormon farming and livestock hamlet of Meadow Valley, north and west forty miles from St. George. In May, the apostle had visited the families

---

19. Hawley, "Autobiography," 20.
20. Wesley W. Craig, Old Pine Valley Cemetery.
21. Brown, *Journal*, 152.
22. Hawley, "Autobiography," 21.

and advised them (1) to stay away from the new mines, especially at nearby Pioche and Panaca, the silver of which had been discovered by William Hamblin with Paiute help, and (2) to allow Samuel Lee, as presiding elder, to select for each family their "inheritances" before property deeds were filed and recorded.[23] Lorenzo Brown noted on June 19th from Pine Valley that "most of the men" were exploring the area "near meadow valley." He added that several Pine Valley families, including "Br Slade & William his son," were hauling to the west, which required Brown to use his own team to bring logs to the mill.[24]

Latter-day Saint worries continued about an alleged Gentile plot led by General Conner in Salt Lake City and fellow government officials to take Meadow and Clover valleys from the Saints and their farming and mineral wealth for themselves and their allies. On June 11th and 12th, Elder John Nebeker took more Latter-day Saint families to reinforce their presence as rumors swirled that new numbers of "apostates and gentiles" were intending to deprive the Saints of their land.[25] By August, the troubles had died down. Lorenzo Brown's journal for August and September that year shows the only interaction between Pine Valley with Meadow Valley and Clover Valley just to its north was that of social interaction. By 1870 and 1871, the new territorial boundaries moved Meadow and Clover valleys and St. Thomas to Nevada. Many of the Saints in those areas began to join with their co-religionists to the east in Utah Territory.[26]

The Saints never wholly abandoned the Upper Muddy and "western valleys." Gentile miners and their operations dominated Pioche; however, Meadow Valley and Panaca would always have a strong Latter-day Saint

---

23. Bleak, *Annals*, 96–97.
24. Brown, *Journal*, 154.
25. Bleak, *Annals*, 97.
26. Brown, *Journal*, 154. Brown's late entries witness the breaking up of the Mormon village. On June 5, 1870, he writes, "Several names were called to go & strengthen the western settlements and endeavor to prevent the aggressions of outsiders & apostate influence and secure this land and farming interests as they are endeavoring to jump our claims and ride the saints or drive them from their homes," 195. In March 1871, Brown reports: "Went to Meadow Valley for Benjamin The settlement is being broken up It has fallen in Nevada State & they claim heavy taxes for 3 or 4 years at which our people demur having them in Utah Benjamin leaves his house & lot that cost him over $1500.00," 197. McArthur, *St. Thomas: A History Uncovered*, 51–59, records in detail the Latter-day Saint town's break-up in the months ending 1870 and beginning 1871 on the south on the Muddy River.

presence. In 1871, President Erastus Snow and the Southern Mission Stake Presidency and merchants from St. George, Santa Clara, and Washington were meeting in order "to regulate the trade of vegetables, fruit and grain to Pioche and the Western Valleys." They estimated that the market could require up to three tons of vegetables plus the excess of the seasonal fruit harvested in the local orchards. Luke Syphus was sustained as the president of the elders' quorum for the Western Valleys to regulate the market so that the highest prices could be obtained.[27]

Once the problems with the western villages waned, the all-too-common incidents of illness and death struck the settlers again. On Founders Day, July 24th, the Brown family was "making grave clothes" for a child of Robert Gardner. The mourners held services at noon and the burial at dark. Brown somberly noted, "This is the third child Bro. Gardner has buried since coming to St George."[28] In August, many people were ill in Pine Valley. The most dangerous of the diseases would be diphtheria or a sore throat if untreated. White pustules would ulcerate the throat, causing the patient to strangle and die within four to six days. The treatment used in Pine Valley for the "strangles" was a mixture of "alum & salt dissolved in vinegar & gurgled in the throat once in 10 or 15 minutes." Plasters with mixed salt and egg yolk would be used on "the neck & throat and renewed occasionally." Brown said the remedies were effective if used in a timely manner and helpful for all the patients.[29]

The members of Pine Valley turned their attention to President Brigham Young, Apostle Erastus Snow, and Orson Pratt Jr. in September 1864. The high council in St. George had earlier been the scene of religious difficulties that involved Orson Pratt Jr. Son of the apostle he was named for, Orson Jr. had moved to Dixie in 1862 as part of the extended family and settled within a few months at St. George. The family lived in a tent for some time. Orson Pratt Jr. lived the privileged life with his father and Erastus Snow, his uncle by marriage, the leading personalities of the Southern Mission. Orson Jr., twenty-seven in 1862, served as the city postmaster, alderman, and a member of the stake high council. John Hawley wrote the younger Pratt had "become dissatisfied with some doctrine taught by the leading men of the church and stepped down and

---

27. Bleak, *Annals*, 238, 248.
28. Brown, *Journal*, 156.
29. Brown, 157.

out of the council and moved back to Salt Lake Valley."[30] There was much more to the story than this simple narrative.

For Pine Valley, it began as Brown excitedly wrote in his journal on September 11th the news announcing the arrival of President Brigham Young the following day. He would preach later in the day. The next day the traveling party arrived from Pinto. The twenty-one wagons carried more than one hundred passengers along with the Nephi Brass band and a quadrille group from Salt Lake City. Nine families in the valley divided and took in the visitors. Thomas Jenkins, Seymour Young, George D. Watt, Philip Margette, and some others supped with the Lorenzo Browns.

According to Brown, Brigham Young felt "first rate and is full of blessings." The company held a meeting at five that afternoon, and the George Hawleys hosted a dance in the evening for neighbors and visitors. Brown believed that "the President and Twelve enjoyed themselves highly." At 9 p.m., President Young stated it "twas time to dismiss kneeled down & offered prayer in which he asked God to bless this settlement and all pertaining to it in the most fervant manner."[31] Then the President began asking questions privately of at least Hawley and Brown.

President Young inquired of John Hawley how the brothers-in-law and apostles Orson Pratt Sr. and Erastus Snow were faring with each other. John said the two apostles "was at peace at present. They was divided at one time in their judgment." Not surprisingly, the matter was over timber and milling. John, as presiding elder, had allowed Robert Forsyth to cut timber in a canyon. John's action ended up in a church trial because Eli Whipple and Erastus Snow, competitors of Forsyth, became wroth. John stood on his priesthood authority and the principle that "a presiding officer had this jurisdiction of managing the country and its surroundings." Orson Pratt Sr., the senior apostle in Dixie, presided in a church court and awarded the decision to Hawley on that principle. The decision caused bad blood between Pratt and Snow. John believed that Whipple and Snow had intended to create a logging and milling monopoly in Pine Valley by removing competition.[32]

John Hawley's interactions with others, whether the president, an apostle, a fellow priesthood holder, or his own brother, seemed to follow an iron rod. His character appeared to be inflexible once he perceived what he thought his action should be. He married his brother's third wife

---

30. Hawley, "Autobiography," 20.
31. Brown, *Journal*, 157.
32. Hawley, "Autobiography," 20–21.

to another man. He ruled against his friend and religious superior Erastus Snow in the matter of timber interests and sought the appellate approval of Orson Pratt Sr. He counseled Lorenzo Brown and others from the pulpit for what he believed was inappropriate behavior. He counseled with President Young on matters involving the Pratt family.

The conversation moved to the namesake of Orson Pratt Sr., who had been having problems with the council and Snow earlier in the year. President Young believed the younger Pratt came by his need for empirical data naturally. Brown wrote that President Young had said that Orson Pratt Sr. "was at heart an infidel." According to Hawley, Young stated Orson Jr.'s "father is sceptical also." Young alleged that the older Pratt "never offers a prayer to God" and that Pratt "was doubtful whether a being of this kind existed or not." John continued, "I thought this strange but he further said the church has had more trouble with this man than any other in the church. For said he, we had to call him home from England at one time for teaching and writing that God had attained to perfection and could not progress further." John was flattered President Young would share private matters with him, writing, "I thought it quite good to thus be honored with a pleasant talk with the Prophet of our Kingdom."[33]

On the 14th, members of the Twelve did most of the preaching. Brown noticed that the president did "not speak a great deal," that he made an exception concerning those who were called to St. George and failed. He believed those who had failed would have action taken against them at the October conference in Salt Lake City. Young then diverted from his topic of apostasy and spoke of a subject near and dear to his heart: cotton.[34] He talked about growing cotton, stating "that his cotton spinner was in successful operation make all sises of yarn from No 8 to No 40," and that "he would exchange" the settler's "raw cotton delivered at the machine at the rate of 5 lbs yarn for [blank] lbs of cotton." Brown continued, writing Young "blessed the people of the mission with future promises wanted them to settle all the nooks and corners up and down the virgin and bye and bye would go beyond the Colorado stopped."[35]

During the next week, matters deteriorated between Erastus Snow and Orson Pratt Jr. Lydia Pratt, Orson Sr.'s first wife and mother of Orson

---

33. Brown, *Journal*, 157; Hawley, "Autobiography," 21.

34. Charles Lowell Walker noted in July 1866 that he was working on the roof of a grist mill for Erastus Snow, on the Virgin River just down the bank from Brigham Young's Cotton Factory. Walker, *Diary*, 265n7.

35. Brown, *Journal*, 157.

Jr., had received permission from Brigham Young for the family to return to Salt Lake City. However, in a sacrament meeting on September 18, Orson Jr. attacked the character of Erastus Snow. He pointed at Snow, calling him "a snake in the grass" who made life so miserable for Orson Sr. that he accepted earlier that year a mission call out of the country. Orson Jr. pointed his finger at Snow for endeavoring unsuccessfully to persuade the younger Pratt's wife "to turn against her husband." He also testified that he did not believe that Joseph Smith came to earth to fulfill the work of the Restoration. Church authorities publicly excommunicated the younger Pratt that evening. The family moved shortly after that to Salt Lake City.[36] In light of Young's conversations in Pine Valley with Brown and Hawley six days earlier, the events of the 18th ending with Orson Jr.'s being struck off from the Church causes one to think the excommunication met the President's approval. Perhaps Snow had been the mover with Young's consent and had also made an attempt to privately turn Orson Jr.'s wife against him.

The Dixie region, as well as Pine Valley, began to develop. In the summer of 1864, "a townsite has been surveyed in Pine Valley, and following the extension of water privilege given by St. George City Council a number of the citizens of St. George have moved part of their families there." John Menzies Macfarlane, a musician and surveyor, laid out the new townsite in Pine Valley at "Lower Town" following the pattern of Joseph Smith and Brigham Young. Macfarlane organized the city "on a grid design with square blocks and straight streets," but not on a straight north and south angle. The new cemetery rested "on an angle when compared to the town."[37] In 1865, Pine Valley's population grew larger. St. George's City Council approval of the limited use of the Santa Clara River to start irrigation farming of thirteen acres began a small diversification of the village economy. Other families took the opportunity to move to the valley. By that summer, the canals stretched about a mile in length with an average four feet wide and about one-and-a-half feet in depth for a cost of $281. In 1868, the community of Pine Valley had spent $1,125 on the updating and maintenance of the canals. By the following summer of 1869, the seven canals stretched some thirteen miles in length at an aver-

---

36. Bleak, *Annals*, 101–3; Richard S. Van Wagoner and Mary C. Van Wagoner, "Orson Pratt Jr.: Gifted Son of an Apostle and an Apostate," 84, 88–90; Hawley, "Autobiography," 20.

37. Bleak, *Annals*, 116; Snow, *William Snow*, 124.

age width of three feet.³⁸ The Hawley houses were moved west to Block 12D and Block 13A on the new townsite. George's house still stands more than 150 years later.³⁹

John finished his entry for 1865 with "all things went off pleasantly this with the exception of the loss of my son," William Nephi, born in January 1864. Sometime in early November, the boy was scalded badly. By February 18, 1865, the wounds had become sorely infected. On the 24th, Brown records that John Hawley took his boy to the doctor at St. George. The snow was so deep that "all hands went two miles with him to help through drifts." The youngster began to improve, but only for a short time.⁴⁰ The following summer, John recalled that the pioneer holiday of July 24th "brought great suffering as well." The infant survived the scalding only to be carried off by scarlet fever. His family buried him as "another son for a glorious resurrection."⁴¹

The 24th of July festival in 1865 was held at the unofficial campground called the "Pinery," a grove of trees three miles up the river. The St. George stake president gave the devotional address at the meeting and then singing followed. "The crowd danced until 5PM" on "a floor made of pieces of newly-sawed timber laid on the ground," which was followed by "speeches, recitations, poems and musical numbers. The evening finished with more dancing." The following day Apostles Amasa M. Lyman, Erastus Snow, and George A. Smith addressed the crowd, followed by "lunch, dancing, supper and more dancing."⁴² Charles Lowell Walker agreed with Hawley that, high "among the towering pines and majestic Mountains, in company with E Snow, G A Smith, A Lyman and large number of Brethren and Sisters," the Saints had a wonderful time. "We enjoyed ourselves the best kind, in having 3 of the Quorum of the Twelve Apostles preach to us besides singing, dancing, jumping, romping, &c &c. The scenery where we were is truly sublime, and imposing." Walker made it home to St. George on the 27th, "pretty well tired out jolting over the rough and rocky roads."⁴³

---

38. Bleak, *Annals*, 99, 113, 116–18, 171, 199–200; Hawley, "Autobiography," 20.
39. Bradshaw, *Under Dixie Sun*, 183; Beckstrom and Beckstrom, *O' Ye Mountains High*, 28, 30.
40. John Hawley, "Experiences of John Hawley," 223; Brown, *Journal*, 159.
41. Hawley, "Autobiography," 21.
42. Snow, *William Snow*, 125–26.
43. Walker, *Diary*, 248.

The death of John and Sylvia's son prevented them from participating in the festivities that day. John knew and liked "Amercy" Lyman and went to listen to his discourse the next day. He thought much of the sermon was "old fashion Mormonism" and "gave us some good instructions." However, as he had for some years, Apostle Lyman continued to teach that the blood of Jesus even as Savior was not necessary for the atonement of any man's sins. According to Hawley, Amasa Lyman argued that "the principle and doctrine of Christ would of [have] saved all mankind should they observed its precept and doctrine whether Christ's blood was shed or not." Church authorities had sternly reproved the errant apostle, but Lyman would not heed counsel and continued his aberrant preaching. John believed that the apostle should have been excommunicated but had not "because of the good he had done."[44] Several days later, on the 28th, Walker went up in the summer heat to the Bowery to hear "Smith, Amasa Lyman and others [give] us some very good teachings and doctrine pertaining to self government, domestic happiness, self preservation &c &c." The speakers "exhorted us to prepare for War. Keep our powder dry, and rifles in shooting order, and be ready at a moments warning. overall we had quite an interesting time of it and felt sorry when they went away."[45] Amasa Lyman, in fact, would be excommunicated a few years later, for such heretical views on the Atonement.[46]

A month later Lorenzo Brown recorded his recollections of the holiday, which was "a big celebration of rather a grand picnic on the 24th of July." The first arrivals came on Saturday the 22nd, with large turnouts from "St. George Santa Clara Washington Pinto & Cedar" and Beaver and Parowan. A large encampment was organized in a "kanyon" a couple of miles "above," possibly Grass Valley. The shade of tall pines covered the "large dancing floor" that "had been constructed." One participant from St. George described the celebration: "We enjoyed ourselves the best kind in having 3 of the Quorum of the Twelve Apostles preach to us besides singing, dancing, jumping, [and] romping."[47] The Sunday morning services including singing and preaching.[48]

---

44. Hawley, "Autobiography," 22.
45. Walker, *Diary*, 248.
46. See Edward Leo Lyman, *Amasa Mason Lyman, Mormon Apostle and Apostate: A Study in Dedication*, about this intriguing character in early Mormon history.
47. Walker, *Diary*, 239, 248.
48. Brown, *Journal*, 162.

The following morning on the 24th, apostles George A. Smith and Amasa Lyman and others arrived about 10 a.m. Brown claimed that the members heard "a good preach." Silas Smith spent the evening with the Browns, and George A. Smith came "after breakfast & dictated a letter for Silas to write." The apostles and their party were able to relax. Silas Smith rode a "skiff on the mill race." The next day Smith came again with Amasa Lyman, William Dame, and others, to the Browns. All attended a moonlight dance at Benjamin Brown's house. George Smith and "sister Lyman led the first set He said twas the first dance for him for four years & enjoyed himself very much." The Browns hosted thirty, including latecomers, for breakfast "till past noon when all had left." Lorenzo's wife collapsed from overworking.[49]

Lorenzo Brown evaluated the prosperity of Pine Valley that fall. The settlers "fenced a large field and raised 2000 bush[els] of small grain besides potatoes & turnips and have built a house for Br [William] Snow and stocked and run three mills beside." Comparing the productivity of Pine Valley with the Pinto settlers, he wrote that the Pinto "raised 700 bush[els] grain & some home[s] had more help than we had their field fenced before which has drove them nearly to death with work we have done more than three times the work that they have and with less hands we have been greatly blessed."[50] The community of Pine Valley under Presiding Elder Hawley's supervision had done well in 1865.

Material and educational improvements continued the next year in Pine Valley. On January 18, 1866, the county appropriated twelve hundred dollars to repair the road from Cedar City through Pine Valley to St. George by the legislature. Erastus Snow would ask at General Conference that year for the Pine Valley road to be improved, and the valley residents subscribed a total of $324.50 for improvement the following year.[51] The burden was considered onerous by many. Charles Lowell Walker, tasked with getting donations from fellow members, griped in his diary:

> I did not feel well in performing the duty, as I had to specify why each one would not pay. It seems to me rather too personal, and a goodly number of the Bretheren [sic] did not feel able to pay anything towards it. Some seemed to say the taxes and calls were rather too heavy, viz the Territorial tax, county tax, city tax, Poll tax, internal revenue tax, school tax, St George Hall tax,

---

49. Brown, 162.
50. Brown, 164.
51. Bleak, *Annals*, 126–27, 146–47, 153.

besides calls to work on the streets, roads, ditches, dams, Public works, &c, &c, &c.⁵²

Lorenzo Brown noted during January 1866 that "our school is decidedly a success The scholars all seem to be improving Lehi Dykes teacher at $3.50 per scholar we are now almost completely shut in to the valley by deep snow much deeper than last winter." On the 17th of February, Brown wrote again: "In the shop P.M. At school This is the last day. The different Classes have made considerable progress." The old log school house was auctioned for $72 along with $30 more for a new school building. Bleak wrote that "the settlers built a new school house" in Pine Valley, with "Sunday School Superintendent, John Hawley" supervising "both regular and ecclesiastical schools" in the new building.⁵³

By 1866, Pine Valley was regularly celebrating the great patriotic and pioneer celebrations. The authorities continued to not neglect their responsibility for "directing and controlling the people. . . . Pine Valley was also visited and instructed in duty."⁵⁴ John did not mention the celebrations that year but noted the birth of Isaac Zimri, yet another son, on the eighth of January. Of Church matters, John remembered that "the church had despaired of Joseph [Smith III], son of the Seer ever doing anything for God or the church," because the young Joseph had become a prophet and revelator to the RLDS defectors of the upper Midwest.⁵⁵

The Hawleys had no idea that future years would bring events that included John Hawley being called on a mission to his RLDS family and friends in Iowa, and that his evaluation of the supposed apostasy of the son of Joseph Smith Jr. would lead to his flirtation with and then conversion to the RLDS Church.

---

52. Walker, *Diary*, 267.
53. Brown, *Journal*, 166–167, 171, 362, 391.
54. Bleak, *Annals*, 129.
55. Hawley, "Experiences," 223.

CHAPTER 9

A Pine Valley Missionary to Iowa

1868

"The thought that I was worthy to officiate in *so* great an endowment as the second was considered, I thought was double honor conferred upon me."

In July 1867, an incident occurred that may have become a festering thorn in John's pride. Misdating the year to 1861 in his autobiography, John recorded that William Snow, selected by his brother Erastus Snow, became the first bishop of Pine Valley. Snow chose Harrison Burgess and John Hawley as counselors, and John "was ordained to the office of High Priest and then set apart as a counselor to our Bishop by Erastus Snow." That evening Samuel Miles preached, and that next day President Erastus Snow came with several others; he had been delayed a day because of the death of one of his children. Lorenzo Brown recorded that Hawley offered his resignation as presiding elder at a meeting held at eight o'clock on the morning of the 11th. The offer was accepted, and William Snow was ordained as bishop with John as the first counselor.[1]

The strain of competing personalities probably made the day uncomfortable for all of them. Several years earlier, John as presiding elder had ruled against Snow and Whipple's attempt to monopolize timber rights in Pine Valley—a ruling that was upheld by Orson Pratt Sr.[2] The preceding year, in April 1866, Lorenzo Brown had gotten into a scuffle with a man named Bryce and was fined $2.50 and $1.00 for court costs. Brown noted that John Hawley "preached about me" four days later, on the 29th. Earlier in January, he had an interview with President Hawley; Brown thought from indirect expressions that he was "considerably prejudiced against me." Nonetheless, Brown and Hawley continued working twelve-hour days together at Brown's mill before Hawley's resignation and after that

---

1. John Hawley, "Autobiography of John Hawley," 19; *The Journal of Lorenzo Brown, 1823–1890*, 180.
2. Hawley, "Autobiography," 20–21.

for a few days. Brown's last notation about John comes in the context of sawing and John being ill on July 31, 1867. After that date, Brown writes nothing more during the three and a half years about John Hawley before the Hawleys moved to Iowa. Brown makes no comment on the Hawleys' conversions to the RLDS Church or the move to Iowa. Apparently, John Hawley's stay in Pine Valley had become strained. John never mentions Brown in his writings, either, although Lorenzo and George Hawley appeared to be close as evidenced by Brown's journal.[3]

A cryptic notation in a federal government publication published decades later closes the year in Pine Valley with a simple comment: "December 3, 1867. Robert Gardiner, a Snow confederate and relative, was given a right to unite the water of Pine Valley and Hawley Springs to run a sawmill." Whether the Hawleys were involved as partners in the mill is unknown.[4] As Gregory Grossman noted, economic and property arrangements were complicated in Utah. Disagreements about property could lead to high excitement in the best of situations. Additionally, Utah property arrangements were "a combination of private, cooperative, chartered, ecclesiastical, and Church property held privately or individually in trust—but all under Church control." The boundaries "between the formally private and the formally common or public shifted back and forth. . . . Precise arrangements on each side were marked by diversity and originality." Some of the social and economic strain in Pine Valley becomes clearer as the reader understands just how fundamental the Church leadership was in common and private property decisions.[5]

The year of 1867 was marked by Latter-day Saint leadership efforts to demonize the missionary efforts in Utah of the RLDS Church, or "Josephites." Hawley wrote that the Salt Lake City leaders told the members that they, the authorities, were sent forth by the Lord "to teach and not be taught," basing Latter-day Saint authority on the revelations of the Doctrine and Covenants. John agreed that it was good to follow Joseph Smith's example of opposing apostates and apostasy. Even if no evidence had been given of RLDS apostasy, Young and other leaders "had said they were apostates and that we took for evidence," John wrote lightly some twenty years later.[6]

---

3. Brown, *Journal*, 146, 153, 169, 171, 180.

4. Elwood Mead, *Bulletin 124: Report of Irrigation Investigations in Utah*, 235.

5. Gregory Grossman, "Central Planning and Transition in the American Desert: Latter-day Saints in Present-Day Sight."

6. John Hawley, "Experiences of John Hawley," 221.

If fortune comes in threes, then the year 1868 was a fortunate year for John Hawley. First, Gazelam, a son, was born to the family on January 31st. Second, John received his second endowment and anointing. Third, he was called to an Iowa mission to "if possible redeem my brothers and mother and sister from the delusion that they had entered into by covenant, for we were taught that by joining these Josephites, they were two-fold more children of hell than they were before." John was to participate in the Utah Church's counter-missionary efforts against those of the RLDS church. Hawley had written that 1868 was marked by "a little excitement about the Josephites and their wild, enthusiastic notions, as" Hawley assumed "them to be at that time. My thoughts were predicated upon what I had read from their own publications, that Sister Maloney, the wife of Stephen Maloney, had sent me from Fort Douglas; but I regarded her as nothing more nor less than an apostate."[7]

Brigham Young had stated as early as 1860 that Joseph Smith III had forfeited his rights because of his association with "those apostates" of the Reorganized Church in Iowa. "David [younger son of Joseph Smith Jr., and brother of Joseph Smith III] would be the leader of the Church," Young said.[8] Joseph Smith III had earlier considered Utah Territory as a field ready for the harvesting of souls. He claimed to receive a revelation in March 1863, which he sent to the RLDS elders and presented for approval at the RLDS annual conference that year. It read, in part,

> And moreover it is expedient in me that my elders in going to declare my gospel to the nations, shall observe the pattern which I have given. Two by two let them be sent, that they may be a help and a support to each other in their ministry. Press onward, ye elders and people of my church, even my little flock, and as I have spoken to you in times past, so will I speak again to you as my friends, inasmuch as you speak in my name; and lo! I am Alpha and Omega, and will be with you unto the end. Amen.[9]

By approval of the semiannual conference, the document was canonized in the RLDS Doctrine & Covenants as Section 115.

Some former Wightites and Hawley friends, such as John H. Taylor and Eleanor Taylor in Weber County, had joined the Reorganization in Utah and stayed to preach to their Latter-day Saint neighbors, a daunting task. RLDS missionary Alexander McCord had converted John H.

---

7. Hawley, "Experiences," 223.

8. Brigham Young, *The Office Journal of President Brigham Young: 1858–1863*, February 28, 1860, and August 15, 1860.

9. Community of Christ, Doctrine and Covenants 115:1c–1e.

Taylor in 1863. E. C. Briggs and Taylor proselytized throughout Weber County in 1864 and 1865. Taylor himself went to Montana and Canada for ten years on behalf of the RLDS church.[10] By 1866, Brigham Young was concerned enough with Josephite preaching in his vineyard to reiterate to the faithful that Joseph Smith III did not "possess one particle of" the "priesthood." However, Young had hopes that "the Lord will speak to [Joseph III's younger brother] David," who must search for forgiveness and "embrace the gospel of life and salvation, and be an obedient son of God, or he never can walk up to possess his right."[11]

Brigham's worries increased during the next two years. The Josephite elders had been steadily recruiting throughout Utah Territory and southeastern Idaho Territory. One example was documented in May 1867 by RLDS Elder J. W. Gillen who wrote from Camp Douglas, Utah:

> Yesterday many of the saints left the land of Salt for the land of Zion. There were thirty-six wagons belonging to the brethren, and fifty-three wagons belonging to the government, accompanied by an escort of forty soldiers, under the command of Captain Gill. The government train goes to Fort Laramie. The government train has taken quite a number of the brethren and some disaffected Mormons, also some Gentiles who had no means of transportation of their own. As near as I can ascertain, the number that have left this season is five hundred. The Brigham City [Box Elder County] branch have all emigrated. There is only one left in Camp Floyd and three in Tooele. Some of the Provo branch have emigrated, and the remaining part have gone to Malad City [Idaho Territory]. So you see it is almost impossible to keep them in Utah after they unite with the church, and indeed they cannot remain without great loss.[12]

John Hawley, as a presiding elder in southern Utah, clearly understood the Church's program was to bias its members against the "Josephites." He believed that the Utah Church held the authority "to teach and not be taught." The authority, according to John, was founded in the Latter-day

---

10. Joseph Smith III and Heman C. Smith, eds., *The History of the Reorganized Church of Jesus Christ of Latter Day Saints*, 4:357; John Taylor, letter to Joseph Smith III, March 2, 1875.

11. See Ronald K. Esplin, "Joseph, Brigham and the Twelve: A Succession of Continuity," 27–28, for a discussion from a Latter-day Saint perspective of the succession concerning Joseph Smith's sons. See the discussion by Jesse L. Embry, "Josephites at the Top of the Mountains: RLDS Congregations in Utah," 57–71, concerning this little-known facet of RLDS missionary work among the members of Utah.

12. Jas W. Gillen, "Pleasant Chat."

Saint Doctrine and Covenants, and such a "ministry . . . was a duty imposed upon us by the Lord."[13]

Like many western Saints, Hawley thought the sons of Joseph Smith, "the posterity of the Seer," certainly "had rights promised to them," but not to priesthood supervisory and organizational authority unless "to enter into these rights they must come to the church."[14] The Utah Saints

> despaired of Joseph, the son of the Seer, ever doing anything for God or the church, as he had connected himself with these apostates, and become their seer and revelator; but our hopes were that David, the child of promise, would eventually see the error of his ways and yet come to the church. I remember hearing Brigham say at one of our conferences (I think it was the fall conference of this year [1866]), that he expected to yet labor under the direction of David Smith as seer and revelator to the church, but as for Joseph he had lost his right to a succession of the Seer and would never lead this people; but he was in hopes David would."[15]

John Hawley had been receiving tracts from Stephen Maloney's wife, the former Mary Jane Hewitt, his neighbors in the Indian Nations. The Maloneys had been rebaptized into the Utah Church about the same time as had the Hawleys. John probably had been hearing from John H. Taylor, his friend from Zodiac and from Weber County. The Taylors and Maloneys had joined the RLDS church in 1863, according to the RLDS:

> *The Herald* for October 15, 1863 contained an encouraging letter from Utah. . . . Bro McCord returned from his mission to Ogden last evening He baptized three up there who were old members in the days of the first Joseph one was Bro John Taylor and one was Stephen Maloney and [they had been re-ordained as] elders and they promised to do what they could to preach the glad news of the Reorganized Church of Christ to all in their vicinity. Sister Taylor with her husband has always held on to their first love and opposed the doctrine of Brigham Young with his accursed polygamous system.

The Reorganized mission was to restore "this people back to God from whom they have strayed in the dark and cloudy day." Hawley's family and friends in the "Josephite" church were obviously in contact with him.[16]

Always willing to follow direction and authority, John and Sylvia Hawley traveled in March 1868 to attend General Conference the following month and to receive "my second anointing and endowment," which

---

13. Hawley, "Experiences," 224.
14. Hawley, 223.
15. Hawley, 223–24.
16. Smith and Smith, *History of the Reorganized Church*, 3:333.

he believed "would give me more power and I could fight the Devil with more force and power." The second anointing made John's salvation secure and unchallenged. He attended the sessions of conference, consisting from four to eight sermons daily. Erastus Snow, following Brigham Young's orders, officiated in the ritual for the second endowments and anointings attended by the Hawleys. Pursuant to Young's earlier directions, Snow called upon several who just had been duly endowed and anointed to assist him with the next set of second endowments and anointings. John wrote that Snow "called upon me to assist in giving others their anointings and endowments." John considered this calling a great "honor conferred upon me." He was set apart with a prediction "that I should be an instrument in the hands of God of doing much good in his cause. . . . As soon as the snow was out of the way I left for the East" in the company of Jesse Crosby.[17]

John drove one of his teams east to the railhead near Cheyenne, where he rented the team out to the Union Pacific working the Salt Lake City connection[18] to help support his mission in Iowa. He took the eastbound train to Omaha, crossed the river to Council Bluffs, and to Dunlap, Iowa. For the first time since 1856, he could visit with and hold his mother, whom he had left in the Indian Nations with his father, who died there in 1858. He found some who had moved to the area from Texas, after the death of Lyman Wight. Among those who had joined the RLDS Church, "this delusion called Josephism; or more, properly speaking, the Reorganized Church of Jesus Christ of Latter Day Saints," were his mother and two brothers and one sister and their families.[19]

John doubted the Reorganized and their claims but found "they were more than willing to converse upon matters of religion, faith, and doctrine, and as this was the case with myself, we soon learned the foundation each stood upon." Knowing his deficiency concerning "the written word," he had hoped that he could "persuade them that the letter killeth but the Spirit maketh alive, and the Spirit said to go to the mountains, where authority of God was." John spoke at the Gallands Grove RLDS meetinghouse several times "with all the liberty I could wish," but discovered "they had gone too far in their darkness; that there was no redemption for them at present."[20]

---

17. James Godson Bleak, *The Annals of the Southern Mission: A Record of the History of the Settlement of Southern Utah*, 162; Hawley, "Experiences," 224–25.
18. Hawley, "Experiences," 225.
19. Hawley, 225.
20. Hawley, 226.

John consented to talk at the home of Uriah ("Father Roundy") Roundy about church history. Neither swayed the other. Although John admitted that Roundy made him "confess some points he made," he remained firm on the on the issue of the authority of the Utah Church. He and his mother visited Alexander McCord "by invitation, and we congenially discussed the issue of patriarchal succession. McCord was well prepared with a table full of books," and he logically argued Joseph Smith III's right to inherit his father's leadership of the church. John admitted that he had "a good many points," but he held on to Latter-day Saint succession and authority.[21]

The issue of tithing troubled at least two RLDS leaders, John A. McIntosh and Apostle Charles Derry. Derry and McIntosh were concerned about an epistle recently released by the RLDS twelve apostles, the first time some members heard the principle mentioned in the local branch. John A. McIntosh stated that he "was afraid of this tithing business; he said it might lead them as it had led the old church, they would grease their heads and want more wives." Hawley believed that Uncle John was having some fun at his expense, but he was willing to bear it "for Christ's sake." The conversations were pleasant and "always in good humor."[22]

John located some members of his "own faith and doctrine" in Magnolia, a few miles from Dunlap and Gallands Grove. Speaking at the schoolhouse, he preached to the members the "need of gathering to the Zion of the West." Moving on to Little Sioux, he had a good reunion and visit with several of the remnants from the Lyman Wight Colony in Texas. Andrew Ballantine, with whom he stayed, told him on that meeting day, "Here, Brother John, You put on my duster, for you will likely be invited to preach, and it looks better than yours. I did so and was invited by Brother Gamet (I think he presided at that time) to talk to the people, and I did so; and while there made and renewed a good many acquaintances."[23]

In June 1868, John attended the Gallands Grove Branch Conference held at Deloit. A sister of former fellow Zodiac resident John H. Taylor was wife to the branch president, Thomas Dobson. John knew her well. He found that

> These Josephites were all clever. They gave me Saturday night of their conference to tell them what they should do to be saved. I wished to get in a warning voice when I could. After I had dismissed my meeting Charles Derry, one

---

21. Hawley, 226.
22. Hawley, 226–27.
23. Hawley, 227.

of their Twelve, called the attention of the congregation and said he would show us the difference between the church he represented and the one I represented the next day. He did so, and I expect the Josephites thought his church was better than mine. I have no idea but had a vote been taken they would have decided in his favor, but still I was not converted, but went on my way rejoicing. Here I made a good many acquaintances and felt well, and I was of the opinion that the Lord would feel after that people, and by and by would emigrate to the Zion of the West.

John and his mother received an offer from a sister in Illinois that the family there would, if John would pay half of the cost, cover the remainder of their travel to visit. They traveled to Naperville, Dupage County, Illinois, just west of Chicago. He had an enjoyable visit with Caroline Scott, his half-sister; he visited "the homestead of my father, where he and mother were baptized into the Church of Christ in the years 1833 and 1834." He spoke with "many acquaintances and renewed a few."[24]

Wanting to visit the prophet's sons, John took the train the eighteen miles distant to Plano, the RLDS headquarters. He visited with Isaac Sheen, the *Herald*'s editor, "Joseph being absent that day." If he had not met Sheen earlier, Hawley certainly knew who he was, that he had been engaged in the failed merger of the Covington church of William Smith with the Wightites of Texas in 1849. The combined leadership, waiting on the young Joseph Smith III eventually to step forward and accept the mantle of his father's presidency of the Restoration, organized itself with William Smith as president and Sheen and Wight his counselors. Several of John's "friends and neighbors had been chosen to serve in the Twelve of Smith's organization." Sheen would be committed to the Joseph Smith's sons until his death in 1874. In the first edition of the Lamoni (IA) *True Latter Day Saints' Herald*, Sheen, while affirming Joseph Smith Jr.'s responsibility for the introduction of polygyny as doctrine and practice to the Nauvoo church, also managed the nimble feat in exonerating him. According to the editor, Smith had atoned for these errors, so that his "salvation and exaltation" were not lost to him.[25]

Joseph Smith III and others later suppressed Joseph Smith Jr. as the founder of Mormon polygamy. Alma R. Blair, an RLDS historian, has written that many early RLDS leaders "accepted as fact that Joseph Smith

---

24. Hawley, 227–28.
25. Hawley, 228; Melvin C. Johnson, *Polygamy on the Pedernales: Lyman Wight's Mormon Villages in Antebellum Texas, 1845–1858*, 127–28, 199–200. "Obituary: Isaac Sheen," 240–41.

had indeed been responsible for the introduction of polygamy at Nauvoo. They included William Marks, Ebenezer Robinson, and Austin Cowles, who were, respectively, the stake president of Nauvoo, an editor of the church newspaper, and a member of the Nauvoo High Council. It has never been a mystery who was the fount of plural marriage in Mormonism." Sheen, however, had opened the way for other Restoration polygamists who had followed Wight or Young or Strang to come and be accepted by the Reorganization.[26]

Sheen and Hawley got along well, and both went to his home for dinner. Mrs. Sheen, when informed that John was a Utah missionary, "reared and pitched." She was a sister of Almon W. Babbitt, then the Secretary of State for Utah, who had been killed by Cheyenne on the plains in 1856, the same year the Croft Company traveled to Utah. Mrs. Sheen, like many in the Church, believed the killers were sent by Brigham Young. Young told a meeting of members of the Twelve and the Salt Lake High Council, on October 4, 1856: "Speaking of Babbitt's death - thank God for that I will acknowledge the hand of the Lord in that at all events."[27] It "took some time before" John "could make [Mrs. Sheen] believe otherwise." He recorded he was willing to bear persecution "for Christ's sake, but I felt sorry for Brother Sheen."[28]

They had a quiet and agreeable visit and after dinner learned that another of Joseph Smith Jr.'s sons, Alexander H. Smith, "was working on his house, which he had just built in Plano. I went over and introduced myself to him and he seemed glad to talk upon religion and it pleased me to do the same. We had a good talk until about sundown." At dusk, the two men walked over to Joseph Smith's pasture, where the head of the RLDS Church was milking cows. Hawley told Joseph, after introductions, that it did "not look much like you were getting the salary it is reported that you get from the founders of the Reorganized Church." Joseph replied that he received no salary. The three men walked to Joseph's house, where John met his wife and their three daughters. The men were but six years apart

---

26. See Johnson, *Polygamy on the Pedernales*, 201; Isaac Sheen, "Polygamy Contrary to the Revelations of God," 6–11; Joseph Smith III, "Opposition to Polygamy," 25–26; Isaac Sheen, ed., "A Revelation, given March 20, 1850, in Covington, Kentucky," 1; Alma R. Blair, "RLDS Views of Polygamy: Some Historiographical Notes," 16–28.

27. David Bigler and Will Bagley, *The Mormon Rebellion: America's First Civil War, 1857–1858*, 197–98; Salt Lake City, Historian's Office, October 4, 1856.

28. Hawley, "Experiences," 228.

in age (John, 1826; Joseph, 1832), yet this was the first time they had met. They shared some common knowledge of the early days in "Nauvoo and still further back than this." They talked more of the past than the present.

A series of questions then ensued. Asked about Mark H. Forscutt, John stated that many Saints thought of, and dismissed, him "as a bitter apostate" because of the many critical letters he published in the *Union Vidette* at Camp Douglas.[29] Joseph then asked John's opinion about Charles Derry and D. H. Bays, former Latter-day Saints who were now associated with the RLDS Church. Bays was nine years old when John converted his father to the Wightite church in 1848. John said that Bays "had gone to studying law . . . and would be worth as much to you as anyone else." John asked Joseph if it was true that he practiced law; Joseph "said he studied law some." Joseph then said he had studied Spiritualism but "found no good in it and threw it to one side as not being profitable."[30] They talked until eleven in the evening.

Joseph told John to spend the night at Alexander Smith's home, and then enjoy breakfast with him. The realization that Joseph and Alexander Smith were poor had dawned on Hawley. He was not sure if Joseph thought of him as a scout for the enemy "Brighamites," but he concluded that due to embarrassment or want of means, Joseph had sent him to sleep at Alexander's home. He discovered that Alexander had a wife and three children, two of them daughters. Sister Smith was "bitter on polygamy, but we got along without much trouble." Hawley came to believe that Alexander felt more concern for his "welfare while at Plano than did Joseph," but he admitted that he liked the brothers.

The next morning, John breakfasted with Joseph in his home, and then the two went to the Herald Office. He recalled: "I had a peaceable visit with Joseph, Sheen, and others in the office, but no one was converted as yet." The visit was concluded with John paying his respect to

---

29. Mark Hill Forscutt, an English LDS convert, emigrated to Utah Territory and served briefly as one of Brigham Young's secretaries. He then moved onto the Mormon dissenter group, the Morrisites, near Ogden. Some years later, he joined the RLDS Church, now the Community of Christ, and came to know Joseph Smith III very well.

30. Bays (or Bayse) would engage in a print conflict with Heman Conoman Smith, a son of Spencer Smith and Anna Wight, on polygamy in the early church. See Heman C. Smith, "The truth defended, or, A reply to Elder D.H. Bays' Doctrines and dogmas of Mormonism," 33; Hawley, "Autobiography," 8–9; Hawley, "Experiences," 229.

William Marks, a powerful leader and friend at one time to Joseph Smith Jr. in Nauvoo, and a good acquaintance of Pierce Hawley, John's father. John himself knew Marks. Now quite feeble and advanced in age, Marks was glad to receive news of his acquaintances in Utah. He thought the Restoration "would not be of much power in the land till the churches came together," but that could not happen with the doctrine of polygamy still being practiced. Concluding his visit with the elderly Marks, John went over to Alexander's and had a good two-hour conversation on the issue of polygamy.

John discovered that Alexander was well-grounded in the Doctrine & Covenants and the Book of Mormon. Alexander pointed out how those scriptures condemned polygamy, but Hawley hung his faith on the revelation of "celestial marriage" (D&C 132), the revelation to Joseph Smith Jr. that the Latter-day Saints believed to authorize plural marriage for worthy members of the church. Hawley wrote that he still believed that God would give revelation for the Church through Brigham Young, that it was Young's mission as Joseph Smith Jr.'s "Successor . . . to teach all that were given through him whom God has appointed." John Hawley had been confronted with the RLDS positions on patriarchal succession and polygamy. However, he still had confidence in "the Successor," Brigham Young, as divinely appointed to lead the Restoration.[31]

On July 28, 1870, John began his return with his mother to Gallands Grove. He said his farewells to his mother and family and started his return "to my mountain home, not having converted anyone, nor was I converted." His brother Aaron and his brother-in-law John Young each gave him ten dollars, and his sister-in-law, the wife of his brother Gideon, gave him three "Josephite" Bibles, the Inspired Version reconstructed by Joseph Smith Jr. more than thirty years earlier: they were for John and his brothers George and William, still in Utah. Hawley rode the railroad and picked up his wagon and team near Cheyenne and drove on to Salt Lake City. He reported his mission events to Apostle George Q. Cannon, the *Deseret News* editor. He had been gone about five months when he arrived in St George on September 12, 1870. He again reported on the events of his mission, most likely to Apostle Erastus Snow. John wrote that his "brethren were glad to think I had run the gauntlet and had not been hurt or converted to their stuff."[32] He most likely spoke about his mission in stake conference.

---

31. William Marks, "Epistle of William Marks;" Hawley, "Experiences," 230–31.
32. Hawley, "Experiences," 231–32.

John, upon his return, once again became involved in the duties of the Pine Valley bishopric with Bishop Snow and fellow counselor Harrison Burgess in looking to the valley's maintenance. By the following summer (1869) the $1,125 spent in 1868 on updating and maintaining the valley's thirteen miles of seven canals, averaging a foot deep and three feet wide, were irrigating nearly 1,200 acres.[33] John Hawley could feel some satisfaction of his stewardship as the one-time leading authority in Pine Valley.

---

33. Bleak, *Annals*, 171, 199–200.

CHAPTER 10

Return to Utah and Conversion to the RLDS Church

1868 to 1870

"'Oh, if you see in me a determination to know that which you have revealed, help me to rightly understand, for I wish to do right and save myself from darkness.'"

Hawley attended a School of the Prophets in 1868, probably in St. George rather than Salt Lake City. James Bleak's annals place it in St. George in November 1868, although Hawley mistakenly placed his entry for attendance in 1865. He attended because he "was considered worthy to be one of that number . . . and I was considered clean from the blood of this generation." The Branch School of the Prophets, on November 2, 1868, was organized in St. George Hall for St. George, Washington and Santa Clara:

> Erastus Snow, President, Jacob Gates and Robert Gardner, Vice Presidents, Henry Eyring, Secretary. Christopher L. Riding and John E. Lloyd, Doorkeepers, and Sam[uel] L. Adams, Chorister. Ninety-four names were enrolled as members of the school.
> On Saturday 7th Nov. School of the Prophets again met and was addressed by President E. Snow, Elder Henry Harriman, Bishop Robert Gardner and Elder Jacob Gates, Elder George A. B. Burgon was appointed Assistant Clerk and Reporter for the School.[1]

Hawley was surprised that the teaching was not "according to the pattern we find in the Book of Covenants." He inquired of Jacob Gates, the priesthood leader responsible for the instruction, and was told that it would be conducted "upon the principle of general instructions." John stayed with the program because he was a believer in education, and he received a certificate that verified his admission "in all schools of this kind."[2]

---

1. James Godson Bleak, *The Annals of the Southern Mission: A Record of the History of the Settlement of Southern Utah*, 171.
2. John Hawley, "Autobiography of John Hawley," 21.

Historian Joseph F. Darowski places the School of the Prophets in the context of its parallels with American and colonial religious training. He explains that Joseph Smith organized the original School of Prophets in Kirtland, Ohio, when the Lectures on Faith of 1834 were linked with

> one hundred "Covenants and Commandments" representing the order and doctrine of the church, a fairly concise course in divinity, theology, and church government was assembled.... Yet there are strong elements of departure. For every hint of an echo, the Kirtland School of the Prophets also offered a new note as well. Joseph Smith incorporated priesthood offices, preparatory or initiatory ordinances, sacramental observances, and covenantal greetings, all leading to a potentially theophanic endowment of power from on high.[3]

Hawley's doubts about taking a plural wife began to take more definite shape after his return from Iowa. He questioned Brigham Young about "whether a man could obtain Celestial Glory with but one wife." President Young replied affirmatively but qualified it with "not the fullest extent of glory." Although disappointed because he desired "to progress in that glory to the fullest extent of light and intelligence," Hawley's mind was somewhat eased. He had believed before "that no man could obtain Celestial Glory" who had not fulfilled the Law of Multiplication. He concluded this entry with "I will now pass this by, and return home cleared and strengthened."[4]

While in Iowa, John missed one of the wonderful Pioneer Day celebrations in Pine Valley. The "cool summer climate" made Pine Valley "a popular meeting place for summer holidays." Local historians recorded the "Pioneer Day celebration lasted two or three days," and homes were "filled with guests." Tables were stretched to capacity. People slept "on floors and in the stack of freshly mowed hay." The day's events included a morning parade of pioneers, a program at the schoolhouse and, after 1868, in the ward house, which was followed by a mid-day community dinner. Alice Gardner Snow, the bishop's wife for many years, once "set her table" in a July celebration "for twenty-eight people three times a day for an entire month. At the end of that time, she knew how people felt who had a plague of crickets."[5]

Grass Valley, where the Hawleys had farming and grazing lands two miles north of Pine Valley, was the location for the great patriotic celebration of Founders Day that year. The men erected "a large dancing floor and

---

3. Joseph F. Darowski, "Schools of the Prophets: An Early American Tradition," 10.
4. Hawley, "Autobiography," 21.
5. *Pioneer Pathways*, 353.

prepared for touring authorities from St. George and other communities as well as many who traveled scores of miles to attend. The Parowan Band aroused the camp site at dawn, and the choirs from Parowan and Pinto opened the festivities at 11AM." The audience knew well the primary themes: the celebrations of trials, tribulations, and triumphs of the Latter-day Saint westward flight and their dispersion into the Great Basin's nooks and crannies.[6] John, away visiting relatives in Iowa, would have thrilled in the celebration, for he had been on that journey for thirty odd years.

Joseph F. Smith, an apostle and counselor to the first presidency, visited the Pine Valley Ward before the year's end. John asked him about an event—a "persecution that Alexander [Hale Smith] had told him . . . while in Salt Lake City." Alexander H. was Joseph F.'s first cousin and had been in Utah during 1866 on an RLDS mission to Utah Territory. Alexander spoke at Provo, and the audience disturbed him more than once during his sermon. Two days later, on Saturday, he preached in Goshen without incident and that afternoon at Camp Floyd, where afterward he was denied further use of the facility. He preached the next evening at Independence Hall, generally pleasing the Gentiles, according to RLDS Elder J. W. Gillen.

On the following Wednesday evening, by previous invitation, he addressed a large congregation at Fox's Gardens. Joseph F. asked after Alexander's speech to address the audience. There, he prophesied that his RLDS cousins, Alexander H. and David H., would come to Utah and approve of the Latter-day Saints' ways. The Twelve, Joseph F. told Alexander, had great friendship for the family of Joseph Smith Jr. In Elder Gillen's report, Alexander H. arose and verbally lashed Joseph F., giving "him one of the worst castigations that I ever saw any person receive." After the meeting, Joseph F. told his cousin that "he had hurt his feelings considerably." Alexander H. did not want to talk it out. He became spooked, worried about enforcers from Brigham Young wanting to punish the wrongdoing to Utah Mormonism, and he left for California by the southern route on September 15.[7]

Hawley asked Apostle Smith to explain what Alexander H. had told John earlier that year in Plano, Iowa:

> He, Alexander, said to me while he was in Salt Lake City, one night after preaching he went part way home with you, and the moon shone bright, and

---

6. Bleak, *Annals*, 168–69.
7. Jas W. Gillen, "Pleasant Chat," 177–78; Joseph Smith III and Heman C. Smith, *The History of the Reorganized Church of Jesus Christ of Latter Day Saints*, 4:455–57, 674–76; Susan Easton Black, *Early Members of the Reorganized Church of Jesus Christ of Latter Day Saints*, 5:436.

while you and him were talking there a man came up and asked him if his name was Smith. He said it was, and the man said, Alexander? and he said that was his name. The man said to him, I have a word of privacy with you; but Alexander said, I have no privacy with any man, and you [Joseph F.] spoke up and said, Who are you? And he said his name was Ross; and you told him to leave; and as he turned to leave Alexander said he could see he had a double barreled shotgun under his cloak. [Hawley] told [Joseph F.] this looked rather suspicious in him, and I knew, too, that name Ross was the name of Brigham's life guard. "Did any such thing as this occur, that you remember of?" Joseph F. said to me, "I know all about it; we did walk together from one of his meetings, as he said; and while we were standing talking together there was a man came up, but his name was not Ross, but sounded so near like Ross that it would easily be taken for that name. But," said he, "it was one of their [RLDS] own clan; a scheme gotten up on purpose to raise the hue and cry of persecution."

Joseph F.'s explanation satisfied Hawley on the subject because it "might easily have been the case," that is, a ploy to start a rumor that the Latter-day Saints were hounding the sons of Joseph Smith Jr.[8]

The year closed with the leadership of the Pine Valley Ward again sustained by the members on December 20, 1868, with William Snow, John Pierce Hawley, and Harrison Burgess remaining as bishop and first and second counselors, respectively.[9] Although sustained as a counselor, John wrote that he had begun the year of 1869 with concerns about various claims for Latter-day Saint authority. However, he was not yet willing to abandon Brigham Young and the Utah church. Once again, tragedy struck the family. Gazelam, born the year before, passed away on February 10, 1869, after a short illness. This was the fourth child of Sylvia and John to be buried in the valley ("planted in Pine Valley," John wrote, "for a glorious resurrection"). Gazelam would be the last.[10]

John Hawley could only hint in his journal about the sorrow that devastated both he and his wife. Erastus Snow, aware of John's losses, had been counseling him to enter "exaltation" through plural marriage. John was quite happy with Sylvia. Expressed in his understated way: "she was as good as I could ask for."[11] However, wishing to follow authority in all spiritual matters, and after having resisted plural marriage for many years, John agreed to take another wife in the summer of 1869. John chose Emily Emmett, a granddaughter of the man who had baptized his father.

---

8. John Hawley, "Experiences of John Hawley," 232–33.
9. Bleak, *Annals*, 175.
10. Hawley, "Experiences," 233; Wesley W. Craig, Old Pine Valley Cemetery, 1.
11. Hawley, "Experiences," 233.

He wrote that Emily would be the woman of "any on earth" who Sylvia could abide.[12] He "wanted [Sylvia] satisfied by all means, as we had lived a long time together and all had been peace and quiet, and I still wished it to exist." John's proposal to Emily was accepted. The newly intended planned to make the trip to Salt Lake City in the fall and seal their marriage "over the altar for time and eternity." The state of Sylvia's (and his own) happiness weighed down on him. When he loaded his wagon with local goods to sell in Salt Lake City, his will began to weaken. John dwelled on the writings "upon the law in the Covenants," and the condemnation of plural marriage recounted in Jacob of the Book of Mormon. He also concluded that Joseph Smith's involvement "was also of a condemning character." John Hawley finally decided against plural marriage.[13]

In 2002, Robert Hawley, a great-grandson, recounted family lore that John never seriously considered entering the doctrine. The narrative recalls that John had loaded the wagon and begun the journey to find Emily. The trail north through Grass Valley to Pinto over the mountains traversed rough terrain. The wagon broke an axle crossing a stream. According to Robert, John took the accident as a sign that the marriage should not take place. Emily supposedly took the news well. He traveled on to Salt Lake City to sell his goods and sent a message to an elated Sylvia.[14]

John's faith in the Brighamite church continued to ebb. He thought of his situation in his patient and phlegmatic way, his wagon moving slowly north to the markets of Salt Lake City, reflecting on the several issues that bothered him. Concerning taking more than one wife, he "concluded to let Erastus Snow's counsel lie idle." He was ready to be persuaded to leave the Latter-day Saint Church and Utah but kept his counsel. His first deliberate, active step in disobeying church counsel occurred once he arrived in Salt Lake City. He wanted another wagon. The church-approved business would sell him an inferior product for forty-five dollars more than a better one offered by the Walker Brothers for eighty dollars. Church counsel was for John to buy the more expensive item.[15] He bought the less expensive

---

12. Emily Dorcas Emmett Eldridge (1846–1916) was a granddaughter of James Emmett, the great Mormon frontiersman, who lived her adult life in Washington County, Utah. Her remains rest in the Pinto Cemetery. James Emmett baptized Pierce Hawley, John's father.

13. Hawley, "Experiences," 233–34.

14. Hawley, 234.

15. Such advice became Number 10 of the Suggested Rules for the Members of the United Order: "10th. We will not knowingly patronize any person engaged in

and better wagon, receiving reproof from "many of my brethren." John had challenged the Church's policy of what Grossman described as "minimizing personal contacts with gentiles, limiting Mormon employment in gentile firms, channeling external trade through selected co-operatives . . . and in other ways." Grossman states that the "disequilibriated" economy of Zion "inevitably spawned system-alien phenomena – creeping privatization, sub rosa dealing with gentiles in Zion." An excellent example was that of Hawley's purchase of the wagon. Though Hawley was chastised for the purchase, his transgression was not severe enough for action to be taken against his membership.[16]

The Hawley brothers began a separation socially and spatially from their neighbors of more than ten years when they moved out to Grass Valley, two miles north of town, where they had purchased a farm that could raise George's branded cattle.[17] Only three families lived there. There, Hawley wrote, "our thoughts were more at liberty to ramble."[18] The rambling would end in defection from Utah territory and emigration to Iowa.

John wrote that even if the Latter-day Saint church was true as he formerly supposed, engaging those who believed differently was profitable. Although he knew that church authorities counseled against the RLDS as an organization and characterized its doctrines as abominations, he began to wonder if the Utah authorities "were afraid of these Josephites."[19] He decided to invite any Josephites in the area to visit with him, and he would be willing to see if their doctrines were better than those of the Latter-day Saint church. When John discovered that two RLDS elders had been shut out from preaching near Mountain Meadows (by the father of one of the elders, no less), he invited them to Grass Valley to discuss Latter Day restoration and authority.[20]

The RLDS elders, a man named "Holt" and Richard C. Gibbons, came to Grass Valley and discussed religion for two hours. By the end, John believed that he had persuaded Gibbons to rejoin Brigham Young's

---

any business who is not a member of the Order, unless our necessities absolutely require us to do so." Bleak, *Annals*, 371.

16. Hawley, "Experiences," 235; Gregory Grossman, "Central Planning and Transition in the American Desert: Latter-day Saints in Present-Day Sight."

17. Department of Animal Industry, *Book of Recorded Marks and Brands*, 134.

18. Hawley, "Experiences," 235.

19. Hawley, 236.

20. Hawley, 235–36.

church. According to Hawley, Gibbons had gone to Southern California and been converted to the Reorganization. This was the same Richard C. Gibbons who, in 1869, Erastus Snow excommunicated at Fort Hamblin for handing out Josephite material and prospecting in metals. John wrote that, in the minds of stauncher Latter-day Saints, any "who would join the Josephites" were treated as if they "had almost committed the unpardonable sin." John did not think that Elder Gibbons had returned to Brigham Young's Church before the Hawleys left the territory. Elder Gibbons did later reconcile with the Latter-day Saint Church and became the presiding elder at Hamblin in the Pinto Ward and was called to a mission in 1877.[21]

Erastus Snow, when he heard that Hawley had been talking to Josephite elders, chided him. John told Snow that the discussion had been about succession of authority to head the church, not about polygamy. Snow felt relieved because he thought the Latter-day Saint position outweighed the Reorganized church on that matter, while the Reorganized church held the higher ground on polygamy. Snow advised, and John agreed, to not seek out the Josephite missionaries, but John told Snow that he intended to talk to the RLDS elders if they came to him. Snow cautioned John once again.[22]

By this time, however, John decided to test the teachings taught by the current Latter-day Saint authorities against the standard books (Book of Mormon, Doctrine and Covenants, and the Bible). He was concerned that church members, even in the days of Joseph Smith, were willing to accept the teachings of men rather than "even studying or thinking what God had revealed direct from heaven for their present and eternal good." According to Hawley, after Smith's death, Brigham Young did "lead the church by his fleshy arm" by relying on his private talks with Joseph Smith rather than the scriptures. John "was determined to get out of this fleshly channel, and in order to do this I must have help from the Lord. So I prayed to him like this: 'Oh, if you see in me a determination to know that which you have revealed, help me to rightly understand, for I wish to do right and save myself from darkness.'"[23] Hawley began to establish scriptural standards to weigh the doctrinal correctness for the principles of baptism for the dead, polygamy, Adam-God teachings, and blood atonement.

Hawley looked for changes made by Brigham Young in the principles of baptism for the dead. He certainly must have remembered Lyman

---

21. Bleak, *Annals,* 187, 105; Hawley, "Experiences," 236.
22. Hawley, "Experiences," 236.
23. Hawley, 237.

Wight's direction to build "a good little Temple to worship in" to perform baptism for their dead, and the washing of feet, and a general endowment.[24] He questioned Young's authority to require new baptisms for family dead where the ancestor and the proxy in an earlier baptism had not been of the same sex. Young taught that the male head of the family and the wife must be proxy for the same sex in each other's family as well, instructing the priesthood holders they had to do the ordinances for the wife's male ancestors and her for the husband's female ancestors. Hawley found no authority for Young's changes, and thus "laid it to 'One side, not considering it scripture profitable for doctrine.'"[25] Young changed the gender policy requirement when the St. George Temple began operation in January 1877.[26]

John dismissed the Latter-day Saint position on polygamy. He wrote that he thought Joseph Smith undoubtedly revealed it and just as readily rejected Smith's teachings. John must have been considering his own reasoning for earlier rejecting Emily Emmett as a plural wife. He had dwelt on Joseph Smith's contradictory character about the matter and that the Book of Jacob in the Book of Mormon, translated by Joseph himself, contradicted his own teachings.[27] John decided against plural marriage, so he "threw it to one side as not being profitable for me," and "passed it by" regardless of how the doctrine came to be.[28]

Hawley next considered the Adam-God doctrine taught by Brigham Young, despite his thinking of it as "too insignificant to talk about." Brigham Young taught Adam-God as early as 1852:

> Now hear it, O inhabitants of the earth, Jew and Gentile, Saint and sinner! When our father Adam came into the garden of Eden, he came into it with a celestial body, and brought Eve, one of his wives, with him. He helped to make and organize this world. He is MICHAEL, the Archangel, the ANCIENT OF DAYS! about whom holy men have written and spoken –

---

24. Hawley, "Autobiography," 7; William Leyland, "The Mormon Colony (Zodiac) Near Fredericksburg, Texas," 21, 25; Melvin C. Johnson, *Polygamy on the Pedernales: Lyman Wight's Mormon Villages in Antebellum Texas, 1845–1858*, 139.

25. Hawley, "Experiences," 237–38.

26. On "Thurs. Jan. 11th Endowments for the dead were first administered in St George Temple. On this day also the first sealing of woman (dead) to man took place, Apostle Wilford Woodruff doing the sealing." Bleak, *Annals*, 447.

27. RLDS Book of Mormon, Jacob 2:30–56; LDS Book of Mormon, Jacob 2:22–36, 3:1–6.

28. Hawley, "Experiences," 234, 238.

He is our FATHER and our GOD, and the only God with whom WE have to do. Every man upon the earth, professing Christians or non-professing, must hear it, and will know it sooner or later![29]

On January 9, 1855, Eliza R. Snow,[30] a plural wife of Brigham Young read a poem extolling "Father Adam, our God" at a gathering in the home of her brother, Lorenzo Snow:

> Father Adam, our God, let all Israel extol,
> And Jesus, our Brother, who died for us all:
> All the praise is imperfect, we *now* can bestow –
> Our expression is weak, and our language *too low*:
> But when Zion that dwells on a plant of light,
> With the Zion perfected on earth, shall unite:
> Sweet, rich, high-sounding anthems, all heaven will inspire,
> As the *pure language* flows from the lips of the choir.[31]

The church membership accepted it with various levels of skepticism or agreement. Historian Polly Aird wrote that George A. Hicks remembered that if Brigham Young said "Adam was the God of this world, the people believed it or pretended to believe it."[32] The day following the President's announcement, Heber C. Kimball, Young's first counselor, was recorded as saying that the "God and Father of Jesus Christ was Adam." Ten years later, he wrote: "the Lord told me that Adam was my father and that he was the God and father of all of the inhabitants of this Earth."[33]

Apostle Orson Pratt, on the other hand, opposed the doctrine for some time. Samuel W. Richards and Wilford Woodruff recorded in their journals for April 11, 1856, of contention in the upper room of the

---

29. Brigham Young, April 9, 1852, *Journal of Discourses*, 1:51. *The Journal of Wilford Woodruff,* May 6, 1855, records Woodruff's private conversation with President Young as the latter explained the principles of doctrine. For further information, consult the Young, *Journal of Discourses*, October 9, 1859, 7:285; October 7, 1857, 5:331; October 8, 1855, 3:119–20.

30. Eliza Roxcy Snow (1804–87), plural wife to Joseph Smith and then Brigham Young, second President of the Relief Society and sister to Lorenzo Snow, fifth President of the Church of Jesus Christ of Latter-day Saints, was a leading writer of religious poetry and prose.

31. Eliza R. Snow, "Address," 320.

32. Quoted in Polly Aird, *Mormon Convert, Mormon Defector: A Scottish Immigrant in the American West, 1848–1862*, 144.

33. Woodruff, *Journal,* April 10, 1852; Solomon F. Kimball, "Sacred History," April 30, 1862.

President's Office. President Young and Apostle Pratt engaged in a quarrelsome discussion about Adam-God. The President, according to Woodruff, said that "Elder Orson Pratt pursued a course of stubbornness & unbelief in what President Young said that will destroy him if he does not repent & turn from his evil ways. For when any man crosses the track of a leader in Israel & tries to lead the prophet—he is no longer led by him but is in danger of falling."[34] The following month Woodruff recorded that

> I met with the Presidency & Twelve in the prayer-circle. Brother G. A. Smith spoke in plainness his feelings concerning some principles of Elder O Pratt's wherein he differed from President Young concerning the creation of Adam out of the dust of the Earth & the final consummation of knowledge & many other things. I am afraid when he come to write he will publish in opposition of President Young's views but he promises he would not.[35]

As late as 1860, Orson Pratt still disagreed with the President, writing "that [the idea that Adam is the Father of our spirits] is revolting to my feelings, even if it were not sustained by revelation."[36] Hawley recognized that Pratt had fought Young "on this, but Brigham had said it, and it was Pratt's business to believe and teach what Brigham taught." John Hawley thought that Pratt, realizing "his living in the church and was liable to be taken from him," submitted in shame to keep his position. So Hawley too "laid that [doctrine] to one side as not being profitable."[37]

Hawley even more quickly dismissed blood atonement, refusing to write about his reasons.

Patrilineal or apostolic succession to lead the church was the final principle with which John struggled. Just as he had turned away from

---

34. Samuel W. Richards, Journals and Family Record, 1846–1876, 113; Woodruff, *Journal*, March 11, 1856.

35. Woodruff, *Journal*, April 20, 1856.

36. Thomas Bullock, "Minutes of the Council of the Twelve in upper room of Historian's Office, April 5, 1860." Joseph Lee Robinson attended General Conference and noted that President Young said, "Adam and Eve were the natural father and mother of every spirit that comes to this planet. . . . Adam was God, our Eternal Father. This as Brother Heber remarked, was letting the cat out of the bag." Robinson wrote: "even our Beloved Orson Pratt told me he did not believe it. He said he could prove by the scriptures it was not correct. . . . I feared least he should apostatize." Joseph Lee Robinson, Autobiography and Journals, 1883–1892, 62.

37. Hawley, "Experiences," 238. Hawley, in an article published "To The Utah Saints," dismisses Adam-God explicitly by appeal to Alma 5:2, 7 in the RLDS Book of Mormon, and develops arguments against Brigham Young's changes to baptism for the dead and against polygamy.

the personal authority of Lyman Wight and rejected Strangite appeals, Hawley also came to discount Brigham Young's authority granted him by the Twelve at Winter Quarters. Hawley fell back on the Wightite belief in the patrilineal succession of Joseph Smith's family as the only proper way to succession to church leadership. As in 1849 with the Wightites, and now twenty-one years later, Joseph Smith III was that man to Hawley—the head of the Reorganized church.[38]

In his crisis of leadership authority in 1870, John used the same tactics for finding his path as he had since 1837: he followed "heaven's commandments." He tried to live a good life. He desired "to understand the doctrines of Christ." He covenanted with God and followed the authority of the Church and its leaders until the issue of leadership and polygamy began undermining his confidence in the Utah leaders. Finally, he bowed "secretly to God in faith" and asked "for blessings" of wisdom to seek the right way on the divergent road of faith that confronted him. Once he had completed his study and prayer, Hawley made his choice and did not look back.[39]

John Hawley, the once presiding elder and current first counselor in the bishopric, preached his last discourse in Pine Valley to a startled congregation, dumbfounding his fellow community members.[40] Other than Hawley's brief comment, no record of the farewell address exists in local journals, diaries, Erastus Snow's letters, or even Bleak's annals. Hawley had come to the position that Joseph Smith III had certain patriarchal rights and was teaching the revelations of the Restoration that had come through his father. Hawley held that Joseph Smith III was the legitimate successor to lead the Restored church. He wrote a letter to Smith III, who published it, in which Hawley informed him that he was ready to join "the reorganization of the church."[41]

An RLDS Elder named John Lawson, living some forty miles from Hawley, read the notice and traveled to interview him. Elder Lawson proved to Hawley that he had authority from the president of the RLDS Utah Mission "to officiate in the ordinances of the church." Lawson, Hawley wrote, "was well known by a large majority in this vicinity, but I had never seen him before. Those that were acquainted with him pronounced him crazy, and I did not think they were far out of the way; but his authority I considered good, and I was under covenant to renew at the

---

38. Johnson, *Polygamy on the Pedernales*, 125–26.
39. Hawley, "Autobiography," 2.
40. Hawley, "Experiences," 238.
41. Hawley, 239.

first opportunity." On February 7, 1870, John was baptized a member of the Reorganized church, as well as for the seventh time for the remission of sins and ordained an elder. Hawley joked that "you will be able by this time to think my sins to have been heavy." Switching from the topic of baptism of himself to that of others, he estimated he had baptized more than two hundred in southern Utah. He thought that he would stop "being baptized for the remission of sins."[42]

Erastus Snow was Hawley's file leader after the bishop and stake president, as well as a colleague and friend. Outraged by hearing of John's defection and baptism, Snow traveled to Pine Valley to cut Hawley "off from the church and kingdom in that land."[43] Snow lectured John and George for three hours at their homesteads in Grass Valley. He said John had received the "seeds of apostasy" during his mission to Iowa from the "Josephites, who were the most bitter apostates the church ever had to meet." He would not let John respond, who was "too vile an apostate to talk in my hearing." George, given the opportunity to respond, said nothing. John wrote a lengthy letter to Snow and corrected the apostle's mischaracterizations. There was no answer. However, Snow and Hawley would meet again. In October, the Hawleys were traveling to catch the train in Salt Lake City for Iowa. They met Snow traveling south after attending the semi-annual conference. This time they talked more quietly and respectfully. John told Snow that he had not apostatized "from any principle of the gospel as I understood it, but I had discarded every doctrine of man that had been added by Brigham, and others; and there is where I stand now, and I expect always to stand on this ground. And I think before you or any other man in this Territory can stand justified before God, you will have to discard the very principles of men that I have done." Snow, according to Hawley, replied, "Well, Brother John, I feel different towards you than I did; after reading your letter my mind has been changed; and now, Brother John, I have this to say to you: when you get tired of stopping out of the kingdom we will gladly receive you back." John answered that he had done nothing that he "was ashamed to meet [in his] record, that I had left or was about to leave. We bade each other good-bye; I going to Salt Lake to take the

---

42. H. A. S., "Rebaptism," 388–93; Hawley, "Experiences," 238–39.

43. Church History Library, email message to author, April 30, 2013; the writer was authorized to state, "A check of the archives in the Church History Library did not reveal any mentions of either John or George Hawley ever being excommunicated from the LDS Church."

train for the east, and he to his home in the south."[44] No records exist that Hawley and Snow ever met or spoke again.

Reports estimated that RLDS converts who immigrated to Iowa that fall numbered two hundred. Elder W. W. Blair wrote from Salt Lake City that prospects for the Reorganized missionary work in Utah "were never brighter, though every obstacle is thrown in the way of our progress by the authorities of the Brighamite Church." He stated that six emigrant companies went east in 1870. The Hawleys were part of that eastward immigration.[45]

John and his companions had to lay over a week in Salt Lake City. While there, he participated in a faith healing. Two elders and Hawley, at the request of an Elder Brand, who had previously attended "many times" an afflicted member but without effect, were directed to minister "to an invalid sister that had not walked for two years." The sister was a member of the Reorganized church, and her husband followed Spiritualism. Once Hawley saw her, he knew that it would require God's interposition to help the sister. He wrote:

> I had faith in doing our duty. She was nothing but a skeleton, as weak as a cripple; but, when my time came to talk I was telling them that God was able to raise her up, and we could only do our duty and leave the result in his hands. The Spirit of prophecy rested upon me and I prophesied that she would be healed. The same moment she was baptized by the Spirit and said she knew she would be healed as I said. We anointed her, and then laid hands on her, and she was healed and arose instantly from her bed and walked across the room.[46]

The husband, who had been at a Spiritualist meeting, returned home before John and the other Reorganized elders had departed. The man "seemed thunderstruck," and Hawley felt that he would never forget his astounded look as he found his invalid wife on her feet. In typical fashion, John ended the story by stating he "would rather someone else had told of this powerful healing, but it is in my history and you must have it."[47]

---

44. Hawley, "Experiences," 239, 240.

45. W. W. Blair, letter to Joseph Smith III, November 21, 1870. Smith and Smith, *History* of the Reorganized Church, 3:601.

46. John Hawley, extract from "My Early Ministerial Life," 232, in Edward Rannie, *Marvelous Manifestations of God's Power in the Latter Days*, 52–53.

47. Hawley, "Experiences," 240–41; Hawley, "My Early Ministerial Life," 53.

EPILOGUE

End of a Trek

1870

"But little sleep, so few of the joys commonly yearned for by men, and pain, pain, always some kind of pain."

John Hawley, greying, broad, and heavily muscled, in black broadcloth and a tieless white shirt buttoned to the neck, waited for his train to Iowa on that chilly November day. Looking at the city from the siding deck finished earlier that year, the Tabernacle and the partially erected temple walls loomed five blocks away north by east. He was probably still pleased with and awed by the city's progress. Since 1856, he had visited Salt Lake City at least once or twice yearly. Having lived his entire life on farms and in tiny hamlets and villages in wilderness forests and western frontier prairies and deserts, he would miss this city and what it was becoming.

John and Sylvia likely did not make their goodbyes to former Wightites and Croft Company members John H. and Eleanor Taylor, who were still on RLDS missions in Colorado and Montana. When the Taylors returned to Utah in 1875, they discovered many of their children had returned to the Latter-day Saint faith, a situation Taylor described "as a state of confusion. Darkness reigns among them; even that same mist that Nephi saw his brethren go into in unbelief and hardness." At least four of his seven sons and one daughter were spouses in polygamous households. Nonetheless, the couple remained in Utah to stay close to their children and grandchildren. John Taylor died in 1896 near Ogden, Utah, and his wife survived him until 1905. None of their children turned to the RLDS church, whereas the children of John and Sylvia Hawley were baptized and remained in the RLDS Church. None returned to the Rocky Mountain church or Utah.[1]

He turned south to stare at a land and people that could be seen in his mind's eye. He must have thought about his life and times. If not gregari-

---

1. Joseph Smith III and Heman C. Smith, *The History of the Reorganized Church of Jesus Christ of Latter Day Saints*, 4:357, 468; John Taylor, letter to Joseph Smith III, March 2, 1875; "Mrs. Taylor Dead," 6.

ous as Lorenzo Brown or his brother George, John Hawley had become appreciated for who he was and what he had become. He had been solid as a Latter-day Saint and a leader. Apostle Erastus Snow told the "apostate" that fellowship waited for him if he returned to the Rocky Mountain Saints. Forty-four years of age, John had been a presiding elder, a bishop's first counselor, a road surveyor, a constable, and a superintendent of secular and religious schools. Four of his little children were interred in Pine Valley's earth. Having been a member in the churches of Joseph Smith, of Lyman Wight, and of Brigham Young for thirty-three years, he had resolved that the patrilineal authority of Joseph Smith III and the companionship of family relations would be his final call. Hawley remained firm in his convictions to his family, his friends, and to the RLDS church.

John Hawley's life was proof of the saying "Land fashions the man." Born in the wilderness of Illinois, raised as a boy in Tennessee and Missouri, and as a teen in the wild Wisconsin pineries, John came of age in Texas and in full manhood in the Cherokee and Choctaw nations. He was thirty when most of the Hawleys immigrated to Utah Territory. Now on his fifth trip across the enormous heartland of America, he traveled for the first time entirely by rail to Iowa from Salt Lake City. Graham St. John Stott in "Zane Grey and James Simpson Emmett" discusses the theme of man molded by the desert's effects, fashioning a man's character for good and bad.[2] Grey wrote that in Utah, he had

> met some real men . . . who live lonely, terrible lives as a matter of course . . . [enduring] loneliness, hunger, thirst, cold, heat, the fierce sandstorm, the desert blizzard, poverty, labor without help, illness without medicine, tasks without remuneration, no comfort, but little sleep, so few of the joys commonly yearned for by men, and pain, pain, always some kind of pain.[3]

Hawley suffered that and more in his frontier life. Such a man's "toughness was the result of . . . life in the wilderness. It was a fierce refusal to yield, which, when linked with a good nature, was the most desirable moral quality of all." Religious conviction had delivered Hawley and other pioneers to Utah, where the religion's singular influence interacting with the desert had cast "in its own ways" the settlers, molding them "in the flaming furnace of [the desert's] fiery life."[4]

---

2. Graham St. John Stott, "Zane Grey and James Simpson Emmett," 491–503.
3. Stott, 493.
4. Stott, 495–96; Zane Grey, *The Heritage of the Desert*, 253.

Zane Grey, without succumbing to the Utah religion, could identify with and admire the settlers as they struggled to live on the southern Utah ranges.[5] Failure in the desert was grounded on inadequacy or greed or lust. Grey described "inadequacy [as] the inability to cope with the demands of Western life." Those who could not cope turned against mankind, such as Belden's failure in *The Young Lion Trainer*, as a forest ranger and his resulting schemes to injure the man who replaced him.[6] Stott believes that "greed is what makes merchants, like Jed and Seth Bozeman in *Shadow on the Trail* or Joshua Sneed in Robbers' Roost, try to 'skin the pants off gentiles who move into town.'"[7] Lust, finally, is what motivates the worst of Grey's infamous villains: Bishop Dyer and Elder Tull of *Riders of the Purple Sage*.[8]

John Hawley matched Grey's vision of how the desert challenged man to cope with and overcome its trials. He undoubtedly wanted to succeed in the affairs of men, but greed did not mar his motivation. The absence of lust undoubtedly affected him and the matter of additional wives. His devotion to Sylvia and the breaking of the marriage contract with Emily Dorcus Emmett, sister to Zane Grey's heroic model, were the roots that would end his journey with the Rocky Mountain Saints and lead him to clasp his Midwest relatives and the Midwest Saints.

Hawley, of course, had imperfections as well as virtues. His writings reveal a typical Euro-American male of the nineteenth century. John sees his wife as a human worthy of acceptance through their shared personal contact and joint suffering, yet he fails to acknowledge equality with indigenous peoples. He touches on American Indians lightly and paternally in his memory, but he refuses to acknowledge the existence of slaves and servants of color whom he must have encountered. He says nothing of his encounters with the natives of Southern Utah. The dark-skinned outliers to his white society had been in his world his entire adult life: he lived in Texas and the indigenous nations from 1845 to 1856. Southerners would be among his companions until 1870. Yet his only recorded interaction with black Americans is as a witness to slave sales recorded elsewhere but never referred to in his personal narratives.

Hawley's personal record does not reveal any distress or compassion about the destruction of Native Americans in Dixie. He had been cared

---

5. Stott, "Zane Grey," 497.
6. Zane Grey, *Young Lion Hunter*, 109.
7. Zane Grey, *Shadow on the Trail*; Zane Grey, *Robbers' Roost*, 30.
8. Stott, "Zane Grey," 499.

for by indigenous women according to his own account, and an uncle had been killed by them. He witnessed, as a small boy, the Black Hawk war in Illinois. He encountered Menominees and others in the Wisconsin pineries, Comanches in Texas, and lived with them in the Indian nations and Utah territory for sixteen years. Hawley does not reveal hatred or a pathetic desire to commit genocide. Some Mormons did have such feelings, such as Captain William McBride, who wrote to his superiors in 1851:

> We wish you without a moment's hesitation to send us about a pound of arsenic we want to give the Indians' well a flavour. Also a spade to dig for water. A little stricknine would be of fine service, and serve instead of salt, to their too-fresh meat.
>
> Most obediently &c &c
> Capt. Wm. McBride
>
> Don't forget the arsenic!
> Don't forget the spade and arsenic!
> Don't forget the spade, stricknine and arsenic![9]

However, unlike Jacob Hamblin's prolific writings about his interaction with the various tribes from Toole to the Las Vegas wash and east beyond the Colorado River, Hawley apparently had no personal reason to write anything about them, because they were not integral to his own world. The destruction of the native habitat along the Santa Clara and Rio Virgin rivers merited not a word from him.[10]

Hawley's love for his wife of almost sixty years contrasts his lack of writing about women. He apparently accepted without question the role of female labor on the wagon road and the frontier. He never notes their overwhelming sacrifices and challenges in the American West. Every successful story of a Sylvia Hawley is balanced by that of a Sarah Hadfield Wight Hawley Earl (Ann's sister and sister-in-law to John and Sylvia Hawley). Born in 1827 and christened in the Cathedral Church of England in Manchester, Sarah immigrated as a Latter Day Saint convert with her family to Nauvoo in 1841. The young girl then went to the wild pineries of western Wisconsin. She sheltered in the rudest of frontier shacks and shanties for more than twenty years, suffering lack of food and enduring desperate winters. A teenage plural wife of Orange Wight, she

---

9. William McBride, Report of Tooele Expedition No 3.

10. For the destruction of Native American habitats near southwest Mormon communities, see Todd M. Compton, *A Frontier Life: Jacob Hamblin, Explorer and Indian Missionary*; Aaron McArthur, *St. Thomas, Nevada, A History Uncovered*; Todd M. Compton, "Becoming a 'Messenger of Peace': Jacob Hamblin in Tooele," 1–29.

walked and rode and floated 1,500 miles down the American borderlands to the Texas frontier. She bore Orange three children: Martenisia, who would be a plural wife herself and die in 1910; Hyrum who was buried as a toddler in the Mormon Mill Cemetery of Hamilton Valley, Texas, in 1851; and Joseph William Wight, who survived until 1881. O. L. Wight joined the home of his son-in-law and daughter Martenisia in his final years and reconverted to the Latter-day Saint church.[11]

Sarah (Martenisia's mother) had joined George Hawley as his second wife and first plural wife when the Hawley clan moved to the Cherokee Nation. She bore a daughter to George named either Amy or Emma who died as an infant. George then took another teenage girl, Jeanette Goudie, as a plural wife. The family immigrated to Utah Territory, settling in Ogden, then later in Lehi, Washington, and finally in Pine Valley, where the Hawleys scrabbled for a rugged backcountry life. Before her death, Sarah left George and married an Earl. She bore a daughter who carried her own name, and within a year both she and her child were buried in the Old Pine Valley Cemetery.[12] John Hawley does not mention Sarah's travails.

Hawley condemned polygamy but is not transparent about his family's plural marriages. After John and George moved to Iowa, they continued to hide George's plural relations. John and George colluded in silence about the latter's wives, which are never mentioned in John's memoirs, RLDS records, or any remarks of George Hawley after his affiliation with the RLDS Church. Neither John nor George mentions that their sister, Mary, had been a plural wife of Lyman Wight. George Hawley, in his later days in Iowa, a solid member and leader in the church's western Iowa congregations, strongly opposed Brigham Young.[13]

Richard Donald Ouellette recognizes the questionable issues with John Hawley's sworn testimony in the Temple Lot Case.[14] The case, in-

---

11. In 1858, Orange Wight had written to Wilford Woodruff inquiring after Sarah and the children, requesting that she reply to his letters. Orange L. Wight, letter to Stephen Wight and Wilford Woodruff, September 17, 1858.

12. Melvin C. Johnson, *Polygamy on the Pedernales: Lyman Wight's Mormon Villages in Antebellum Texas, 1845–1858*, 84; John Hawley, "Autobiography of John Hawley," 20; Wesley W. Craig, Old Pine Valley Cemetery.

13. Brigham Young, letter to Bishop Zadok K. Judd, Feb 24, 1860; Brigham Young, letter to Bishop Z. K. Judd, May 2, 1860; Freddijo Burk, *Joseph Hadfield Story: An Incredible Odyssey*, 188, 362.

14. Richard Donald Ouellette, "The Mormon Temple Lot Case: Space, Memory, and Identity in a Divided New Religion."

stituted by the RLDS Church, claimed ownership of certain lands in Independence, Missouri, important to Restoration believers. The RLDS complaint was eventually denied at the appellate court level.

The Abstract reported that Hawley believed Lyman Wight to be the first Mormon to teach and practice the doctrine, as Hawley testified that he had never heard word of the subject in Nauvoo. In fact, Hawley recounted an 1868 conversation wherein William Marks, former president of the Nauvoo Stake, told him the prophet sought to bring up charges against Nauvoo's polygamists shortly before his 1844 murder. As depicted in the Complainant's Abstract, Hawley's deposition seemed quite helpful to the plaintiffs, as he absolved Joseph Smith as founder of polygamous practices in the Church.[15] Hawley's testimony permitted the RLDS Church to argue that the "true church" had been practicing monogamy, while Brigham Young and company had falsified Smith's original teachings on plural marriage.

However, Hawley contradicted the above testimony in his autobiography, which predated his testimony. Writing about his struggle to reject the Brighamite church, he concluded that polygamy "was a contradiction to what was revealed before through Joseph Smith, and I threw that to one side as not being profitable for me, let it come through what channel it may have come to the people. *I really believed that it was given by Joseph Smith*, but my understanding was then and now that I could not in reality served two masters, so I passed it by."[16]

Hawley's lived for another thirty-nine years, and the world around him continued to change. The world of his childhood had been one of animal and human muscle and sweat labor. Many of his neighbors in the backcountry of Illinois never traveled more than fifty miles from home. They lived by the seasons, by rise and fall of the moon, by sweep and ebb of the creeks and streams and rivers, by heat and cold and snow and drought. They knew those who made their shoes and saddles and holsters, their barrels and wagons, ground their corn and wheat, tailored their clothing and hats and gloves and whips, repaired their weapons and clunky timepieces. They would know the person who built their coffins, the clergy who preached the funeral eulogy, the diggers who opened the earth and lowered them into the ground and closed their final resting place in mortality. Humankind had lived in this manner for millennia. A man could travel no more quickly than the fastest sailing ship or by

---

15. Ouellette, "Temple Lot Case," 681–82.
16. John P. Hawley, "Experiences of Elder John Hawley," 238; emphasis added.

horseback or animal-drawn conveyance. Hawley spent most of his life outside the cultural mainstream of American technological development. Then it all changed.

He had, by that day in Salt Lake City, already traveled the interior's modern passenger railroads. He had seen the telegraph and knew of the transatlantic cable. More would come to pass: the invention of the telephone, the death of Custer and his troops at Little Big Horn, professional baseball, 10,000 horsepower steam engines and the manufacturing revolution, the end of the Indian Wars at Wounded Knee, the rise of Jim Crow and segregation, the motion picture camera and beginning of the film industry, powered flight, and the end of Mormon polygamy. He would continue into the twentieth century as an RLDS priesthood holder and missionary.

In 1837 he had been baptized a member of the Church of Jesus Christ of Latter Day Saints and later became a Wightite. He had been proselytized by the Strangites, became a member of the Latter-day Saints again, and finally for his final thirty-nine years, a staunch follower of the RLDS Church under Joseph Smith III. John had learned the craft of a logger in Wisconsin, and as a woodworker helped to erect the first post-Joseph Smith temple in the Texas Hill Country. He did missionary service from the upper reaches of the Missouri to the East Texas forests and Texas Gulf coast for the Wightites, and in Utah and Iowa for the Latter-day Saints, and throughout the Midwest, Kansas, Oklahoma, and Texas for the RLDS.

For thirteen years the Hawleys had pioneered in Dixie alongside a thousand other followers of the Restoration. They created a community in the sage and sand brush, below mountain crags and above flooding streams, under the burning sun and the savage storms. They lived in dugouts and tents and shanties and wagons, built homes, schools, and churches. They worshipped their god as they believed and, for a time, achieved the lyrics of the pioneer hymn: "We'll find the place which God for us prepared, far away in the west, where none shall come to hurt or make afraid; There the Saints will be blessed."

Hawleys and Relatives Buried in Pine Valley[17]

Name	Age	Birth/Death	Parents
John	1	1858/1859	Sylvia Johnson/John Hawley
Sylvia Amelia	1	1862/1863	Sylvia Johnson/John Hawley
Sarah Earl	infant	1863	Sarah Hadfield/Sylvester H. Earl
Sarah Hadfield Wight Hawley Earl	37	1827/1864	Mary Ann Godby/ Samuel Hadfield
William Nephi	1	1864/1865	Sylvia Johnson/John Hawley
Hiram Hadfield Wight	17	1850/1867	Sylvia Johnson/John Hawley
Gazelam	1	1869/1869	Sylvia/John Hawley
Joseph William Wight	28	1881	Sarah/Orange Wight

After the Hawleys left for Iowa, the town of Pine Valley divided into two factions: Mormons and Gentiles. Work at the sawmills lured rough and tough millers and loggers as well as saloon keepers and gamblers and the women who serviced their needs. Local historian Wanda Snow Petersen wrote: "[O]ne man said that 'Pine Valley had the two greatest extremes for settlers: one group who were so pious and sanctimonious, they would hesitate to even say 'sand paper' lest it might sound rough, and another group who prided themselves on how rough and tough they could be.'"[18]

---

17. The Hawley clan deaths starkly illustrate how poor living conditions not only in Pine Valley but also in nearby Pinto and Hamblin contributed to child mortality. Cemetery records in northern Washington County, although incomplete, confirm that fact. The Old Pine Valley graveyard in Upper Town has been called "The Children's Cemetery" because twelve of the thirteen interred there were children. Sarah Hadfield Wight Hawley Earl is the only adult buried there, identified as Sarah Wight Hawley. Presumably, Wilber Earl buried her. If so, it is not clear why he left off her Earl name. Sarah's fate at the end of her life underlines the melancholy that stalked Utah polygamy: a fourteen-year-old convert who lived almost twenty-five years in the far west of America as the third wife to a succession of three men. Another nine burials are recorded in the records of Pine Valley Cemetery by 1871, seven of them children. Eleven of the twelve buried in the graveyard at Pinto by 1868 were children. Just to the west at the tiny village of Hamblin, by 1893, the dozen recorded graves were all children. See Craig, Old Pine Valley Cemetery; Hawley, "Autobiography," 18, 20, 22.

18. Wanda Snow Petersen, *William Snow, First Bishop of Pine Valley, A Man Without Guile*, 124–25.

Family and friends of John and Sylvia remained behind in Pine Valley. Four were their own children, another was the infant daughter of Sarah Hadfield Wight Hawley Earl and Sylvester H. Earl. Another son of Sarah, Hiram Hadfield Wight, born in 1850 and died in 1867, probably rests in Pine Valley.

The Hawleys, like all the pioneers of southern Utah, had reasons to remember with melancholy their sojourn in Pine Valley. They would have sympathized with their co-religionist of decades and former Texan, Seth Blair, who wrote on November 9, 1867, that only by experience and time may one find wisdom:

> A hasty judgment is not always true. Few men unsurprised of God can judge completely his fellow. Smiles often hide a soul filled with inward sorrow. The rose that seems to be your[s] may yet be my thorn. The more distant your home the more pleasant things seem. Few will . . . create or help to make [w]hat they most envy in others. A true wife, a true husband, or a friend is at last found by contrasts.[19]

The Dixie histories of the Hawleys' experiences and accomplishments remain understated if not altogether forgotten. The dispositions of Hawley Springs in Pine Valley, as well as Hawley Canyon in Grass Valley, were recorded in government reports before and just after the turn of 1900. The final holdings were extinguished earlier: "In 1881, government investigations resulted in the awarding to others of the irrigation rights to the 'Hawley and Carr' springs, in Pine Valley" and "all in Hawley Canyon, Grass Valley." T. J. Jeffrey received the award for the springs, and Hawley Canyon went to J. and T. H. Gardner.[20]

John Hawley and his companions boarded the train. John recalls:

> After four days' ride we landed in Omaha and then took the Northwestern train for Dunlap, landing, all safe, and soon shook hands with mother and all our Josephites, being one in faith and doctrine, which made it more agreeable. This meeting took place on November 11, 1870. My family, all that were old enough, were baptized. [John's brother] Aaron Hawley had died just before we arrived, so we will have to wait till the resurrection before we meet each other.[21]

From 1871 to 1909, John Hawley remained active in the RLDS Church and made his living by farming around Gallands Grove, Iowa, for almost a decade. All the members of the Hawley families were bap-

---

19. Seth M. Blair, Diary and Autobiography, 1853–1868.
20. Frank Adams, "Agriculture Under Irrigation in Basin of Virgin River," 235, 242.
21. Hawley, "Experiences," 240–41; Hawley, "Autobiography," 32.

tized as members of the RLDS Church. John renewed his acquaintance with Joseph Smith III and "learned that business was not conducted on the same principle as it was in Salt Lake City, which I thought an improvement in the liberty of each member's rights." By 1873 the farm was improving economically, and the family increased as Mary Caroline was born, a healthy girl child. 1875 witnessed growth in the family farms (John now farming with his two oldest sons, Abinadi and Alma), as well as the final son for Sylvia and John: Francis Aaron.[22] In 1876 John and George Hawley were ordained as elders by Joseph Smith III.[23]

By 1881 Hawley was working "in the district as an elder" for the Church, often preaching at congregations in Iowa. For many years, he was a delegate to the annual conference of the RLDS Church. The members church-wide felt his effort. The *Saints' Herald* reported in 1883 that "Charles Derry and John Hawley presented a resolution stating that this General Conference does authorize the holding of yearly meetings in the Fall of each succeeding year, at such time and place, or times and places, as shall be deemed wisdom in the mind of the conference, such meetings to be called Annual Reunion Meetings of the Latter Day Saints. The body adopted this resolution and reunions were born."[24]

From 1887 to 1902, John Hawley served as an RLDS missionary. In 1887, he was sent on a full-time mission to Kansas and Missouri for three months, which ended up lasting seven. He crossed into the Indian Nations and proselytized at Tahlequah in the Cherokee Nation where the Wightites had journeyed so many years earlier. He "preached 27 discourse[s]" and baptized six and confirmed eight new members. In 1888, he was "recommended as a counselor to I. N. Roberts by the First Presidency," to labor in the Southern Mission, which encompassed the Indian Territory and Texas. That year he preached in Iowa, northern Missouri, Kansas, and the Indian Nations. Hawley baptized five persons, ordained one to the office of priest, "confirmed 6 members . . . blessed 8 children," and felt he had "received addition of light on the Holy Scriptures." He performed a marriage for one of his nephews on December 24, 1888.

John Hawley's Autobiography ended that year, and little is recorded of his missionary years in Texas from 1889 to 1902. At the age of 76, because of declining health, John and Sylvia returned to Dow City and spent most of their final years there and, finally, at the home of a daughter in Ravenwood,

---

22. Hawley, "Autobiography," 32, 34–35.
23. Joseph Smith III, letter to Bertha M. Smith, January 27, 1893.
24. "General Conference Minutes," 284; Hawley, "Autobiography," 36, 38.

Missouri. John and Sylvia were traveling by train to attend conference in Lamoni, Iowa, when a train wreck and exposure to the elements "brought pneumonia which terminated [John's] life." He passed away at the home of his son, Eber Pierce Hawley, at 83 years of age. Seven weeks later, Sylvia passed at 77 years "to join her husband in the paradise of God."[25]

While the death of Joseph Smith Jr. led to dissension and spreading clusters of opposing communities, his impact also transcended this division by creating a unique culture among his followers. Smith imbued believers with a willingness to overcome sectarian antagonism and cross-sectarian bonds to retrieve and rejoin family members and friends. The life of John Hawley demonstrates this great legacy. A diverse web of family and friendly relations was spun across the American territories covering plains and mountains all the way to California and back again to the Mississippi and Missouri River valleys.

John Hawley is a Mormon Ulysses, a singular and unique individual in the understanding of this important facet of the pioneers' and settlers' expansion to the West Coast before and after the Civil War. Mormonism turned the story of the West into an extraordinary tale of religious devotion, pioneer struggle, and familial connections. John Hawley illustrates Joseph Smith's legacy, and Hawley's story is so exceptional that it becomes a vehicle for telling a larger story than his own: that of the Mormon diaspora.

John Hawley climbing the passenger car steps in Salt Lake City bound for Iowa could not have possibly known that his trek throughout the vast Restoration vineyard of America was far from complete. He still had half of his adult life to live and serve the cause of his faith. Historian Dale Morgan observed: "The flow of time has been of paramount importance in the Mormon experience; there has never been a day when Mormonism has attained a state of finality about anything—it has always been, and continues today, in a state of becoming. So also with its principal personalities."[26]

When John stepped down from the train in Iowa, his life would repeatedly change in the years ahead. He adjusted his biography and his testimony, and in doing so revealed his mutability in the larger story of Mormonism. The Restoration today remains in motion, in flux, altering those who consciously and unconsciously define themselves by it as they bob and weave along that stream sweeping into the river called humanity.

---

25. Hawley, "Autobiography," 32–41.

26. Dale Morgan, *Dale Morgan on the Mormons: Collected Works, Part 2, 1949–1970*, 479–80.

APPENDIX A

John Hawley, Letter to Joseph Smith III, June 12, 1884

Printed in *The Saints' Herald*, Vol. 31, No. 26 (June 28, 1884), 412.

Dow City, Iowa, June 12, 1884.

Bro. Joseph: – As I often hear my brethren say that endowments and garments introduced by Lyman Wight were the same as those introduced by Brigham Young, I wish to state that they were not. And, as I was considered worthy by both these men to receive my endowments, I consider myself a competent witness, and will proceed to tell the difference as I understand it. Both claimed authority to seal men and women together for time and eternity; in this they were alike. Lyman Wight gave no endowments of secrecy. The washing of feet, anointing with oil, ordaining kings, queens, and priests, are the sum and substance of Lyman's endowments. The garment and robe he introduced, was a loose frock, made according to the pattern of one worn by Moroni when he first appeared to Joseph Smith, as given in his history. This was not worn[,] only on certain occasions. No marks indicating the priesthood were on this garment. Brigham's garment was a tight garment, made like drawers with sleeves and body connected, with marks on the knee and breast. This was to be worn always. Our instructions were even in washing of the body to keep one leg in the garment. In Brigham's endowments both feet and body were washed and anointed with oil; but he did not ordain kings and priests and queens, as did Lyman. He brought all under oath and covenant to avenge the blood of the prophets, and gave us a name we would be called forth from the grave by. This is about the extent of his endowment, with the addition of a second endowment, and I am a witness of this also; which was an anointing and setting apart for the resurrection and power conferred to the rise from the dead, and to raise others. Saints, you see no similarity between the endowments of these men. The robe that Lyman introduced was an entire covering of linen, with the exception of the head, hands and feet; added to this he had an apron, imitating the one made by Adam and Eve in the Garden of Eden; but no mark. This we were to be laid away in after death, and be worn when sealed for eternity. Brigham's robe was the same as Lyman's with the exception of the marks of the priesthood, and used for the same purpose, hence we see some similarity in the robes of these two men—alike, only the marks. This ends the history I set out to make.

Now let me place myself on record concerning the Mountain Meadows Massacre. I have been asked the question a number of times, "Were you in that massacre?" Those asking the question, seeing the name of John Hawley in John D. Lee's history, thinking that he had made a mistake when he said, "This John Hawley went to Indian Territory, and died there." And, as I lived in southern Utah at the time of this massacre, they have thought that I must be the man. Now, let me say to all, that I was not the John Hawley that Lee speaks of; neither was I there, nor do I know any thing of how it was conducted only from hearsay. Let me relate a few things that took place at the time, or after the massacre. Those that went to the Mountain Meadows, and as I suppose took part in the killing, (this is supposition only upon my part), on their return, three of the men spoke with a great deal of zeal, and declared to us that the dividing line was then drawn between Jew and Gentile, and all must die that passed through the Territory who were not of our faith. The work of death they applauded very much. As I had just returned from Salt Lake City with my family, they called upon me to talk; and I continued the subject of death; and proclaimed with as much zeal against the work of death (done by them as I then supposed) as they did for it. For this they took me to task, but all in secret; but as I had a balance of power in their meeting, the vote stood in favor of my living. However, they sent a delegate to inform me that I must be more on my guard in what I said, and the man interrogated me thus: "Bro. John, you came very near losing your life for what you said yesterday; and I have been sent to tell you to be more on your guard." I remember very well the answer I gave him, and that was this: "Bro. Young, (Wm. Young was the man), I don't know but I am as well prepared to die now as ever I will be; and if you take my life for proclaiming against that deed of murder, you will kill an innocent man; but you may tell your brethren that I still stand on what I said." That day brought Brigham's message to the people, concerning the company just killed; but too late to do them any good. It read as follows: "Let them pass, and treat them as you would like to be treated were you passing through their own land." When this was read, I had friends. This testimony I must meet some time.

JOHN HAWLEY.

Although the RLDS Journal of History published an autobiographical sketch of Elder John Hawley in its issue for April 1911, the editors removed the portion relating his 1850s residence in Utah. For the suppressed section, see the 1889 transcript entitled, "Autobiography of John Hawley" in the Community of Christ Library-Archives.

APPENDIX B

Temple Lot Case

THE CIRCUIT COURT OF THE U.S., WESTERN DIVISION, AT KANSAS CITY. THE REORGANIZED CHURCH OF JESUS CHRIST OF LATTER DAY SAINTS VS. THE CHURCH OF CHRIST AT INDEPENDENCE, MISSOURI. 1893, P. 451–62.

PLAINTIFF'S EVIDENCE IN REBUTTAL.

JOHN HAWLEY, of lawful age, being produced, sworn, and examined on the part of the Plaintiff in rebuttal, testified as follows:

I was sixty-six years old the fourth day of last March. I reside at Sheridan, Worth County, Missouri.

I am a member of the Reorganized Church of Jesus Christ of Latter Day Saints. I was baptized by Wm. O. Clark in the year 1837 into the church of which I am now a member. William O. Clark was an elder in the church at the time I was baptized. I was baptized in Ray county, Missouri. There was a branch of the church close to where I lived at that time.

I was ordained a teacher in the church about 1842 at a place called Ambrosia, in Lee county, Iowa, about four miles from Montrose. There was an organization of the church at that place. That branch of the church at Ambrosia was presided over by John Smith, who was a cousin I think of the first Joseph Smith, I think that was the [452] way it was, but I would not swear positively to that. That organization continued there at Ambrosia until 1843, and from there it was moved to what was called Zarahemlah, close to Montrose in Iowa.

I pursued my occupation as a teacher for six or seven years and then I received a higher ordination as an elder. I was ordained an elder in Texas; disremember the county, but it was about the central part of the State, about eighty miles from the Capital, and about sixty-five miles from San Antonio. There was an organization of the church there of which Lyman Wight was the head. Lyman Wight was one of the Twelve Apostles in the original church, —one of the original Twelve. He became one of the Twelve to fill a vacancy in old Joseph's day.

I remained in Texas until about 1853, and during my stay there, the organization was kept up. When I left Texas, I came to the Cherokee

Nation and wintered there in 1853. Remained there until 1856 and then went to Utah.

I remember the time and the circumstances attending the death of Joseph Smith the Martyr. I was in Wisconsin at the time.

My father went to Wisconsin in company with Lyman Wight, and George Miller, and others for the purpose of obtaining lumber for finishing the Temple at Nauvoo. I was in Wisconsin on this lumber expedition at the time I heard of the death of Joseph Smith. That did not deter us, we went right ahead and finished our labors and brought the lumber down the next spring after the death of Joseph Smith; that would be in the spring of 1845. In the summer of 1845, we went back to Wisconsin.

I was acquainted with the requirements of the church at that time and its doctrines, as much so as anyone of my age was at that time. I was acquainted with the teaching of the church and the requirements of its officers.

There were no teachings of the church, nor requirements with reference to the question of endowments at the time that I was an officer in it. There was no teaching of endowments to my knowledge at any time until after we went into Texas. That was the first time I ever knew anything about endowments.

Lyman Wight was the first person that taught anything about endowments according to my best recollection. He taught us that it was necessary for men and women to be sealed together in order to enjoy each other's society in eternity.

That is, he taught that husband and wife were to be sealed together in order to enjoy each other's society in eternity. Lyman Wight was the first person I ever heard teach that doctrine.

There was no particular difference between that sealing and the ordinary ceremony of marriage, except it was done as we understood it by the power of the priesthood.

It was used instead of the legal form of marriage and at that time we looked upon it as being more binding for eternity than the other form of marriage. One was performed through the requirements of [453] the law of the land; and the other through the requirements of the spiritual law. That was the understanding we had.

I passed through that ceremony myself. I was married in 1851. Lyman Wight became the head of the church there in Texas from the fact as we understood it that he had a mission given him by Joseph Smith the Seer, to go to Texas and preach the gospel to that people, and raise up a branch of the church there.

That appointment was made in 1843. At least that was the time that Lyman Wight received his commission to go into Texas. That was the statement he made to us at the time. He made the statement to us that his commission was given him in 1843.

I do not know that I could enumerate all of the Twelve, at the time Lyman Wight went into Texas, but there was Brigham Young, Heber C. Kimball, Willard Richards, George A. Smith, Wilford Woodruff, Orson Hyde, William Smith, Orson and Parley P. Pratt.

In 1844 the Twelve were scattered throughout a good deal of territory. In 1848 they were scattered a good deal more, but the most of them I think were in Utah. Most of them had gone to Utah with the branch of the church that went there.

I don't believe I can state how many of the Twelve went to Salt Lake City, but there was quite a large number of them, quite a large number of that branch of the church, and some of the Twelve went with them of course. I think most of the Twelve went to Salt Lake City with the exception of William Smith, Lyman Wight, and John E. Page.

I went to Salt Lake City in 1856, from the Indian Territory. I identified myself with the church there in Salt Lake, as did my wife.

I took the endowments there. The endowments that I took at Salt Lake were not the same endowments that I took under Lyman Wight's administration. They differed in the manner of the sealing, and in the manner of conferring the endowments.

Lyman Wight only gave the endowments in respect to the matter of the washing of the feet, and (in Utah) they gave the endowments of washing and anointing, and then there was an oath taken in Utah to avenge the blood of the prophet. That was a part of the endowment that was given in Salt Lake City.

The endowments in Salt Lake City were given in the endowment house as they called it, which was arranged especially for conferring these ceremonies, reserved entirely for that service.

The endowments that Lyman Wight gave us were the washing of feet, and sealing a man's wife to him for eternity. I can't repeat that ceremony, but it was sealing in the name of the Lord Jesus Christ, for time as well as eternity.

There were no other obligations than that, nothing more than sealing for time and eternity, that was all there was to it. It related purely to matrimonial affairs and that was all the endowments that Lyman Wight ever gave.

[454] In 1848 was the first time I ever heard of endowments being given in the church. That was after the death of Joseph Smith certainly, because he died in 1844. At the time I lived at Nauvoo, I did not hear or know anything about endowments.

I never heard of it at the time I was a resident of Nauvoo, or before the time that I was in Texas under Lyman Wight, no further than I heard that there was an endowment of the Spirit at Kirtland. That was in 1833 as I understand it, but I had never heard anything about endowments in Nauvoo.

The endowment at Kirtland was the washing of feet and the endowment with power, that the elders might go forth with greater power to preach the word. That endowment was given to the elders through the Holy Spirit.

After that, the next I heard of endowments was from Lyman Wight in Texas, where it was applied to the marriage relation.

And after that, I went to Salt Lake City, Utah, and there I found the ordinance, as it is called, of endowments, in force, only with a greatly extended application.

The endowments that I received in Texas were not conferred secretly. There was nothing secret about it. They were conducted openly and all had the privilege of seeing them performed. Everyone could go that felt like going.

That was not the case in Salt Lake. In Salt Lake City it was done secretly and no one was permitted to see them only the officers and the ones taking the endowments. No one else was present or permitted to be present simply because no one else had any business there and they were not permitted to be there. That was the reason there was no one else there.

That was the rule at the time I received my endowments at Salt Lake City at least. Of course I don't know what happened afterwards.

Wilford Woodruff did the anointing and washing and Brigham Young did the sealing at the time I received my endowments at Salt Lake City.

At the time I received my endowments in Texas, Lyman Wight did the sealing and my father was a high priest in the church in old Joseph's time and he did the washing of the feet and the anointing of the head.

When my wife and I received our endowments in Salt Lake City, we were in different rooms while we were washing and anointing, but when we were sealed, we were together.

In Texas when we received our endowments, we were not separated at all, it was simply the washing of the feet there.

My father's name was Pierce Hawley. I have attended church at Nauvoo many a time. My father lived near Montrose, that was across the river in Iowa, and we often went over on the Sabbath to Nauvoo, and attended church.

At the time I attended church at Nauvoo and while I was a teacher [455] in the church there, there was no such thing then taught, or practiced, as endowments or any endowments that I have spoken of.

I heard nothing of that kind at all there at Nauvoo. That was from 1841 to 1844 that we attended church services or meetings there at Nauvoo. It was while we lived across the river at Montrose.

If there was ever any such a thing as endowments practiced in the church at Nauvoo, during this period from 1841 to 1844, I never knew it and I don't think there was. It was in 1848 when I first heard of it.

I knew something about what went on in Salt Lake City, after I got there of course, with reference to the endowments. There was such a thing known as endowments being administered to those who had not been joined in marriage as husband and wife.

There were several single men went through and got their endowments, —unmarried men. Of course they did not receive the ordinance of sealing for eternity. That ordinance was not administered to them.

They were anointed and when they got their wives, if they ever did get any, they then got the rest of the endowments. That was the way it was done in Utah. That was never practiced in Texas, with reference to single men, to my knowledge. In Texas it was confined exclusively to husband and wife.

I went to Utah in 1856 and remained there until 1870. The first indications that ever came to my knowledge that polygamy was being practiced in the Mormon Church was in 1845 in Wisconsin, after we went to Wisconsin the second time from Nauvoo. That was where I first heard of polygamy or plurality of wives. It was at Prairie Lacrosse.

There was a church organization there at that time. Lyman Wight was there with his little band. He was the head of the organization of the church there at that time. Lyman Wight went from Wisconsin to Texas and his organization went with him, most of them did.

I first heard of the practice of polygamy when I was just starting for Texas in the summer of 1845 and we were on the move for Texas. Lyman Wight had performed the ceremony and had sealed a young lady, near us, to a man who had another wife. He had just done it a short time before we started. I know this is so for at the time I was paying my regards to the young lady myself and I didn't know for some time that she was another man's wife.

When we got to Davenport, Iowa, was where I came into possession of the knowledge that she was another man's wife, and of course I dropped her mighty quick. That was the first intimation that I had that there was anything of the kind practiced. That was the first case of spiritual marriage that ever came to my knowledge.

Spiritual wife marriage as it is termed. Those that were in spiritual marriage were said to be in polygamy, as well as those that were not. The understanding was that they would enjoy the same [456] glory as the others, but the ones that had more than one wife would enjoy a greater portion of it.

It was not a necessary and logical sequence if they were spiritually married that they would practice polygamy. The theory was that the man that had more than one spiritual wife, would enjoy a greater measure of glory than the man that had only one, enjoy the glory hereafter; the glory which was in eternity would be greater. I mean that that would be applicable if they practiced polygamy.

Lyman Wight taught that in Texas, and practiced it there. According to my understanding, Lyman Wight was the first man to teach and practice polygamy in the Mormon Church.

I was pretty well acquainted with Joseph Smith the Seer, from 1838 to 1843. I was pretty well acquainted with him during all that time. I was ordained a teacher in 1842 and if polygamy had been taught or practiced in the church at that time at Nauvoo or anywhere else, I think I should have heard of it.

I have my reasons for thinking so and they are these: My father was one of the first elders in the church, and if he had heard of any such thing, I think he would have said something about it, and we would all have heard about it; but I didn't hear of it. That is, of the teaching and practice of polygamy prior to the death of Joseph Smith.

I never knew of Joseph Smith teaching or preaching or practicing polygamy. The first time I heard of it was in 1845, and I never heard of it before that time from anybody.

Q. —I now hand you Plaintiff's Exhibit D, on the title page of which appears the following: "A few choice examples of Mormon practices and sermons," and I will ask you whether or not you recognize the cuts of the garments and implements contained within the first eight pages as being of the character and description used in the ordinances of the endowments at the time you took them at Salt Lake?

A. —I have not used them or seen them since 1870, but I recognize this garment on the front page here as being the complete garment with sleeves and dress and all as being the same as the garment used at Salt Lake, at the time I received my endowments. I recognize the aprons and the emblems on the aprons as shown on page two of Exhibit "D." I remember the leaves there on the apron and the form of the apron, I remember that very well. That was the form of the apron worn and used at the time of the endowments at Salt Lake. The apron is used at the time of the sealing, —that particular stage of the proceedings.

I don't know that I can recognize the building with all its compartments and forms, but still I remember it had a good many departments. It had a reception room, a small stairway to the veil, and it was pretty much all on the ground floor. Had dressing rooms, washing rooms, a prayer circle, and an altar.

This square room here marked "Peter," "John," "James," "altar," [457] and "world" is intended to represent the three apostles, Peter, John, and James. It represented the Melchizedekal priesthood that they held. The Garden of Eden part of it was more fully practiced and carried out when I received my endowments.

When I received mine there was only an offering made and the ones it was offered to would receive it, and we expected that for accepting it, they would be cast out as a representation of the truth. I mean the ones that would accept the fruit that would be offered to them would be cast out the same as Adam was.

We expected that the man would be cast out and then you would go out with your wife. Then there was another room which was entitled "heaven."

There was an altar where we were all sealed for time and eternity, the jumping off place, so to speak; that is what they called it. That was the last room and was the last act in the ceremony.

The room below it in the diagram where the square and compass is marked and is designated "instruction room," the name indicates what it was. It was a room where we received general instruction. The instruction related to garments and robes and teaching people how to wear them.

The undergarment to be worn continually and the robe that was worn at the time of the prayer circle was to be the same in which you were to be buried. If you died, you were to be buried in a robe like the one you wore at the time you were sealed.

I recognize the drawing on page six of Exhibit "D" as the robe that was worn on that occasion. I remember the bows on the side. It was a robe that came down over our shoulders and had a bandage across. That was a robe that was worn outside of the garments.

I recognize the representations on page seven of Exhibit "D" as the woman's cap and moccasins and the man's cap. I recognize them as part of the paraphernalia that was used on that occasion. These were used at the time of the sealing.

I left Salt Lake in 1870. During the time I was there, I was a member of the church in Utah. Was not a member of any other church during the time I was there. I am now a member of the Church of Christ denominated the Reorganized Church.

The Reorganized Church does not have any endowments of the kind I have mentioned. If they have, I never have seen them or heard of them. They teach nothing of the kind.

In taking the endowments at Salt Lake there was an oath required, and the oath that was required was to avenge the blood or death of the prophet.

No such an oath was required in the administration of the endowments under Lyman Wight. There was nothing of that kind required.

I severed my connection with the Mormon Church in Utah in 1870 and that is the year that I came away from there. The occasion for my severance from that organization was, that the doctrine taught there [458] was not in keeping with that which is written in the inspired books, the Bible, the Book of Mormon, and the Book of Doctrine and Covenants.

I left because the doctrine and teaching of the church in Utah did not conform to the teaching set forth in the books of the church acknowledged to be inspired.

I think the doctrines of the church were presented there in Utah about the same when I came away as when I went there. There was one doctrine and that was about Adam being our God. I can't say about when that was introduced. That was a doctrine that I never agreed to and couldn't understand for the reason that I couldn't understand how he could be our God, and have fallen under condemnation the way he did, but however that was, Brigham Young sent a proclamation to that effect to the people, but whether it was in '52 or '54 or 56, I couldn't say; but at any rate, I objected to that doctrine and would not accept it.

And polygamy was another doctrine. I was baptized after I went to Salt Lake City. The occasion of being rebaptized after I went to Salt Lake City was, it was supposed that the people in crossing the plains at that time, would naturally commit sins, and it was considered beneficial to be rebaptized.

At the time I took my endowments in Salt Lake City, I don't remember of taking any oath except for avenging the death of Joseph the martyr and his brother Hyrum Smith. I find here in the Exhibit to which my attention is called, that we are to teach our children to do likewise. Now it might have been all in there at the time I took it, but I don't remember it if it was.

I am satisfied from what I had heard before I took my endowments that there were many things done in the endowment house that were not done at the time I received mine.

I recognize the oath that I took here in Exhibit "D," but I can't say that I took it all. I recognize parts of it all right though. We were made to swear to avenge the death of Joseph Smith the martyr, together with that of his brother Hyrum, on this American nation, and that we would teach our children and childrens' children to do so. The penalty for this grip and oath was disembowelment.

CROSS-EXAMINATION.

I became a member of the Plaintiff church in this case in 1870, in Utah, and I left Utah in the fall of the same year. It was probably about four months after I became a member of the Plaintiff church, before I left Salt Lake City.

After I left Utah, I went to Shelby county, Iowa. Stayed there eighteen or nineteen years. Was a member of the Plaintiff church there. I lived at Galland's Grove in Shelby county, Iowa. I left there when I moved into Missouri about four years ago. There is a branch of the Plaintiff church where I now live in Worth county, Missouri, of which I am a member, — the branch of "Sweet Home." [459]I came here to Independence yesterday evening on the application of E. L. Kelley. He requested me to come.

At the time I took my endowments at Salt Lake everybody was excluded except the ones taking endowments and those who were officiating in the ceremonies. I belonged to and was baptized into the original church that was organized April 6, 1830.

I was directed not to disclose the method of the endowments. I I agreed not to do so in certain places. One of the places where I could divulge the endowments, was not in a court room where depositions were being taken.

I would not have discussed the methods of these endowments when I was a member of the Utah Church. The penalty for revealing or disclosing these secrets was disembowelment.

The grips and tokens of the priesthood were what we were not to disclose. When I took the endowments I took this oath. All who took the endowments took the same oath. I didn't make any halves of anything in this business; I generally saw the whole thing through, and therefore I say I took that oath, the whole thing; and I kept the obligations while I was living in Salt Lake City.

There is nothing to compel me to divulge anything. I don't recognize any obligations to disclose anything at all; there was nothing said about it, and I have not disclosed the grips nor the tokens; and that is what we were not to disclose.

I did not know that the church at the time I took these endowments practiced polygamy. I heard it did and I suppose as a matter of fact it did. I have no reason to doubt it. The greater part of the membership of the Utah Church did not practice polygamy, nothing like the greater portion of them. I was acquainted with some people who did practice polygamy, and was acquainted with a great many men that they said had more wives than one. I can't tell you the number.

I objected to the practice of polygamy then, never liked or approved of the idea that it was practiced, and that was the main reason that I left the church. I objected to the practice of it all the way through, in every way.

From what was written in the standard books of the church, I saw that it was condemned by these standard books and therefore I did not approve of it and I objected to it for that reason, and because I considered it did not tend to good morals.

I received my first lesson in polygamy in Texas. Aside from the lesson I mentioned in my examination in chief, which I received in Wisconsin, or on the road from Wisconsin to Davenport.

I knew a man by the name of George Miller while I was in Wisconsin. He didn't practice polygamy at that time that I am aware of. But afterwards while in Texas he did. This man Miller joined the branch in Texas of which I was a member.

I understood that George Miller and Lyman Wight had received their instructions to go on this mission to Texas from Joseph Smith. [460] That is what I understood, I don't know anything about it. That is what they said.

The instructions were that George Miller and Lyman Wight were to take the Black River Country and take a mission there, and afterwards it was changed to Texas and we were all coupled together to go on that mission.

I said that the endowments given at Salt Lake were not like those that Lyman Wight gave, and I haven't seen anything like them since I left Salt Lake.

I have been taught since I left Salt Lake that all these things that lead to polygamy and these things that are not in keeping with the law, are not of God. That is what I have been taught.

I have never received any endowments, with reference to feet washings since I left Salt Lake. I don't know anything about endowments in the Plaintiff church, except endowments of the Spirit, that is all.

I have been baptized three times. I was baptized into the Reorganized Church of Jesus Christ of Latter Day Saints in Utah before I left there; and have never been baptized since. That is the baptism that I was received upon. I was baptized into the Utah Church in the Indian Territory, and then I was baptized again when I got to Utah. I was baptized originally in 1837 in Ray county, Missouri. I was baptized in the Cherokee Nation by an elder in the Utah Church, by the name of Miller.

I don't know that I could explain the reason why it was necessary for me to be rebaptized into the Reorganized Church of Jesus Christ of Latter Day Saints, any more than it seemed to be a practice among the people.

Those that had been baptized into the Utah Church were rebaptized before they were admitted into the Reorganization. But I understand that that is not necessary in the case of parties who were baptized into the original church before the death of Joseph Smith, and who had never been identified with the Utah Church, or any other faction of the original church after the death of Joseph Smith. That is my understanding. The church in Salt Lake or Utah was called by a good many the Brighamite Church, or the Utah Church, and of course was called the Church of Jesus Christ of Latter Day Saints also.

I suppose the reason I was baptized into the Utah Church, or the Salt Lake Church, was because of a certain class claiming authority to be leaders, and the membership were to be baptized when they came into that organization. Lyman Wight claimed to be a leader, and Brigham Young claimed to be a leader, and there was a lot more of them claimed to be the true leaders of the church after Joseph Smith died.

Q. —Well, now, if the church you joined in 1837 was the same church that you joined in 1870 the last time, what use was there in your being confirmed at all? What was the necessity of your confirmation in the Reorganized Church?

[461] *A.* —Well I think I have answered that question. I think I told you it was because of the different leaders leading off a portion of the church, that had their institution and those that came in, after being with these different leaders, must come in through the door, by being baptized and reconfirmed and I was one that had to do that.

I was confirmed a member of the Reorganized Church of Jesus Christ of Latter Day Saints,—the Church of Christ—denominated the Reorganized Church of Jesus Christ of Latter Day Saints. When I was confirmed the language used was something like this: "I confirm you a member of the Church of Christ."

I don't know that the word *reorganized* was used when I was confirmed. I have confirmed people myself. I confirmed them members of the Church of Christ denominated the Latter Day Saints. That is the language I used.

I went back to Wisconsin the second time to get the outfit to go down to Texas. There was nothing said about polygamy in Nauvoo at the time I left there in 1844; nothing said about it to my knowledge.

Lyman Wight broke off from the church at Nauvoo, because he became dissatisfied with Brigham Young. He thought that Brigham was usurping authority that did not belong to him. He was going to Texas, which was a long way from Nauvoo, and he concluded from the way Brigham, and the church there were acting, without authority, that he would refuse to have anything to do with them and that was what he did.

I was acquainted with William Marks when I was a boy in Nauvoo. I knew him in Plano after we left Nauvoo; that was in 1868 that I saw him in Plano. I never saw him after that.

Yes, sir, I talked with him about the church, talked with him some in Nauvoo. I never introduced the subject of polygamy to him or he to me, but there was something said about it between us.

He said that he knew polygamy was practiced, but that he didn't know how far it was practiced there at Nauvoo. I don't know that he stated when it was first practiced there at Nauvoo

He told me that Joseph Smith carne to him at one· time and said to him: —

Brother Marks, I am glad that you have not received the teaching of this doctrine, for now we have to go to work and put down this wicked practice, and I want you to call the High Council together and I will prefer charges against these members of the church who have entered into this practice of plural marriage, and if they do not repent, they will be expelled from the church.

That was what he said to me, and shortly after that he was arrested and taken to Carthage.

He said that he had been approached about this matter, this matter of plural marriage, and he had refused to have anything to do with it, and he wanted the High Council called together to take action on the cases of the members of the church who had violated the marriage law, in taking plural wives, and that he would [462] prefer charges against them. That was what William Marks told me in 1868. He said that was what Joseph Smith told him before his death.

He didn't say anything further than that he and Joseph Smith had this conversation that I have detailed, and that Joseph Smith said there were persons practicing it, and that they would be cut off from the church if they did not stop it at once and repent of their wicked practice, and that he would prefer charges against them before the High Council; but he was murdered before he had time to do it. That is what Marks told me. There was no revelation spoken of at that time between Marks and I. It was never spoken of between us at all at any time.

———

APPENDIX C

Chronology of John Pierce Hawley

Year	Event	Notes
1826 (March 4)	Birth to Sarah Schroeder Hawley and Pierce Hawley	Tazewell County. One of eleven siblings. Fifth child, third son in birth order. Lived in Hawley and Pekin, east of the Illinois River.
1832	Moved to DuPage, Illinois, west of Chicago	Forted in Chicago during Black Hawk War. Gideon Hawley, an uncle, was killed in the conflict.
1833–34	Parents baptized as members of Church of Jesus Christ of Latter Day Saints.	Parents baptized winter of 1833–34 by James Emmett.
1834	Family moved to Sangammon County, Illinois	Pierce Hawley bought a farm to wait out the events of being forced from Jackson County.
1836	Family moved to Missouri	Pierce Hawley had property in Ray and Caldwell counties.
1837	Baptized into the Church of Jesus Christ of Latter Day Saints	John with brothers George and Aaron were baptized by William O. Clark.
1838–43	Driven from Missouri by enemies of the Church	The Hawley family survived Mormon-Missouri War. Crossed over the Mississippi River at Tipton. Settled across the river from Nauvoo, in Hawley's Grove then Ambrosia. John P. Hawley ordained a teacher.
1843–45	Black Falls and Mormon Coulee, Wisconsin Territory	John worked as a logger and learned woodworking. Pierce Hawley served in bishopric and was ordained a patriarch by Lyman Wight.

1845–46	Wightite Colony moves to Texas	The Wight company journeys from Wisconsin Territory to the Republic of Texas, the move taking sixteen months, requiring wintering on the Red River before arriving in Austin, Texas.
1846 (July 4)	Marriage to Harriet Hobart near Austin, Texas	Harriet Hobart is John Pierce Hawley's first wife. She went with a group of defectors from the company and was never heard from again. Lyman Wight declared John and Harriet divorced.
1847–51	Zodiac, Texas	John P. Hawley grew to manhood. Helped to build the Zodiac Temple, the first temple of the Mormon Diaspora west of the Mississippi.
1849 (October 22)	Marriage to Sylvia Johnson	Lyman Wight and Pierce Hawley officiating.
1851–54	Mormon Mills, Burnet County, Texas	Moved with Lyman Wight Colony from Zodiac. Joined his father and mother in Cherokee Nation.
1854–56	Spavinaw, Cherokee Nation, Indian Territory	Worked at salt and lumber mills. Explored southern Kansas but rejected homesteading there. Joined the Utah LDS Church and immigrated to Utah Territory.
1856–57	Ogden, Utah Territory	Contracted to buy Farr sawmill but was called to Washington County in April 1857.
1857–70	Washington, then Pine Valley (1858), Utah Territory	Farmed. Worked in logging and lumber and mill businesses. Served as presiding elder, bishop's first counselor, school superintendent, constable.
1870 (November)	Pine Valley to Salt Lake City, then by rail to Iowa	Moved to Iowa with his and George Hawley's families to join with relatives and friends in the RLDS Church.

Appendix C: Chronology of John Pierce Hawley

1870–1909	Iowa, Missouri, Indian Territory, Kansas, and Texas	Lived as a farmer and missionary. Served the RLDS Church in various capacities as elder and high priest and missionary.
1909 (April 17)	John Hawley dies in Lamoni, Decatur County, Iowa	Passes in train accident in route to attend a conference of the RLDS Church. Place of Burial: Oak Lawn Cemetery, Ravenwood, Missouri.

Bibliography

Adams, Frank. "Agriculture Under Irrigation in the Basin of Virgin River." In *Report of Irrigation Investigations in Utah*, edited by Elwood Mead, 207–65. U.S. Department of Agriculture, Office of Experiment Stations, Bulletin No. 124. Washington: Government Printing Office, 1903.

Adams, Henry. *The Education of Henry Adams*. Boston: Houghton Mifflin, 1918.

"Agreement with Arthur Morrison and Others, 15 June 1844." The Joseph Smith Papers. Accessed November 29, 2018. https://www.josephsmithpapers.org/paper-summary/agreement-with-arthur-morrison-and-others-15-june-1844/1.

Aird, Polly. *Mormon Convert, Mormon Defector: A Scottish Immigrant in the American West, 1848-1862*. Norman, OK: Arthur H. Clarke, 2009.

———. *Playing with Shadows: Voices of Dissent in the Mormon West*. Norman, OK: Arthur H. Clark Co., 2011.

Alexander, Thomas G. "Wilford Woodruff and the Mormon Reformation of 1855–57." *Dialogue: A Journal of Mormon Thought* 15, no. 3 (Summer 1992): 25–39.

Anderson, Emma L. "An Incident of the Past," *Autumn Leaves* 8, no. 7 (July 1895): 315–16.

"Arrived." *The Deseret News* 6, no. 32 (October 15, 1856): 253.

Avard, Sampson. Testimony of Sampson, Avard, Cause 91, State of Missouri vs. Jos. Smith et al. November 12–13, 1838, folder 2, Eugene Morrow Violette Collection, 1806–1921. Western Historical Manuscript Collections, University of Missouri, Columbia.

Bagley, Will. *Blood of the Prophets: Brigham Young and the Massacre at Mountain Meadows*. Norman: University of Oklahoma Press, 2004.

———. "'One Long Funeral March': A Revisionist's View of the Mormon Handcart Disaster." *Journal of Mormon History* 35, no. 1 (Winter 2009): 50–116.

———. *So Rugged and Mountainous: Blazing the Trails to Oregon and California, 1812–1848*. Norman, OK: University of Oklahoma Press, 2010.

Barlow, Oswald. "History of Oswald Barlow, St. George Pioneer." The National Society of the Sons of Utah Pioneers. http://www.pioneerstories.org/story/history-oswald-barlow-st-george-pioneer.

Barton, Pierson. "Journal of Pierson Barton Reading, In His Journey of One Hundred Twenty-Three Days Across The Rocky Mountains From Westport On the Missouri River, 450 Miles Above St. Louis, To Monterey, California, On The Pacific Ocean, In 1843." *Quarterly of The Society of California Pioneers* 7, no. 3 (September 1930): 148–98.

Bashore, Melvin L., H. Dennis Tolley, and the BYU Pioneer Mortality Team. "Mortality on the Mormon Trail, 1847-1868," *BYU Studies Quarterly* 53, no. 4 (2014): 109–23.

Bayse, Henry. Henry Bayse, Record of Service Card, Mormon War, 1838. Soldiers' Records: War of 1812—World War I. https://s1.sos.mo.gov/records/archives/archivesdb/soldiers/Detail.aspx?id=S1194&conflict=Mormon%20War.

Beck, James. Notebooks, 1859–1865. LDS Church History Library, Salt Lake City.

Beckstrom, Elizabeth, and Bess Beckstrom. *O' Ye Mountains High: The Story of Pine Valley Utah*. St. George, UT: Heritage Press, 1980.

Beckstrom, Ella Lloyd. "Dorinda Melissa Moody's History." Michael Roup Goheen and Dorinda Melessa Moody. Revised May 2, 2006. http://freepages.rootsweb.com/~genjengi/genealogy/personalinfo/michael_dorinda.html.

Bennett, Richard E. "'The Upper Room': The Nature and Development of Latter-day Saint Temple Work." *Journal of Mormon History* 41, no. 2 (April 2015): 1–35.

Bennion, Lowell C. "Mapping the Extent of Plural Marriage in St. George, 1861–1880." *BYU Studies* 51, no. 4 (2012): 27–42.

Berkhofer, Robert F. *The White Man's Indian: Images of the American Indian from Columbus to the Present*. New York: Vintage Books, 2004.

Bidwell, John. *A Journey to California*. Newberry Library Microfilm 1–12. Newberry Library, Chicago, IL.

Bigler, David L. *Forgotten Kingdom: The Mormon Theocracy in the American West, 1847–1896*. Logan: Utah State University Press, 1998.

Bigler, David L., and Will Bagley. *The Mormon Rebellion: America's First Civil War, 1857–1858*. Norman: University of Oklahoma Press, 2011.

Black, Susan Easton, comp. *Early Members of the Reorganized Church of Jesus Christ of Latter Day Saints*, 6 Vols. Provo, UT: Religious Studies Center, Brigham Young University, 1993.

Blair, Alma R. "RLDS Views of Polygamy: Some Historiographical Notes." *John Whitmer Historical Association Journal* 5 (1985): 16–28.

Blair, Seth M. Diary and Autobiography, L. Tom Perry Collections, Harold B. Lee Library, Brigham Young University, Provo, Utah.

———. Letter to General Samuel Houston, December 1, 1857. Historian's Office Letterpress Copybooks, Vol. 1, 1854–1861, LDS Church History Library, Salt Lake City.

———. Letter to President Brigham Young, January 7, 1855. Brigham Young Office Files, LDS Church History Library, Salt Lake City.

Blair, W. W. Letter to Joseph Smith III, November 21, 1870. In *The True Latter Day Saints' Herald* 18, no. 1 (January 1, 1871): 20.

Bleak, James A. Letter to George Albert Smith, April 13, 1866. George A. Smith Collections, LDS Church History Library, Salt Lake City.

Bleak, James G. *The Annals of the Southern Mission: A Record of the History of the Settlement of Southern Utah*. Edited by Aaron McArthur and Reid L. Neilson. Salt Lake City: Greg Kofford Books, 2019.

Bradshaw, Hazel. *Under Dixie Sun: A History of Washington County by Those Who Loved Their Forebears*. St. George, UT: Washington County D.U.P., 1978.

Briggs, Robert H. "The Mountain Meadows Massacre: An Analytical Narrative Based on Participant Confessions." *Utah Historical Quarterly* 74, no. 4 (2006): 313–33.

Brooks, Juanita. *The Mountain Meadows Massacre*. 3rd ed. Norman: University of Oklahoma Press, 1993.

Brown, Lorenzo. The Journal of Lorenzo Brown, 1823–1890. Typescript. Mesa Family History Center, Mesa, AZ.

Brown, Thomas D. *The Southern Indian Mission Diary of Thomas D. Brown*. Edited by Juanita Brooks. Logan: Utah State University, 1972.

Bullock, Thomas. "Interesting from our Missionaries on the Plains." *The Mormon*, November 15, 1856, 2. https://history.lds.org/overlandtravel/sources/8733/bullock-thomas-interesting-from-our-missionaries-on-the-plains-the-mormon-15-november-1856-2.

———. "Minutes of the Council of the Twelve in upper room of Historian's Office, April 5, 1860." Brigham Young Office Files. LDS Church History Library, Salt Lake City.

Burk, Freddijo Passey. *Joseph Hadfield Story: An Incredible Odyssey*. Scottsdale, AZ: Concept Management Corporation, 2008.

Burton, Don E. Burton. *The History of Faithful John Burton*. LDS Church History Library, Salt Lake City.

Campbell, Alexander. "Delusions." *The Millennial Harbinger* 2, no. 2 (February 7, 1831): 85–96.

Campbell, Eugene E. "Brigham Young's Outer Cordon: A Reappraisal." *Utah Historical Quarterly* 41, no. 3 (Summer 1973): 220–53.

———. *Establishing Zion: The Mormon Church in the American West, 1847–1869*. Salt Lake City: Signature Books, 1988.

Campbell, Eugene E., and Bruce L. Campbell. "Divorce among Mormon Polygamists: Extent and Explanations." *Utah Historical Quarterly* 46 (Winter 1978): 4–23.

Cedar City Ward Relief Society Minute Book. LDS Church History Library, Salt Lake City.

Clark, David L. "Mormons of the Wisconsin Territory: 1835–1848." *BYU Studies* 37, no. 2 (April 1997): 57–85.

———. "Violence and Disruptive Behavior on the Difficult Trail to Utah, 1847–1868." *BYU Studies Quarterly* 53, no. 4 (December 2014): 81–108.

Cluff, Harvey Harris. Harvey H. Cluff Autobiography, Journals, and Scrapbook, 1868–1916. LDS Church History Library, Salt Lake City.

Compton, Todd. "Becoming a 'Messenger of Peace': Jacob Hamblin in Tooele." *Dialogue: A Journal of Mormon Thought* 42, no. 1 (Spring 2009): 1–29.

———. *A Frontier Life: Jacob Hamblin, Explorer and Indian Missionary*. Salt Lake City: University of Utah Press, 2013.

———. Email to Melvin C. Johnson, September 30, 2016. In author's possession.

Corrill, John. *A Brief History of the Church of Christ of Jesus Latter-Day Saints (Commonly Called Mormons)*. Bountiful, UT: Restoration Research, 1983.

Craig, Wesley W. Cemetery Indexes for Washington County, Utah (1852–1996). http://sites.rootsweb.com/~utwashin/cemetery/pine1.html.

Crampton, C. Gregory. *Mormon Colonization in Southern Utah and in Adjacent Parts of Arizona and Nevada (1965)*. Special Collections, C. Gregory Crampton

Papers, Box 7, Folders 1 to 3, J. Willard Marriott Library, University of Utah. Salt Lake City, Utah.

Cropper, Thomas Waters. "The History of Thomas Waters Cropper." In Armis J. Ashby, *The Robert L. Ashby and Hannah Cropper Family Book of their Descendants and Ancestors*. Salt Lake City: Ashby-Cropper Family Organization, 1991.

———. "The Life and Experience of Thomas Waters Cropper." In Robert L. Ashby, *Family History of Thomas Waters Cropper and Hannah Lucretia Rogers*, 22–26. Self-published, 1957.

Curtis, Meacham. Letter to Joseph Smith III, September 15, 1884. Community of Christ Library and Archives, Independence, MO.

Darowski, Joseph F. "Schools of the Prophets: An Early American Tradition," *Mormon Historical Studies* 9, no. 1 (Spring 2008): 1–13.

Daughters of Utah Pioneers. *Grand Memories*. Grand County, UT: Daughters of Utah Pioneers, 1972.

Department of Animal Industry. *Book of Recorded Marks and Brands, Embracing All of the Marks and Brands From the First Orginazation of the Territory to December 9th, 1874, Near Five Thousand in Number, Except Those Voluntarily Relinquished And A Few For Which the Recording was not Paid*. Salt Lake City: Deseret News, 1874.

Drinnon, Richard. *Facing West: The Metaphysics of Indian-hating and Empire-building*. Norman: University of Oklahoma Press, 1997.

Earl, Joseph Ira. Journals From the Life and Times of Joseph Ira Earl and His Wives: Elethra Calista Bunker, Agnes Viola Bunker. Compiled by Owen Ken Earl. LDS Church History Library, Salt Lake City.

Elk Mountain Mission Journal, 1855 May–October. MS 2204. LDS Church History Library, Salt Lake City.

Embry, Jesse L. "Josephites at the Top of the Mountains: RLDS Congregations in Utah," *John Whitmer Historical Association Journal* 16 (1996): 57–71.

Enders, Donald L. "The Steamboat Maid of Iowa: Mormon Mistress of the Mississippi," *BYU Studies* 19, no. 3 (July 1979): 320–36.

Esplin, Ronald K. "Joseph, Brigham and the Twelve: A Succession of Continuity," *BYU Studies* 21, no. 3 (1981): 301–41.

Eyring, Henry. The Journal of Henry Eyring, 1835–1902. LDS Church History Library, Salt Lake City.

Farnsworth, Stephen. Stephen M. Farnsworth Vision, 1844. MS 3081. LDS Church History Library, Salt Lake City.

Fish, Joseph. *Life and times of Joseph Fish: Mormon Pioneer*. Danville, IL: Interstate Printers & Publishers, 1970.

Fletcher, Rupert J., and Daisy Whiting Fletcher, *Alpheus Cutler and the Church of Jesus Christ*. Independence, MO: Church of Jesus Christ, 1973.

Foreman, Carolyn Thomas. "Dr. William Butler and George Butler, Cherokee Agents," *Chronicle of Oklahoma* 30, no. 2 (1952): 160–77.

Foreman, Grant. "Missionaries of the Latter Day Saints in Indian Territory," *Chronicles of Oklahoma* 13, no. 2 (June 1935): 196–213.

———. *The Five Civilized Tribes*. Norman, OK: University of Oklahoma Press, 1938.

"General Conference Minutes." *The Saints Herald* 30, no. 17 (April 28, 1883).

Gillen, Jas W. "Pleasant Chat." *The True Latter Day Saints' Herald* 12, no.1 (July 1, 1867): 11–12.

Gillespie, Emily Hawley. *'A Secret to Being Buried': The Diary of Emily Hawley Gillespie, 1858–1888*. Edited by Judy Nolte. Iowa City: University of Iowa Press, 1989.

Gossett, Thomas F. *Race: The History of an Idea in America*. New York: Oxford University Press, 1997.

Greene, John Portineu. *Facts Relative to the Expulsion of the Mormons or Latter Day Saints, from the State of Missouri: Under the "Exterminating Order."* Cincinnati: R. P. Brooks, 1839.

Gressman, Asher, and Effelinda [Essilinda] Gressman. Letter to Levi Moffet, November 6, 1844. In Albert Hart Sanford, "The Mormons of Mormon Coulee," *Wisconsin Magazine of History* 24, no. 2 (December 1940): 129–42.

Grey, Zane. *The Heritage of the Desert*. Roslyn, NY: Black, 1938.

———. *Robber's Roost*. New York: Collier & Son, 1935.

———. *Shadow on the Trail*. Roslyn, NY: Black, 1946.

———. *Young Lion Hunter*. New York: Harper & Row, 1939.

Grossmann, Gregory. "Central Planning and Transition in the American Desert: Latter-day Saints in Present-day Sight." *Economics Systems* 24, no. 4 (2000): 385–90.

Grow, Matthew J., Ronald K. Esplin, Mark Ashurst-McGee, Gerrit J. Dirkmaat, and Jeffrey D. Mahas, eds. *Council of Fifty, Minutes, March 1844–January 1846*. Vol 1. of the Administrative Records series of *The Joseph Smith Papers*, edited by Ronald K. Esplin, Matthew J. Grow, and Matthew C. Godfrey. Salt Lake City: Church Historian's Press, 2016.

Hafen, Arthur Knight. "A Sketch of the Life of Samuel Knight, 1832–1910." Washington County Historical Society. March 1960. http://wchsutah.org/people/samuel-knight1.pdf.

———. *Dixie Folklore and Pioneer Memories*. St. George, UT: N.p., 1964.

Halliburton, R. *Red over Black: Black Slavery among the Cherokee Indians*. Westport, CT: Greenwood Press, 1977.

Hansen, Klaus J. *Quest for Empire: The Political Kingdom of God and the Council of Fifty in Mormon History*. East Lansing: Michigan State University Press, 1967.

Hartley, William G. *My Best for the Kingdom: History and Autobiography of John Lowe Butler, a Mormon Frontiersman*. Salt Lake City: Aspen Books, 1993.

H. A. S. "Rebaptism." *The True Latter Day Saints' Herald*, 17, no. 13 (July 1, 1870): 388–93.

Hawley, John. "Autobiography of John Pierce Hawley." Edited by Robert Hawley. Hamilton, MO: Robert Hawley, 1981.

———. "Experiences of John Hawley." *Journal of History* 4, no. 2 (April 1911): 223–45.

———. Letter to Lyman Wight, August 28, 1853. Lyman Wight Letterbook. Community of Christ Library and Archives, Independence, MO.

———. Letter to Bro. Joseph, June 12, 1884, Dow City, Iowa. Community of Christ Library and Archives, Independence, MO.

———. "My Early Ministerial Life." *Autumn Leaves*, 4 (1891): 232.

———. "To the Utah Saints." *The Saint's Advocate* 2, no. 1 (July 1879): 1–3.

Hawley, Pierce. Letter to Jacob Croft, June 6, 1856. George Wise Cropper Collection, 1823–1898, LDS Church History Library, Salt Lake City.

Heninger, Suzanne. "Building a New Jerusalem: Comparison of the Anabaptists in Münster with the Latter Day Saints in Missouri & Nauvoo." *John Whitmer Historical Association Journal* 38, no. 2 (Fall/Winter 2018): 140–64.

Hicks, George Armstrong. *Family Record and History of George Armstrong Hicks, Containing the Principle Events of Life Among the Poor of Utah and the "Rants" Generally*. N.p, 1938. http://www.scribd.com/doc/18344493/Family-Record-and-History-of-Geo-A-Hicks.

Higginson, George B. Letter to Andrew Kimbal, March 1892. MS 87, LDS Church History Library, Salt Lake City.

"History of Lyman Wight." *Latter-Day Saints' Millennial Star* 27, no. 29 (July 22, 1865): 455–57.

Hixon, Adrietta Applegate. *On to Oregon! A True Story of a Young Girl's Journey into the West*. Edited by Waldo Taylor Hixon. Weiser, ID: Signal-American Printers, 1947.

Hunter, Marvin J. *The Lyman Wight Colony in Texas: Came to Bandera in 1854*. Bandera, TX: Frontier Times Museum, 1925.

"Improvements in the South." *Deseret News* 5, no. 52 (March 5, 1856): 413.

Iron Military District, 1856–1857; Muster Rolls. Territorial Militia Records, Series 2210. Utah State Archives, Salt Lake City.

Ivins, Anthony W. Letter to Mrs. G. T. Welch, October 18, 1922. MS 4222, LDS Church History Library, Salt Lake City.

"Jacob Croft Company Reports, 1856." CR 1234 5, Brigham Young Office Emigrating Companies Reports, 1850–1862. LDS Church History Library, Salt Lake City.

J[aques], J[ohn]. "Some Reminiscences." *Salt Lake Herald-Republican* 9, no. 175 (December 29, 1878): 1.

Jennings, James H. "Sketch of James H. Jennings Historical Sketch, 1935." USU_COLL MSS 18, Federal Writer's Project, Mormon Diaries, 1820–1936, Utah State University Special Collections and Archives, Logan, UT.

Jeffrey, Julie Roy. *Frontier Women: The Trans-Mississippi West, 1840–1880*. New York: Hill and Wang, 1998.

Jenson, Andrew. "The Elk Mountain Mission." *The Utah Genealogical and Historical Magazine* 4 (1913): 188–200.

Jesse, Dean C., and David J. Whittaker. "The Last Months of Mormonism in Missouri: The Albert Perry Rockwood Journal." *BYU Studies* 28, no. 2 (Winter 1988): 5–41.

Johnson, Clark V., ed. *Mormon Redress Petitions: Documents of the 1833–1838 Missouri Conflict*. Provo, Utah: Religious Studies Center, Brigham Young University, 2017.

Johnson, Joel H. Joel H. Johnson Autobiography, Circa 1882. MS 15025, LDS Church History Library, Salt Lake City.

Johnson, Melvin C. "Bishop George Miller: A Latter Day High Priest and Prince on the High Plains." *John Whitmer Historical Association Journal* 34, no. 1 (Spring/Summer 2014): 85–106.

———. "John Hawley, Mormon Ulysses: His LDS Mission to Iowa and Eventual RLDS Conversion." *John Whitmer Historical Association Journal* 35, no. 2

(Fall/Winter 2016): 43–72.

———. "The Mormon Cowboys of Bandera County and the Texas Hill Country," *West Texas Historical Association Year Book* 80 (2004): 159–77.

———. *Polygamy on the Pedernales: Lyman Wight's Mormon Villages in Antebellum Texas, 1845–1858*. Logan: Utah State University Press, 2006.

———. "'So We Built a Good Little Temple to Worship In': Mormonism on the Pedernales–Texas, 1847–1851," *John Whitmer Historical Association Journal* 22 (2002): 89–99.

———. "Wightites in Wisconsin: The Formation of a Dissenting Latter Day Community (1842- 1845)." *John Whitmer Historical Association Journal* 32, no. 1 (Spring/Summer 2012): 63–78.

Jones, Christopher C. "The Power and Form of Godliness: Methodist Conversion Narratives and Joseph Smith's First Vision," *Journal of Mormon History* 37, no. 2 (Spring 2011): 88–114.

Journal of Discourses. 26 vol. London and Liverpool: LDS Booksellers Depot, 1854–86.

Journal History of The Church of Jesus Christ of Latter-day Saints. LDS Church History Library, Salt Lake City.

Kelly, Alfred H., Winfred A. Harbison, and Herman Belz. *The American Constitution: Its Origins and Development*. New York: Norton, 1991.

Kimball, Solomon F. "Sacred History." MS 3220, LDS Church History Library, Salt Lake City.

King, Henry. Letter to John Chambers, July 14, 1843. Iowa Superintendency, 1838–1849, Letters Received by the Office of Indian Affairs, 1824–1881, BIA Microfilm #363, 357–60.

Knight, Newel. Newel Knight Autobiography, circa 1871. MS 19156, LDS Church History Library, Salt Lake City.

"Lady Brings A.W., The." *Northern Islander* 6, no. 5 (May 22, 1856): 4.

Larson, Gustave O. "The Mormon Reformation." *Utah Historical Quarterly* 26, no. 1 (January 1958): 45–63.

Launius, Roger D. *Alexander William Doniphan: Portrait of a Missouri Moderate*. Columbia: University of Missouri Press, 1997.

Lee, John Doyle. *Confessions of John D. Lee: A Photomechanical Reprint of Mormonism Unveiled; or, The Life and Confessions of the Late Mormon Bishop; John D. Lee, 1880 ed.* Salt Lake City: Modern Microfilm, 1970.

———. *A Mormon Chronicle: The Diaries of John D. Lee 1848 –1876*. Edited and annotated by Robert Glass Cleland and Juanita Brooks. San Marino, CA: Huntington Library, 2003.

Lensink, Judy Nolte, and Christine M. Kirkham. "'My Only Confidant'—The Life and Diary of Emily Hawley Gillespie." *The Annals of Iowa* 45, no. 4 (1980): 288–312.

Leonard, Glen M. *Nauvoo: A Place of Peace, A People of Promise*. Salt Lake City: Deseret Book, 2002.

LeSueur, Stephen C. *The 1838 Mormon War in Missouri*. Columbia: University of Missouri Press, 1987.

———. "The Danites Reconsidered: Were They Vigilantes or Just the Mormon Version of the Elks Club?" *John Whitmer Historical Association Journal* 14 (1994): 35–51.

Levi Moffet vs. Charles Ross, 1844–1845. Des Moines District Court, Iowa County. MS 12681. LDS Church History Library, Salt Lake City.

Leyland, William. "The Mormon Colony (Zodiac) Near Fredericksburg, Texas." In Heman Hale Smith, "The Lyman Wight Colony in Texas." Community of Christ Library and Archives, Independence, MO.

Lund, Terry, and Nora Lund. *Pulsipher Family History Book*. Salt Lake City: Ivin L. Holt, 2007.

Lyman, Edward Leo. *Amasa Mason Lyman, Mormon Apostle and Apostate: A Study in Dedication*. Salt Lake City: University of Utah Press, 2009.

———. "Southern Paiute Relations with Their Early Dixie Mormon Neighbors." Proceedings of the 27th Annual Juanita Brooks Lecture Series, Dixie State University, St. George, UT. https://library.dixie.edu/special_collections/Juanita_Brooks_ lectures/2010.pdf.

MacKinnon, William P, ed.. *At Sword's Point, Part 1: A Documentary History of the Utah War to 1858*. Vol. 10 of *Kingdom in the West: The Mormons and the American Frontier*. Norman, OK: The Arthur H. Clarke, 2008.

———. "'Lonely Bones': Leadership and Utah War Violence," *Journal of Mormon History* 33, no. 1 (Spring 2007): 121–78.

Marks, William. "Epistle of William Marks." *Zion's Harbinger and Baneemy's Organ* 3, no. 7 (July 1853): 52–54.

Martineau, James H. Parowan Utah Stake History, 1851–1980. M277.9247 P257 1981, LDS Church History Library, Salt Lake City.

Mattes, Merrill. *The Great Platte River Road: The Covered Wagon Mainline via Fort Kearny to Fort Laramie*. Lincoln: University of Nebraska Press, 1988.

McArthur, Aaron. *St. Thomas: A History Uncovered*. Reno: University of Nevada Press, 2014.

McBride, William. Report of Tooele Expedition No 3, June 24, 1851. Territorial Militia Records, Series 2210, Reel 1, Utah State Archives, Salt Lake City.

McCourt, Tom, and Wade Allinson. *The Elk Mountain Mission: A History of Moab, Mormons, the Old Spanish Trail and the Sheberetch Utes, 1854–1855*. Price, UT: Southpaw Publications, 2017.

Mead, Elwood. *Bulletin 124: Report of Irrigation Investigations in Utah*. Bulletin (United States. Office of Experiment Stations) no. 124, Washington Government Printing Office, 1905.

Miles, Zaidee Walker. "Pioneer Women of Dixie." Library of Congress Manuscript Division, WPA Writer's Project Collection, 2. http://www.forefamilies.org/washington/wpa/women.html.

Miller, A. W. "The Cherokee Nation." *Latter-Day Saints' Millennial Star* 17, no. 40 (October 6, 1855): 637–38.

Miller, George. *Correspondence of Bishop George Miller with the Northern Islander from his first acquaintance with Mormonism up to near the close of his life. Written by himself in the year 1855*. Burlington: W. Watson, ca. 1915.

Miller, Henry W. Diary, 1855 April–1862 October. MS 1888, LDS Church History Library, Salt Lake City.

———. Letter to George A. Smith, August 8, 1855. MS 1322, George A. Smith

Papers, LDS Church History Library, Salt Lake City.
Mills, H. W. "De Tal Palo Tal Astilla." *Annual Publication of the Historical Society of Southern California* 10, no. 3 (1917): 86–174.
Minutes of Missionary Meeting, Salt Lake City, Seventies Hall, April 8, 1855. CR 100 318, Historian's Office General Church Minutes, 1839–1877, LDS Church History Library, Salt Lake City.
Montague, George. "Reminiscences." *Autumn Leaves* 9, no. 9 (September 1896): 388–89.
———. "Reminiscences No. 2." *Autumn Leaves* 10, no. 1 (January 1897): 73.
Morgan, Dale. *Dale Morgan on the Mormons: Collected Works, Part 2, 1949–1970*, Richard Saunders ed. Norman, Oklahoma: The Arthur H. Clark, 2013.
"Mrs. Taylor Dead." *Ogden Daily Standard*, June 12, 1905, 6.
Munkres, Robert L. "The Plains Indian Threat on the Oregon Trail Before 1860." *Annals of Wyoming* 40, no. 2 (October 1968): 193–221.
Murphy, Thomas W. "Imagining Lamanites: Native Americans and the Book of Mormon." PhD diss., University of Washington, 2003.
Newell, Linda King, and Valeen Tippets Avery. *Mormon Enigma: Emma Hale Smith*. 2nd ed. Urbana: University of Illinois Press, 1994.
"News From Elders." *The Deseret News* 6, no. 14 (June 11, 1856): 5.
Novak, Shannon A. "The Mountain Meadows Massacre." *Archaeology*, September 16, 2003. https://archive.archaeology.org/online/features/massacre/meadows.html.
———. *House of Mourning: A Biocultural History of the Mountain Meadows Massacre*. Salt Lake City: University of Utah Press, 2008.
Novak, Shannon A., and Derinna Kopp. "To Feed a Tree in Zion: Osteological Analysis of the 1857 Mountain Meadows Massacre." *Historical Archaeology* 37, no. 2 (2003): 85–108.
Novak, Shannon A., and Lars Rodseth. "Remembering Mountain Meadows: Collective Violence and the Manipulation of Social Boundaries," *Journal of Anthropological Research* 62, no. 1 (Spring 2006): 1–25.
"Obituary: Isaac Sheen." *The True Latter Day Saints' Herald* 21, no. 8 (April 15, 1974): 240–41.
Olch, Peter D. "Treading the Elephant's Tail: Medical Problems on the Overland Trails," *Bulletin of the History of Medicine* 59, no. 2 (Summer 1985): 196–212.
Oullette, Richard Donald. "The Mormon Temple Lot Case: Space, Memory, and Identity in a Divided New Religion." PhD diss., The University of Texas at Austin, 2012.
Pace, William B. William B. Pace Autobiography, 1904. MS 13067, LDS Church History Library, Salt Lake City.
Parowan Utah Stake Melchizedek Priesthood Minutes and Records, 1855–1973. Vol. 1, 1855–1887. LR 6778 13, LDS Church History Library, Salt Lake City.
Parowan Ward General Minutes, 1851–1926. LR 6775 11, LDS Church History Library, Salt Lake City.
Perdue, Theda. *Slavery and the Evolution of Cherokee Society, 1540–1866*. Knoxville: University of Tennessee Press, 1993.
Petersen, Wanda Snow. *William Snow, First Bishop of Pine Valley, A Man Without Guile*. American Fork, UT: N.p., 1992.

Peterson, Paul H. "The Mormon Reformation of 1856–1857: The Rhetoric and the Reality." *Journal of Mormon History* 15 (1989): 59–87.

Pioneer Pathways. 11 vols. Compiled by the Lesson Committee of the International Society of the Daughters of Utah Pioneers. Salt Lake City: International Society of the Daughters of Utah Pioneers, 1998–2008.

Platt, Elsie Hawley, and Robert Hawley. *House of Hawley*. Port Huron, MI: N.p., 1909.

Porter, Nathan Tanner. "Nathan T. Porter Reminiscences, circa 1879." MS 618, LDS Church History Library, Salt Lake City.

Pratt, Orson. "Celestial Marriage." *The Seer* 1, no. 11 (November 1853): 169–76; *The Seer* 1, no. 12 (December 1853): 183–92.

Pulsipher, Zerah. "History of Zera Pulsipher, As Written by Himself." BX 8670.1.P969, Harold B. Lee Library, Brigham Young University, Provo, UT.

Quinn, D. Michael. *The Mormon Hierarchy: Origins of Power*. Salt Lake City: Signature Books, 1994.

———, ed. *The New Mormon History: Revisionist Essays on the Past*. Salt Lake City: Signature Books, 1992.

Rannie, Edward. *Marvelous Manifestations of God's Power in the Latter Days*. Independence, MO: Ensign Publishing House, 1910.

Rea, Tom. *Devil's Gate, Owning The Land, Owning The Story*. Norman: University of Oklahoma Press, 2006.

Reorganized Church of Jesus Christ of Latter Day Saints. *The Reorganized Church of Jesus Christ of Latter Day Saints, Complainant, Vs. the Church of Christ at Independence, Missouri: Richard Hill, Trustee; Richard Hill, Mrs. E. Hill, C.A. Hall [and Others] . . . as Members of and Doing Business Under the Name of The Church of Christ, at Independence, Missouri, Respondents. In Equity Complainant's Abstract of Pleading and Evidence*. Lamoni, IA: Herald Publishing House, 1893.

"Report of the Returned Elders," *Northern Islander* 6, no. 4 (May 1, 1856): 2.

Reeve, W. Paul. *Making Space on the Western Frontier: Mormons, Miners, and Southern Paiutes*. Urbana: University of Illinois Press, 2006.

Richards, Franklin D., and Daniel Spencer. "Journey from Florence to G. S. L. City." *The Deseret News* 6, no. 33 (October 22, 1856): 2.

Richards, Samuel W. Journals and Family Record, 1846–1876. MS 8495, LDS Church History Library, Salt Lake City.

Richards, Willard. Diary Entries, December 2–11, 1842. Joseph Smith's Office Papers, 1835–1844. MS 21600, LDS Church History Library, Salt Lake City.

Riddle, Isaac. Letter to Brigham Young, December 9, 1858. Brigham Young Office Files, 1832–1878, General Correspondence, Incoming, 1840–1877, General Letters, 1840–1877, Pen-R, 1858. CR 1234 1, LDS Church History Library, Salt Lake City.

Roberts, Brigham H. *A Comprehensive History of the Church of Jesus Christ of Latter-day Saints: Century I*. 6 vols. Salt Lake City: Deseret Book, 1930.

Roberts, David. *Devil's Gate: Brigham Young and the Great Mormon Handcart Tragedy*. New York: Simon & Schuster, 2009.

Robinson, Joseph Lee. Autobiography and Journals, 1883–1892. MS 1920, LDS Church History Library, Salt Lake City.

Rogers, Jedediah S, ed. *The Council of Fifty: A Documentary History*. Salt Lake City: Signature Books, 2014.
Rowley, Dennis. "The Mormon Experience in the Wisconsin Pineries, 1841–1845." *BYU Studies* 32, no. 1 (1992): 119–48.
"Rules for Teachers." On display at Fort Croghan Museum, Burnet, TX.
Schlissel, Lillian. *Women's Diaries of the Westward Journey*. New York: Shocken Books, 2013.
Seventh Census of the United States, 1850, NARA microfilm publication M432, Record Group 29. Washington, DC: National Archives and Records Administration, n.d.
Sharp, Cornelia A. "Diary of Mrs. Cornelia A. Sharp: Crossing the Plains from Missouri to Oregon in 1852." In *Transactions of the Thirty-first Annual Reunion of the Oregon Pioneer Association*, 171–88. Portland, OR: Peaslee Bros. Company, 1904.
Sheen, Isaac, ed. "A Revelation, given March 20, 1850, in Covington, Kentucky." *Melchisedek & Aaronic Herald* 1, no. 9 (April 1850): 1.
———. "Polygamy Contrary to the Revelations of God." *The True Latter Day Saints' Herald* 1, no. 1 (January 1860): 6–11.
Shepard, William, and H. Michael Marquardt. *Lost Apostles: Forgotten Members of Mormonism's Original Quorum of Twelve*. Salt Lake City: Signature Books, 2014.
"Sketch of the Life of Bishop William Davis." Book of Abraham Project. Accessed February 7, 2019. http://www.boap.org/LDS/Early-Saints/WDavis.htm.
Smart, William B., and Donna T Smart. *Over the Rim: The Parley P. Pratt Exploring Expedition to Southern Utah, 1849–1850*. Logan: Utah State University Press, 1999.
Smith, Anna C. Letter to Spencer Smith, 1850. Typescript prepared by author, original in possession of Ron Fox, Salt Lake City.
Smith, Christopher C. "'The Whites Want Everything': Mormon Conquest of the Wasatch Front and Range, 1847–1851." PhD diss., Claremont Graduate University, 2016.
Smith, George A. and Ezra T. Benson. Letter to Brigham Young, October 7, 1878. Brigham Young Office Files, 1832–1878, General Correspondence, Incoming, 1840–1877, Letters from Church Leaders and Others, 1840–1877, George A. Smith, 1848-1849. CR 1234 1, LDS Church History Library, Salt Lake City.
Smith, Heman C. "The Truth Defended, or, A Reply to Elder D. H. Bays' Doctrines and Dogmas of Mormonism." Lamoni, IA: Board of Publication of the Reorganized Church of Jesus Christ of Latter Day Saints, 1905.
Smith, Heman Hale. "George Miller." *Journal of History* 2, no. 2 (April 1909): 225–32.
Smith, Joseph. Blessing given by Joseph Smith Jr. to Lyman Wight, Kirtland, Ohio, 29 December 1835, recorded 1 January 1836, with Oliver Cowdery, recorder, and Frederick G. Williams, clerk. Patriarchal Blessings, Vol. 2 (transcript 53): 56. Community of Christ Library and Archives, Independence, MO.
———. Contract with Arthur Morrison and Pulaski S. Cahoon. In Helen B. Flemmin Collection, 1836–1963. MS 9670, LDS Church History Library, Salt Lake City.

Smith, Joseph, et al. *History of the Church of Jesus Christ of Latter-day Saints*. Edited by B. H. Roberts, 7 vols., 2nd ed. rev. Salt Lake City: Deseret Book, 1948 printing.

Smith, Joseph III. Letter to Bertha M. Smith, January 27, 1893. Miscellaneous Letters and Papers, Community of Christ Library and Archives, Independence, MO.

———. "Opposition to Polygamy." *The True Latter Day Saints Herald*, 1 (January 1860): 25–26.

———. "Statements of Joseph Smith." Compiled by Heman Hale Smith. *Journal of History* 12, no. 4 (October 1919): 400–47.

Smith, Joseph III, and Heman C. Smith. *The History of the Reorganized Church of Jesus Christ of Latter Day Saints*, 4 Volumes. Lamoni, Iowa, 1896–1903.

Smith, Vida E. "Two Widows of the Brick Row." *Journal of History* 3, no. 2 (April 1910): 202–12.

Smithwick, Noah. *Evolution of a State: or, Recollections of Old Texas Days*. Salem, MA: Higginson Book Company, 2007.

Snow, Eliza R. "Address." *The Latter-day Saints' Millennial Star* 17, no. 20 (May 19, 1855): 320.

Snow, Erastus. Letter to Brigham Young, January 5, 1862. Brigham Young Office Files, 1832–1878, General Correspondence, Incoming, 1840–1877, Letters from Church Leaders and Others, 1840–1877, Erastus Snow, 1860–1863. CR 1234 1, LDS Church History Library, Salt Lake City.

———. Letter to Brigham Young, September 9, 1862. Brigham Young Office Files, 1832–1878, General Correspondence, Incoming, 1840–1877, Letters from Church Leaders and Others, 1840–1877, Erastus Snow, 1860–1863. CR 1234 1, LDS Church History Library, Salt Lake City.

———. Letter to Brigham Young, February 12, 1863. Brigham Young Office Files, 1832–1878, General Correspondence, Incoming, 1840–1877, Letters from Church Leaders and Others, 1840–1877, Erastus Snow, 1860–1863. CR 1234 1, LDS Church History Library, Salt Lake City.

———. Letter to Brigham Young, September 28, 1863. Brigham Young Office Files, 1832–1878, General Correspondence, Incoming, 1840–1877, Letters from Church Leaders and Others, 1840–1877, Erastus Snow, 1860–1863. CR 1234 1, LDS Church History Library, Salt Lake City.

———. Letter to Brigham Young, February 24, 1867. Brigham Young Office Files, Letters from Church Leaders and Others, 1840–1877, box 42 fd. 19. CR 1234 1, LDS Church History Library, Salt Lake City.

———. Letter to Brigham Young, November 7, 1869. Brigham Young Office Files, 1832–1878, General Correspondence, Incoming, 1840–1877, Letters from Church Leaders and Others, 1840–1877, Erastus Snow, 1867–1869. CR 1234 1, LDS Church History Library, Salt Lake City.

———. Letter to Daniel H. Wells, May 28, 1866. Roll 3, Item # 1,527. Territorial Militia Records, Series 2210. Utah State Archives, Salt Lake City.

Snow, Minerva White. "Temple Workers: Biographical Sketch of the Life and Labors of Minerva White Snow." *The Young Women's Journal*, Vol 4, no. 7 (April 1893): 300–302.

Snow, William. Excerpts From the Diary of William Snow. M270.1 S6748s, LDS Church History Library, Salt Lake City.

Sperry, Kip. "Migration, Emigration and Immigration Records." In *A Guide to Mormon Family History Sources*, 61–68. Provo, UT: Ancestry Publishing, 2007.

Stott, Graham St. John. "Zane Grey and James Simpson Emmett," *BYU Studies* 18, no. 4 (October 1978): 491–503.

Stubblefield, Laurel Hawley. *Pierce Hawley 1788–1858: A History of His Family and Their Conversion to The Church of Jesus Christ of Latter-Day Saints*. Yuba City, CA: L. H. Stubblefield, 2000.

Swartzell, William. *Mormonism Exposed, Being a Journal of Residence in Missouri from the 28th of May to the 20th of August, 1838*. Salt Lake City: Utah Lighthouse Ministry, circa 1992.

Symes, M. Shane. "Robert Cowan Petty, 1812–1856." Find A Grave. Accessed January 1, 2019. https://www.findagrave.com/memorial/55977822/robert-cowan-petty/.

Taylor, John. Letter to Joseph Smith III, March 2, 1875. In *The True Latter Day Saints Herald* 22 (April 15, 1875): 249.

Taylor, Lori Elaine. "Telling Stories about Mormons and Indians." PhD diss., State University of New York at Buffalo, 2000.

Thomas, Daniel H. *Preston Thomas, 1814–1877, a Biography*. N.p., 1940.

Turk, Toni R. *Mormons in Texas: The Lyman Wight Colony*. Port Lavaca, TX: N.p., 1987.

Tom, Gary, and Ronald Holt. "The Paiute Tribe of Utah." In *A History of Utah's American Indians*, edited by Forest S. Cuch, 123–65. Logan: Utah State University Press, 2014.

Van Cott, John W. *Utah Place Names: A Comprehensive Guide to the Origins of Geographic Names: A Compilation*. Salt Lake City: University of Utah Press, 1990.

Van Wagoner, Richard S. *Sidney Rigdon: A Portrait of Religious Excess*. Salt Lake City: Signature Books, 2006.

———. "Mormon Polyandry in Nauvoo." *Dialogue: A Journal of Mormon Thought* 18, no. 3 (Fall 1985): 67–83.

Van Wagoner, Richard S., and Mary C. Van Wagoner. "Orson Pratt Jr.: Gifted Son of an Apostle and an Apostate." *Dialogue: A Journal of Mormon Thought* 21, no. 1 (Spring 1988): 84–94.

Van Wagenen, Michael. *The Texas Republic and the Mormon Kingdom of God*. College Station, TX: Texas A&M University Press, 2002.

———. "The Texas Republic and the Mormon Kingdom of God: The Attempt to Establish a Theocratic Nation in the Texas-Mexico Borderlands in 1844," Master's thesis. University of Texas at Brownsville and Texas Southmost College, 1999.

Vaughan, Alden T. *Roots of American Racism: Essays on the Colonial Experience*. New York: Oxford University Press, 1995.

Walch, Tad. "New study: Mormon Pioneers Were Safer on Trek than Previously Thought, Especially Infants," *Deseret News*, July 20, 2014.

Walker, Charles L. *Diary of Charles Lowell Walker*. Edited by A. Karl Larson and Katharine M. Larson. Logan: Utah State University Press, 1980.

Walker, Ronald W., Richard E. Turley Jr., and Glen M. Leonard. *Massacre at Mountain Meadows*. New York: Oxford University Press, 2011.

Wardell, Morris L. *A Political History of the Cherokee Nation, 1839–1907*. Norman: University of Oklahoma Press, 1977.

Webb, Loren. "Southern Utah Memories: Newspapers of Washington County, Utah, 1864 to 1994 - Part 1 of a two-part series." Aired December 15, 2012, on KCGS, Saint George, UT.

Weberhistory. "Home Page & 1849–1869 Chronology." *History of 2nd Street, Ogden, Utah: Stories of Bingham's Fort, Lynne, Five Points*, April 27, 2012. https://binghamsfort.org/category/1-home-page-1849-1869-chronology/.

Weeks, Sue Jensen. *How Desolate Our Home Bereft of Thee: James Tillman Sanford Allred and the Circleville Massacre*. Thornbury: Clouds of Magellan, 2014.

Wiggins, Rhea Farr. "Lorin Farr." Family Search. Accessed January 9, 2019. http://www.familysearch.org/photos/stories/1110511/lorin-farr.

Wight, Levi Lamoni. "Autobiography of Levi Lamoni Wight." *Journal of History* 9, no. 3 (July 1916): 259–88.

Wight, Lyman. *An Address by Way of an Abridged Account and Journal of My Life from February 1844 up to April 1848, with an Appeal to the Latter Day Saints*. Pamphlet, 2. M270.1 W657w, LDS Church History Library, Salt Lake City.

———. Letter to Cooper and Chidester, July 1855. Lyman Wight Letterbook, Community of Christ Archives, Independence, MO.

———. Letter to William Smith, July 26, 1849. In *Melchisidek and Aaronic Herald* 1, no. 6 (September 1849): 2.

Wight, Orange Lysander. Letter to Stephen Wight and Wilford Woodruff, September 17, 1858. Wilford Woodruff Collection, 1831–1905. MS 19509, LDS Church History Library, Salt Lake City.

———. "Recollections of Orange L. Wight: Son of Lyman Wight." M270.1 W657wig, LDS Church History Library, Salt Lake City.

Willes, William, and Gilbert Clements. "Great Reformation." *Deseret News* 6, no. 29 (September 24, 1856): 4.

Wilson, William A. "Folklore of Dixie: Past and Present." Paper presented at the 22nd Annual Lecture, The Juanita Brooks Lecture Series, St. George, UT, March 2, 2005.

Winkler, Albert. "The Circleville Massacre: A Brutal Incident in Utah's Black Hawk War." *Utah Historical Quarterly* 55, no. 1 (Winter 1987): 4–21.

Winn, Kenneth H. *Exiles in a Land of Liberty: Mormons in America, 1830–1846*. Chapel Hill: University of North Carolina Press, 1990.

Woodruff, Wilford. Journal of Wilford Woodruff. M270.1 W893j, LDS Church History Library, Salt Lake City.

Woods, Fred. "Immigration to Utah and Early Settlement of Spanish Fork." In *Fire on Ice: The story of Icelandic Latter-day Saints at Home and Abroad*, 31–46. Provo, UT: Religious Studies Center, Brigham Young University, 2005.

WPA. *Oklahoma: A Guide to the Sooner State*. Compiled by the Workers of the Writers' Program of the Works Progress Administration in the State of Oklahoma. Norman: The University of Oklahoma Press, 1945.

Young, Brigham. Letter to Bishop Zadok K. Judd, Fort Clara, February 24, 1860. Brigham Young Office Files and Transcriptions, 1974–1978, Letterbook, Vol. 5, 1859 December 6–1860 March 8. MS 2736, LDS Church History Library, Salt Lake City.

———. Letter to Elder Erastus Snow, June 30, 1855. Brigham Young Office Files and Transcriptions, 1974–1978, Letterbook, Vol. 2, 1855 May 16–August. MS 2736, LDS Church History Library, Salt Lake City.

———. Letter to Elder Henry W. Miller, November 28, 1855. Brigham Young Office Files and Transcriptions, 1974–1978, Letterbook, Vol. 2, 1855 November 30–1856 March 7. MS 2736, LDS Church History Library, Salt Lake City.

———. Letter to Jacob Croft, December 2, 1857. Brigham Young Office Files and Transcriptions, 1974–1978, Letterbook, Vol. 3, 1857 August 15–1858 January 6. MS 2736, LDS Church History Library, Salt Lake City.

———. Letter to John Taylor, January 26, 1857. Brigham Young Office Files and Transcriptions, 1974–1978, Letterbook, Vol. 3, 1857 January 3–March 1. MS 2736, LDS Church History Library, Salt Lake City.

———. *The Office Journal of President Brigham Young, Book D, 1858–1863*. Edited by Fred C. Collier. Hanna, UT: Collier's Publishing, 2006.

Young, Priscilla. Statement, Holden Stake, 1923. Miscellaneous Collection. P13 f1515, Community of Christ Library and Archives, Independence, MO.

Index

A

Adair, Samuel, 71
Adair Springs, 71
Adam–God doctrine, vii, 17, 148, 150n37
Alger, John, 89
Alley, John, viii
Allred, James T., 96
Ambrosia, 12, 171, 185

B

Babbitt, Almon, 59–60, 137
Bagley, Will, viii, xvi, 49, 51–52
Ballantyne, Andrew, 135
baptism for the dead, xv, 12, 22, 147, 150, 181
Barkdull, Jen, ix
Barlow, Oswald, 115
Barron, Alexander, 34
Berry, Isabella, 102
Berry, Joseph, 102
Berry, Robert, 102
Bateman, William, 77
Bayse (Bays), Henry, 22, 30, 138
Bennett, Richard E., xv,
Benson, Ezra T., 36, 85
Bertice, Sam, 53, 56
Bingham, Erastus, 63
Bird, Phineas, 17–18
Black Hawk War, 4, 158, 185
Black River lumber mission, 13–14, 16–18, 36, 41
Blackburn, Jehu, 82
Blair, Alma R., 136
Blair, Seth Millington, 91, 108, 163
Blair, W. W., 153
Bleak, James Godson, 82, 96, 99, 100–103, 106, 108–9, 128, 141, 151
Blythe, Chris, vii
Boggs, Lilburn W., 7
Booth, Ty, viii
Borkhoefer, Robert F., 97
Brand, [Elder], 153
Bricker, William, 39
Briggs, E. C., 132
Brighamites, xiii, 37, 42, 138, 145, 153, 160, 181
Brooks, Juanita, vii, xvi, 78n53
Brown, John, 119
Brown, Lorenzo, 79, 89, 114–16, 118–20, 122–23, 126–29, 156
Brown, Sarah, 119
Bryce, George, 115
Burgess, Harrison, 129, 140, 144
Burgess Mill, 89–90, 118
Burgon, George, 90, 141, 159
Burton, John, 105–6
Butler, George, 40–41
Butler, William F., 68

C

Campbell, Alexander, 14
Cannon, D. H., 115
Cannon, George Q., 138
Carleton, James M., 78–79
Case, James, 39
Chatterley, John, 65–66
Circleville Massacre, 96–97
Clapp, Benjamin L., 42, 49,
Clark, William O., 5–6, 9, 82, 171, 185
Clayton, William, 51
Cluff, Harvey Harris, 50, 59
Coats, William, 34–35
Community of Christ, vii, xii–xiii, 138n29, 169
Compton, Todd, viii, 103
Cook, Washington N., 38, 40,
Corrill, John, 4
Council of Fifty, 13, 87
Covington, Robert, 71
Cowdery, Oliver, 32
Cowley, William, 115
Cradlebaugh, John, 79

Craigham, Jesse, 118
Croft, Frances, 38
Croft, Jacob (Jacob Croft Company) xvi, 33–42, 45, 47–49, 52–59, 61, 64, 73, 105, 118, 137
Croft, Sebrina Cropper, 33–34, 51
Cropper, George, 53
Cropper, Leigh, 53
Cropper, Thomas Waters, 35, 46, 51–57
Crosby, J. W., 115
Crosby, William, 109
Crouch, George, 38
Curtis, Patience, 20, 23
Curtis, William, 26, 70
Cutler, Alpheus, 8n28, 9, 14n4, 16

D

Dame, William Horne, 77, 96, 105, 109
Dan (slave), 51, 105
Davidson family tragedy, 93
Derry, Charles, 135, 138, 164,
Dixie College, vii, viii
Dobson, Thomas, 135–36
Doniphan, Alexander W., 7
Drake, Cynthia Parker Johnson, 32
Drake, Daniel Newell, 32
Drake, Saminay, 38
Duggins, John, 54
Duggins, Stephen A., 36, 37, 42, 53

E

Earl, Harriet Martenisia Wight, 30n3, 37, 70
Earl, Mary Langley, 70
Earl, Sarah Wight, 162–63
Earl, Wilbur Bradley, 70
Egan, Howard, 72, 93
elephant, the (saw), 89
Emmet (Eldridge), Emily Dorcas 144, 145n12, 148, 157
Emmett, James, 81, 145n12, 185
Emmett, James Simpson, 156
endowment, xv, 22, 26–27, 67, 73, 129, 131, 133–34, 142, 148n26, 167, 172–75, 177–81
Enos (Indian), 100
Eyring, Henry, 36, 39–40, 141

F

Family, The, 14–15
Fancher–Baker Wagon Train, 74, 77
Farnsworth Stephen, 113, 134

Farr, Lorin, 63
Fife, Alta S., viii
Fife, Austin E., viii
Fish, Joseph, 97
Flavel, William O., 39
Forscutt, Mark H., 138n29
Forsyth (Forsythe), Robert, 11
Forsythe, Thomas, 89–90, 118
Fredericksburg, 21, 22
Freestone, 81

G

Garberry (Sister), 24
Gardner, Robert, 88–89, 118, 121, 141
Gardner, William, 88
Gardner's Mill, 89
Gates, Jacob, 109, 115, 141
Gerland, Jonathan L., viii
Gibbons, Richard C., 110, 146–47
Goodale (Choosdale) Joseph D. 32, 38
Gossett, Thomas F., 98
Goudy (Goudie), Jeannette, 40, 61, 84, 159
Grant, Jedidiah M., 64–65
Gray, Benjamin, 118
Grey, Zane, 156,–57
Grossman, Gregory, 50n18, 107, 130, 146
Gurley, Zenos, xi, xiii,

H

Hacksaw, Enoch, 39, 40, 53
Hacksaw, Rebecca Hewitt, 40
Hadfield (Hatfield), Joseph, 37, 71, 84, 117
Hadfield, Sarah, 20, 30n3, 38, 55, 61, 70, 71n29, 84, 117, 119, 158, 159n11, 162n17
Hall, J. A., 106
Hamblin, Jacob, 72n37, 74–75, 79, 81, 89, 100, 102, 104, 118, 158
Hardy, Augustus P., 96, 104
Hardy, Pansy, vii
Hamblin, Oscar, 77
Hamilton, Samuel, 86
Harriman, Henry, 109, 141
Haskell, Thales H., 104
Hatch, Ira, 78
Haun's Mill, 7, 79
Hawley, Aaron (brother of John Pierce Hawley), xv, 6, 9, 29, 31, 139, 163, 185
Hawley, Aaron (brother of Pierce Hawley), 4
Hawley, Aaron (Major), 1

Hawley, Abinadi, 29–30, 64
Hawley, Alma, 29–30
Hawley, Ann Hadfield, 38, 84
Hawley, Eber Pierce, 30, 165
Hawley, Francis Aaron Frank, 30, 164
Hawley, Gazelam, 30, 131, 144, 162,
Hawley, George, vii–viii, xvi–xvii, 30, 31n3, 37–38, 51, 67, 70, 75n47, 82, 84, 89, 113, 116–17, 119, 122, 130, 152n43, 159, 164, 186
Hawley, Gideon (brother of John Pierce Hawley), 139
Hawley, Gideon (brother of Pierce Hawley), 2–3, 5, 139, 185
Hawley, Gideon (uncle of Pierce Hawley), 1
Hawley, Isaac (brother of John Pierce Hawley), 38, 53
Hawley, Isaac Zimri (son of John Pierce Hawley), 30
Hawley, John (son of John Pierce Hawley), 30
Hawley, Joseph, 1
Hawley, Lavinia Darrough, 1–2
Hawley, Lucy Lovina, 30
Hawley, Mary (wife of Lyman Wight), 6, 8, 20, 21, 30, 159,
Hawley, Mary Caroline Carrie (daughter of John Pierce Hawley), 30, 164
Hawley, Nancy Matheny, 40, 53
Hawley, Pierce, xi, xv, xvi, 1–6, 8,–12, 17–18, 21–22, 25, 29–30, 32, 38, 41–42, 139, 145n12, 175, 185, 186
Hawley, Sarah (daughter of John Pierce Hawley), 30, 40
Hawley, Sarah Schroeder, 2–4, 12, 162
Hawley, Sylvia Amelia (daughter of John Pierce Hawley) 30, 119, 162
Hawley, Sylvia Johnson, xii, xv, 24–26, 29, 38, 67, 74, 84, 133, 155, 158, 162, 186
Hawley, William (brother of John Pierce Hawley), xvi, 6, 38, 40, 53, 71, 75n47
Hawley, William Nephi (son of John Pierce Hawley), 30, 119, 125, 162
Hawley's Grove, 12, 185
Haws, Peter, 16
Hewitt, Richard, 32, 33n11
Hicks, George Armstrong, 65, 149
Hicks, Jefferson, 40
Higbee, John M., 77
Higginson, George B., 39–40
Hobart, Harriet, 15, 23–24, 186

Houston, Sam, 19, 108
Huffman, Andrew, 26
Hunt, Jefferson, 72, 93
Hutchins, James C., 37
Hyde, Orson, 173

I

Indian Bill, 102
Ivins, Anthony W., 79, 103

J

Jacques, John, 47–48
Jeffrey, Julie, 99
Johnson, Eber (Heber), 24, 38, 46
Johnson, Sally, 24, 46
Johnson, Sarey Jane, 38
Johnson, William, 38
Johnston, Albert Sydney, 79
Johnstun, Joseph, viii
Josephites, xiii, 33, 129–33, 135–36, 139, 145–47, 152, 163
Judd, Mary Dart, 93
Judd, Zadok Knapp, 93

K

Kelting, Lucy Johnson, 73
Kimball, Heber C., 19, 149, 171
Klingensmith, Philip, 77–78
Knight, Newell, 107–8
Knight, Samuel, 83, 104

L

Lawson, John, 151
Leavitt, Michael, 78
Lee, Hector B., viii
Lee, John D., xiii, 13, 74 78, 82
Lee, Samuel, 120
Leithead, James, 93
Lensink, Judy Nolte, xvii,
Leyland, Eliza (Lyzia Salona), 24
Lloyd, John E., 141
Loyd (Lloyd), Robert L., 34, 53, 89, 118
Lucas, Samuel D., 7
Lund, Jenny, ix
Lyman, Amasa, 87, 126, 127
Lyman, Edward Leo, 103–4, 121
Lynch, Joseph Martin, 35, 40

M

MacFarlane, John Menzies, 123
Mackay, Lach, ix
Maid of Iowa, xvi, 17, 20, 41, 87
Maloney, Mary Jane Hewitt, 33, 133
Maloney (Molloy), Stephen, 33, 133
March, Abraham, 38
Marks, William, 138–39, 160, 182
Marquardt, Mike, viii
Martineau, James Henry, 106
Matheny, Ellen B. Ray, 92
Matheny, Sim B., 71, 73
McDonald, Archie, viii, 95
McIntyre, William P., 102, 115, 158
Meeks, Melissa, 33
Miles, Jennie B., 116
Miles, Joel S., 22, 24
Miles, Samuel, 129
Miller, George, xi, xv, 14n4, 16–18, 25, 32, 88, 111, 172, 180–81
Miller, Henry W., 16, 33, 36, 42, 118
Molloy (Maloney), Stephen, 33, 133
Moqueak (Moquetus), 96
Morgan, Dale, 165
Mormon Coulee, 14n2, 17, 20n22, 21, 185
Mormon Mill Cemetery, viii, xiv, 30, 159, 186
Mormon–Missouri War, 6–11
Moroni (angel), 167
Morris, William Thomas, 106
Morse, Larry, ix
Mountain Meadows Massacre, vii, xii, xvii, 67, 72–74, 75n47, 76–78, 82, 109, 168
Murdock, John, 8
Murphy, Thomas F., 97

N

Navajo, 100, 102–3
Nebeker, John, 120
Novak, Shannon, 78

O

Okus, 101
Orton, Joseph, 90
Ouellette, Richard, 160
Our Dixie Times, 90

P

Paiutes (Pi-ute), 81, 83, 95n1, 97, 100–103
Pearce, Harrison, 71, 77
Pearce, J. D. L., 101
Petersen, Wanda Snow, 83, 91, 116, 162
Petty, R. C., 36, 38, 40n35
Phelps, Morris, 5–6
Phelps, W. W., 68
Piatt, Elsie Hawley, 3
Pi-edes (Piedes), 73, 96, 102–3
Pine Valley, vii, xvi–xvii
Ponca Camp, 107
Porter. A. J., 37
Pratt, Lydia, 124
Pratt, Orson Jr., 90, 121, 124
Pratt, Orson Sr., 69, 109, 117, 122–24, 129, 149, 150n36, 173
Pratt, Parley P., 72
Prince, Phoebe Jane Boggs, 92
Prindle, Anson, 37
Prindle, L. T. (Luther), 37
Pulsipher, Zerah, 69–70

Q

Quan-tun, 104

R

Reagan, James B., 71
Reeve, W. Paul, viii, 95, 101
Reorganized Church of Jesus Christ of Latter Day Saints (RLDS), vii, xvii
Rich, Charles C., 4–5
Richards, Franklin D., 57, 60
Richards, John, 34, 82
Richards, John (Jonathan) A., 36, 38–40
Richards, Samuel W., 149
Richey, Robert, 72, 82
Richey, William, 36, 40
Riddle, Isaac, 81–82, 88
Riding, Christopher L., 141
Rigdon, Sydney, 13–15
Riggs, Carol, viii
Rio Virgin Times, The, 90
Robinson, Joseph Lee, 114
Rogers, Lewis, 32, 41,
Romig, Ron, viii
Ross, John, 38
Ross, Robert Daniel, 40
Roundy, L. W., 72
Roundy, Uriah (Father), 135
Russell, Bill, viii

S

Sangiovanni, Guglielmo Gustavo Rosetti (Ego), 90–91
School of the Prophets, 141–42, 159
Scott, Caroline Hawley, 136
second anointing, 131, 133–34
Sessions, Gene, 78
Shebits (Paiutes), 99, 104
Sheen, Isaac, 136, 137, 138
Shepard, Bill, viii
Skabelund, Dean, viii
Slade, 'Dorinda' Melissa Moody 33, 52
Slade, William Rufus, 33–34, 37–38, 42, 54, 71, 73, 77, 84, 117, 120
slaves, 51, 57, 105–6
Smith, Alexander Hale, 137–39, 143–44, 161
Smith, Christopher C., viii, 98–99
Smith, David Hyrum, 143
Smith, George A., 38, 80, 85, 100, 109, 125, 127, 173
Smith, George A., Jr., 100
Smith, John, 12, 25, 87, 171
Smith, Joseph, Jr., xiii–xiv, xvi, 4–5, 32, 43, 87, 97, 110, 128, 131, 136–37, 139, 143, 171, 174, 176, 179, 181–83
Smith, Joseph III, xvii, 42, 110, 128, 131–32, 136, 151, 156, 161, 164, 167
Smith, Joseph F., 142–43
Smith, Robert M., 105
Smith, Silas S., 97, 127
Smith, Spencer C., 17, 25, 26n36, 46, 67, 138n30
Smith, William, xv, 27, 136, 173
Smithwick, Noah, 31
Snow, Alice Gardiner, 142
Snow, Eliza R. (Roxcy), 149n30
Snow, Erastus F., 42, 63, 68, 83, 89, 92–93, 96, 102, 109–10, 117, 112–125, 127, 129, 134, 139, 141, 144–45, 147, 151–52, 156
Snow, Steven E., ix
Snow, William, 83n10, 86, 117, 127, 129, 144
Snyder, Gary, viii
Southern Indian Mission, 104
Spavinaw Creek, 32, 35, 39, 40n35, 41, 50, 53–54, 186
Spencer, Daniel, 57, 60
St. George Temple, 148
Strang, James J., xiii, xv, 33n10, 36–37
Strangites, xv, 32, 137, 151

Stout, Hosea, 5
Stucki, John, 103–4
Sutherland, Marion, 70
Syphus, Luke, 121

T

Taylor, Eleanor, 131, 155
Taylor, John, 49
Taylor, John H., 63, 70–71, 131–33, 135, 155
Taylor, Tom, 39
Temple Lot Case, v, xv, 15, 21, 171
Texas Epidemic, 88
Thomas, Preston, 34, 57, 71
Tolkien, Barry, viii
To-o-no-quints, 103–4
Turley, Richard E., ix
Tutegabits Charley, 104
Tyler, Daniel, 86

V

Veprecula, The (*Little Bramble*), 90

W

Walker, Charles Lowell, 90, 115, 125–27
Walker, Thomas, 103
Webb, Loren, 90
Wells, Daniel H., 96, 109
West, John Anderson, 106
Whipple & Gardner Mill, 90, 118
Whipple, Eli, 88–90, 118, 122, 129
Whitney, Brian, viii
Wight, Lyman, viii, xiii–xvi, 4, 6–7, 13, 16–18, 20–21, 23, 25–27, 29, 32, 36–37, 57, 67, 70–71, 85, 88, 110, 134–35, 148, 151, 156, 159–60, 167, 171, 176, 178, 180–82, 185–86
Wight, Joseph William, 159
Wight, Orange Lysander, 20, 30n3, 37, 70, 119, 159n11, 162
Willie and Martin Companies, 45, 48–49
Wilson, William A., 115–16
Woodruff, Wilford, 36, 67, 104, 149, 150, 173–74
Woods, C. M., 10

Y

Young, Brigham, xiii–vii, 14, 17, 20, 32, 36, 38, 41–42, 46, 63, 65–69, 73–74, 79, 81, 85, 87, 89, 92, 95, 102–3, 107–10, 114, 117–18, 121–22, 124, 131–34, 137, 139, 142–44, 146–50, 156, 159–60, 167, 173–74, 178, 182

Young, John W., 18, 30, 32, 110, 139

Young, Priscilla Hawley, xiii, 3, 30–31

Young, William (Uncle Billy), xiii

Z

Zodiac Temple, xv, 22n27, 25–27, 88, 133, 161, 186,

Zodiac, Texas, xv

Also available from
GREG KOFFORD BOOKS

Joseph Smith's Polygamy, 3 Vols.

Brian Hales

Hardcover
Volume 1: History 978-1-58958-189-0
Volume 2: History 978-1-58958-548-5
Volume 3: Theology 978-1-58958-190-6

Perhaps the least understood part of Joseph Smith's life and teachings is his introduction of polygamy to the Saints in Nauvoo. Because of the persecution he knew it would bring, Joseph said little about it publicly and only taught it to his closest and most trusted friends and associates before his martyrdom.

In this three-volume work, Brian C. Hales provides the most comprehensive faithful examination of this much misunderstood period in LDS Church history. Drawing for the first time on every known account, Hales helps us understand the history and teachings surrounding this secretive practice and also addresses and corrects many of the numerous allegations and misrepresentations concerning it. Hales further discusses how polygamy was practiced during this time and why so many of the early Saints were willing to participate in it.

Joseph Smith's Polygamy is an essential resource in understanding this challenging and misunderstood practice of early Mormonism.

Praise for *Joseph Smith's Polygamy*:

"Brian Hales wants to face up to every question, every problem, every fear about plural marriage. His answers may not satisfy everyone, but he gives readers the relevant sources where answers, if they exist, are to be found. There has never been a more thorough examination of the polygamy idea."
—Richard L. Bushman, author of *Joseph Smith: Rough Stone Rolling*

"Hales's massive and well documented three volume examination of the history and theology of Mormon plural marriage, as introduced and practiced during the life of Joseph Smith, will now be the standard against which all other treatments of this important subject will be measured." —Danel W. Bachman, author of "A Study of the Mormon Practice of Plural Marriage before the Death of Joseph Smith"

Mormon Thunder: A Documentary History of Jedediah Morgan Grant

Gene A. Sessions

Paperback, ISBN: 978-1-58958-111-1

Jedediah Morgan Grant was a man who knew no compromise when it came to principles—and his principles were clearly representative, argues Gene A. Sessions, of Mormonism's first generation. His life is a glimpse of a Mormon world whose disappearance coincided with the death of this "pious yet rambunctiously radical preacher, flogging away at his people, demanding otherworldliness and constant sacrifice." It was "an eschatological, pre-millennial world in which every individual teetered between salvation and damnation and in which unsanitary privies and appropriating a stray cow held the same potential for eternal doom as blasphemy and adultery."

Updated and newly illustrated with more photographs, this second edition of the award-winning documentary history (first published in 1982) chronicles Grant's ubiquitous role in the Mormon history of the 1840s and '50s. In addition to serving as counselor to Brigham Young during two tumultuous and influential years at the end of his life, he also portentously befriended Thomas L. Kane, worked to temper his unruly brother-in-law William Smith, captained a company of emigrants into the Salt Lake Valley in 1847, and journeyed to the East on several missions to bolster the position of the Mormons during the crises surrounding the runaway judges affair and the public revelation of polygamy.

Jedediah Morgan Grant's voice rises powerfully in these pages, startling in its urgency in summoning his people to sacrifice and moving in its tenderness as he communicated to his family. From hastily scribbled letters to extemporaneous sermons exhorting obedience, and the notations of still stunned listeners, the sound of "Mormon Thunder" rolls again in "a boisterous amplification of what Mormonism really was, and would never be again."

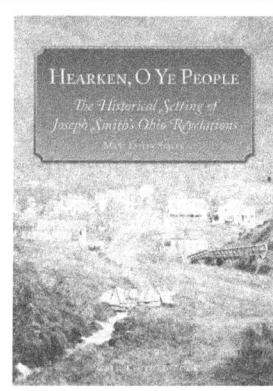

Hearken, O Ye People: The Historical Setting of Joseph Smith's Ohio Revelations

Mark Lyman Staker

Hardcover, ISBN: 978-1-58958-113-5

2010 Best Book Award - John Whitmer Historical Association
2011 Best Book Award - Mormon History Association

More of Mormonism's canonized revelations originated in or near Kirtland than any other place. Yet many of the events connected with those revelations and their 1830s historical context have faded over time. Mark Staker reconstructs the cultural experiences by which Kirtland's Latter-day Saints made sense of the revelations Joseph Smith pronounced. This volume rebuilds that exciting decade using clues from numerous archives, privately held records, museum collections, and even the soil where early members planted corn and homes. From this vast array of sources he shapes a detailed narrative of weather, religious backgrounds, dialect differences, race relations, theological discussions, food preparation, frontier violence, astronomical phenomena, and myriad daily customs of nineteenth-century life. The result is a "from the ground up" experience that today's Latter-day Saints can all but walk into and touch.

Praise for *Hearken O Ye People*:

"I am not aware of a more deeply researched and richly contextualized study of any period of Mormon church history than Mark Staker's study of Mormons in Ohio. We learn about everything from the details of Alexander Campbell's views on priesthood authority to the road conditions and weather on the four Lamanite missionaries' journey from New York to Ohio. All the Ohio revelations and even the First Vision are made to pulse with new meaning. This book sets a new standard of in-depth research in Latter-day Saint history."
    -Richard Bushman, author of *Joseph Smith: Rough Stone Rolling*

"To be well-informed, any student of Latter-day Saint history and doctrine must now be acquainted with the remarkable research of Mark Staker on the important history of the church in the Kirtland, Ohio, area."
    -Neal A. Maxwell Institute, Brigham Young University

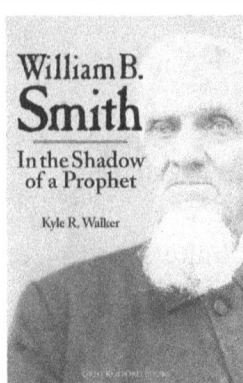

William B. Smith: In the Shadow of a Prophet

Kyle R. Walker

Paperback, ISBN: 978-1-58958-503-4

Younger brother of Joseph Smith, a member of the Quorum of the Twelve Apostles, and Church Patriarch for a time, William Smith had tumultuous yet devoted relationships with Joseph, his fellow members of the Twelve, and the LDS and RLDS (Community of Christ) churches. Walker's imposing biography examines not only William's complex life in detail, but also sheds additional light on the family dynamics of Joseph and Lucy Mack Smith, as well as the turbulent intersections between the LDS and RLDS churches. *William B. Smith: In the Shadow of a Prophet* is a vital contribution to Mormon history in both the LDS and RLDS traditions.

Praise for *William B. Smith*:

"Bullseye! Kyle Walker's biography of Joseph Smith Jr.'s lesser known younger brother William is right on target. It weaves a narrative that is searching, balanced, and comprehensive. Walker puts this former Mormon apostle solidly within a Smith family setting, and he hits the mark for anyone interested in Joseph Smith and his family. Walker's biography will become essential reading on leadership dynamics within Mormonism after Joseph Smith's death." — Mark Staker, author *Hearken, O Ye People: The Historical Setting of Joseph Smith's Ohio Revelations*

"This perceptive biography on William, the last remaining Smith brother, provides a thorough timeline of his life's journey and elucidates how his insatiable discontent eventually tempered the once irascible young man into a seasoned patriarch loved by those who knew him." — Erin B. Metcalfe, president (2014–15) John Whitmer Historical Association

"I suspect that this comprehensive treatment will serve as the definitive biography for years to come; it will certainly be difficult to improve upon." — Joe Steve Swick III, Association for Mormon Letters

www.ingramcontent.com/pod-product-compliance
Lightning Source LLC
Chambersburg PA
CBHW031435160426
43195CB00010BB/742